M

EVANSTON PUBLIC LIBRARY

P9-DGF-678

346.0166 Mille.K 2007
Miller, Kathleen,
Fair share divorce for women :

Fair
Div
for Women

MAR 1 5 2007

346.0166
Mille. K
2007

Fair Share Divorce for Women

The Definitive Guide to Creating a Winning Solution

Second Edition

Kathleen Miller, CFP®, MBA

EVANSTON PUBLIC LIBRARY
1703 ORRINGTON AVENUE
EVANSTON, ILLINOIS 60201

St. Martin's Griffin ⚘ New York

FAIR SHARE DIVORCE FOR WOMEN, SECOND EDITION. Copyright © 2007 by Kathleen Miller. All rights reserved. Printed in the United States of America. No part of this book may be used or reproduced in any manner whatsoever without written permission except in the case of brief quotations embodied in critical articles or reviews. For information, address St. Martin's Press, 175 Fifth Avenue, New York, N.Y. 10010.

"The Hardship of Accounting" from *The Poetry of Robert Frost*, edited by Edward Connery Lathem. Copyright © 1969 by Henry Holt and Company. Copyright © 1936 by Robert Frost, copyright © 1964 by Lesley Frost Ballantine. Reprinted by permission of Henry Holt and Company, LLC.

www.stmartins.com

Design by Nancy Singer Olaguera

Library of Congress Cataloging-in-Publication Data

Miller, Kathleen, 1946–
    Fair share divorce for women : the definitive guide to creating a winning solution / Kathleen Miller.—2nd ed.
        p. cm
    Includes index.
    ISBN-13: 978-0-312-35432-9
    ISBN-10: 0-312-35432-0
    1. Equitable distribution of marital property—United States. 2. Divorce settlements—United States. 3. Divorced women—United States—Finance, Personal.

KF532.7.M54 2007
346.7301'664—dc22

                                                                        2006051266

First published in the United States by Miller Advisors, Inc.

First St. Martin's Griffin Edition: March 2007

10 9 8 7 6 5 4 3 2 1

Author's Note

This book is intended as a resource and offers guidance and information for women going through the process of divorce who seek to safeguard marital assets and create a sound financial plan for their future. Examples of typical situations and solutions to common problems encountered by divorcing women are included for illustrative purposes only. I have changed the names and identifying characteristics of people mentioned in the book to protect their privacy.

If the reader needs advice concerning the evaluation and management of specific legal or financial risks or liabilities, such as bankruptcy or tax matters, he or she should seek the help of a licensed, knowledgeable professional.

Contents

Divorce Is Like Riding an Escalator . . . • . . . While Also Climbing Up Some Very Steep Stairs • Divorce Comes in Many Different Forms • Get Organized as Soon as Possible • The Corporate Wife • The Wife as Alpha Earner • What Is the First Step?

The Emotional Stages of Divorce • A Maze of Emotions: Depression, Anger, and Lack of Control • 1. Pre-Divorce • 2. Decision • 3. Final Acceptance • 4. Mourning • 5. Re-Equilibrium • Most Often Asked Questions About Divorce

Differences Between States Are Important • Which Method Is Best for Your Situation? • Frequently Asked Questions About Hiring an Attorney • Checklist for the Initial Meeting with Your Attorney • Janice's Decision: Mediation

Why We Get Divorced • Contemporary Relationships • Lessons Learned

No Fraternization! • Don't Talk to Him About the Divorce Case on Your Own • Don't Let Him Come Between You and Your Lawyer • Watch Out

Acknowledgments

Fair Share Divorce for Women is the result of not just my twenty-five years of experience, but more important, the contributions and support of many fine people. Without them, this book would still be just a vision. I am deeply grateful for their efforts in helping make the vision a reality.

To my friends and family, I wish to express my appreciation for their ongoing support, encouragement, and belief in my work. They share my passion about the importance of getting the tools for equitable divorce into the hands of my readers.

I especially want to thank my husband, Don, for his help in preparing the manuscript, as well as researching much of the statistics and data on divorce. His dedication to the project and unwavering personal support has helped keep me on track.

My daughter, Nicole, has been an inspiration and devoted supporter. She represents the Generation X women of today who will build financial awareness and equality into their marriages.

The staff at Miller Advisors has gone beyond the call of duty in taking on many of the tasks involved in preparing the book, in addition to their already demanding jobs in my wealth-management practice. I am truly thankful for their patience and dedication in the face of daunting challenges. Each year the tools and decision-making models they have helped create are enhanced by our experiences working with clients, attorneys, and other professionals. I want to thank John Twitchell, CDFA, for his commitment and expertise in this area. Patricia Doran has worked closely with me to create realistic postdivorce financial plans for many clients. Cherryl Franco has managed our office with efficiency and calmness when emotions have been particularly intense around a divorce settlement.

Renee Gastineau has helped develop presentation materials and provided guidance in taking my message to the public. She has kept my message visible and focused on fair share divorce.

I met Denise Marcil, my agent, when I was completing the first edition in 1994. Although I had decided to self-publish that book, Denise was very supportive of my message. We agreed to meet again if I did a second edition, and she has been a marvelous source of insight, encouragement, and understanding throughout the publication process.

Diane Reverand, my editor, and Regina Scarpa, her assistant at St. Martin's Press, have taken a raw manuscript and turned it into a professional publication. Readers will unquestionably benefit from their sharp pencils and experienced direction.

Vicki McCown's dedicated local editorial assistance ensured the book incorporated the required changes. Her expertise as a writer and freelance editor was invaluable in meeting publication deadlines.

Elizabeth Lyon, a nationally recognized author and editor in her own right, gave me the impetus to actively pursue publishing *Fair Share Divorce for Women*. Her guidance and enthusiasm in editing the initial book proposal got me energized.

Jan Reha is an outspoken advocate of equitable dissolution and has worked with me in developing effective career plans for women who are economically disadvantaged in divorce. In addition to her contribution to this book, we have collaborated on articles addressing such issues as the disparity of spousal earnings and the use of experts in divorce.

Divorce is, first and foremost, a legal process that is most often managed by the attorney. I have been fortunate to work closely with many of the leading family attorneys in our area and around the country. The field of family law is changing. Thanks to a growing number of supportive attorneys, the knowledgeable financial planner is now an important advisor for divorcing clients.

Most of all, I want to thank the women and men who have shared their divorce processes with me. They have helped pioneer a new way of looking at divorce. Together we will leave a legacy for those who seek their own fair share divorces.

Introduction

Why I Wrote *Fair Share Divorce for Women*

This book was inspired by the needs of women and by their often frustrated efforts to obtain financial equity in divorce in order to create a secure financial future for themselves and their families. I have worked with divorcing couples for the past twenty-five years, and I have seen a profound need for professional, compassionate guidance on the financial aspects of divorce.

Although I have an intimate knowledge of the divorce process, I am neither an attorney nor a therapist. I am a financial planner and wealth manager. My career has focused on a desire to help people achieve financial independence and security.

I have a special interest in seeing women educated to use their money wisely. Women are the nurturers in our society, and they have a profound impact on the money values they pass along to children.

> **An empowered woman is able to create, protect, and preserve her wealth for herself, her children, and her grandchildren.**

When children see their mothers standing up for their fair share at the time of divorce to protect themselves and their families, it inspires wise money-management decisions in future generations of girls and boys.

Women who develop confidence in managing their own financial affairs find themselves setting new life goals and releasing the emotional baggage of the past. Professional experience has shown me that when women protect themselves in divorce, they increase their self-assurance and become engaged in many other areas of their lives. Ultimately, they move forward into a positive financial future and a secure life.

Know What to Expect

Reaching those goals while struggling with divorce is one of the most difficult challenges of contemporary life. I wrote this book to help make the transition from marriage to divorce easier.

What might otherwise have been a textbook approach to divorce is enriched in these pages by the personal perspectives of many of my clients. The material draws upon the expertise of hundreds of professionals with whom I have worked as a financial planner, expert witness, mediator, and consultant.

Fair Share Divorce for Women will help you understand the emotional stages and legal phases of divorce. From predivorce preparation to the intricacies of the dissolution process itself to the critical elements of postdivorce financial planning, this book will provide you with detailed information on every issue you need to consider.

UNDERSTANDING CONTEMPORARY DIVORCE

Studies show that the divorce rate is holding steady in the United States, but the adult population is increasing in this country, so the actual number of people getting divorced has probably increased during the past fifteen years. More important, the increasing economic complexities of life have intensified the problems associated with divorce.

I am seeing many more women who earn higher incomes than their husbands; more husbands who are stay-at-home dads; many women who enter into "starter" marriages lasting five years or less, and who face divorce much sooner than previous generations; and the percentage of second marriages that end in divorce has skyrocketed.

The media has popularized numerous high-profile divorces involving corporate wives, who are aggressive in standing up for their financial fair share of the marriage. These are women who are not ashamed of their marriage, divorce, or fighting for what they believe is their marital right and the rights of their children and grandchildren. Divorce is also generating attention in corporate boardrooms, because the perks corporations give their executives have been made public in divorce court in some rather embarrassing ways.

Today, divorce is not as stigmatic as it has been in the past. The way the media and society view and treat divorce has changed profoundly. These trends affect how people handle money in their marriages and relationships.

What has not changed is that divorce continues to place many women at a significant financial disadvantage compared to their male partners. I wrote this book to try to change that condition by providing a positive approach to a traditionally fearful, negative topic and to give you the tools you need to create your own win-win financial strategy.

Control Your Own Destiny

My goal is to remove the mystique of the divorce process. Once you understand the emotional and legal dimensions of divorce, you will be better prepared to take control of your own divorce, rather than leaving it in someone else's hands. That does not mean you should act as your own attorney, financial planner, career advisor, or therapist. It means you must guide the process by providing the goals, making the decisions, telling the experts what you want and need, and helping to gather the information they will need to implement your goals. You must be an involved, sophisticated, and active participant, not an observer. This book will show you how.

> Although I have great respect for many of the family law attorneys with whom I have worked through the years, there are emotional and financial issues in divorce that the legal process does not address.

The case studies and examples I've included cover a wide range of my clients' experiences. You are likely to find a scenario with aspects similar to your own situation. With these examples, I hope you can find some ideas with which to build your own solution.

Who Should Read This Book?

This book is written for the 1.1 million women actively involved in divorce every year, and those who are considering divorce in the near future. The majority of divorce cases in this country are initiated by women—national surveys estimate between 60 and 75 percent. You are not alone in divorce, nor should you feel left out of the process.

I tell former clients, friends, and attorneys who refer divorce clients to me that I don't take on shrinking violets. This book is designed to help those who want to take control of their future. Getting a divorce takes time. There are many details involved in earning your fair share, including organizing your records; managing your spending; making tough choices about home, children, and career; and perhaps fighting for what is rightfully yours.

You may not feel you are emotionally ready to tackle these challenges right now. Not everyone is. It is important to be realistic about where you are in your own process. If you need more time to prepare, I encourage you to find a counselor, friend, minister, or family member who can get you through the first emotional steps of your divorce. Then refer to this book. It is never too late to take charge of your own divorce, no matter where you are in the process.

If you are ready to start planning your new life and creating a winning strategy for life after divorce, then read on!

Fair Share
Divorce
for Women

1

What Should You Do First?

Fair share divorce does not always mean equal.

—Kathleen Miller

If you are a woman considering divorce or are being forced to think about divorce because your husband has declared his intention to separate from you, you are no doubt wondering what first steps you should take. If you are like most people, you will think of calling an attorney to help you navigate this difficult process. Though you will certainly need legal advice, there is another professional you should consult, perhaps even before you make that call to the lawyer: a Certified Financial Planner™. A CFP® can be invaluable to you during this time because when a marriage fails, money issues often dominate the divorce proceedings.

The financial aspects of breaking the marital bonds are among the most important decisions you will ever make during your lifetime. You have to protect yourself, and that means you have to make financial plans to preserve what you have contributed to the marriage early on in the divorce negotiating process—even while the shock is still sinking in. These are marital assets you have a right to share.

> Trusting that the legal process will take care of you is the worst assumption you can make.

Divorce Is Like Riding an Escalator . . .

The not-so-funny illustration in Figure 1.1 represents the dissolution process. Those going into divorce face two types of challenges: legal and emotional.

Going through the legal process of getting a divorce is like stepping

FIGURE 1.1   The Divorce Escalator

on an escalator. The escalator doesn't stop. Once you're on, you are going to get off—whether under your own power or by being thrown off by the unrelenting process of the legal system. Ready or not, you will be divorced.

The legal process consists of five separate phases you will have to navigate:

1. Preparation
2. Initiation
3. Analysis and Planning

4. Negotiation and Settlement
5. Implementation

Each phase has its own unique set of activities, tasks, documents, participants, and challenges.

. . . WHILE ALSO CLIMBING UP SOME VERY STEEP STAIRS

As if the legal problems were not enough to deal with, you must negotiate the five emotional stages of divorce at the same time:

1. Pre-Divorce
2. Decision
3. Acceptance
4. Mourning
5. Re-Equilibrium

Again, each of these stages presents its own hurdles that have to be overcome.

As you approach divorce, you will find yourself being dragged up the legal escalator while you must struggle up the emotional staircase on your own. That is a tough balancing act!

We will look at the five emotional stages of divorce in the next chapter; a detailed discussion of the five legal phases of divorce will come later on in chapter 6.

My experience shows that most women urgently need divorce advice. Many women dislike confrontation, shy away from conflict, and traditionally have taken a backseat to men with regards to money management. After the legal complexities and emotional nasties have been exhausted, money is what divorce is all about.

Money issues are critical when you go through the divorce process. If you ignore them, you will suffer financially. When the divorce is over, regrets won't provide solace for the financial assets you've lost.

The good news is that you can emerge from divorce with your fair share. That's why I've written this book. I will show you, by instruction and through examples of what other women have experienced—both the good and the bad—how important the first steps in a divorce can be to the final financial outcome.

DIVORCE COMES IN MANY DIFFERENT FORMS

Sean is a good example of how and why women come to me when divorce has become a certainty in their lives. She left an urgent message for me after learning my name from another client.

When Sean presented herself, her distress was obvious. As she bit her lip, she told me her husband had left the previous weekend after informing her he wanted a divorce. Sean had three children ages fifteen, eleven, and seven, and she and the children were trying to understand what was happening to them. Sean was calm with the children and attempted to keep them on their regular schedules at school and involved in all the things they would normally do. Her personal agony was intensified by the fact that she had no previous indication of a problem in her marriage.

Panicky, twisting a handkerchief with her fingers, Sean related the events of the weekend.

"After working late at the office on Friday, Jim got up earlier than usual on Saturday and told me he wanted to talk. We sat down and had a cup of coffee. He said he was leaving. Just like that. He had found an apartment and was going to move in on Sunday. He needed time away from me and the family. He was feeling overwhelmed at work and needed to be by himself. That's what he said.

"I asked if he was involved with someone else, and he told me that was not why he was leaving, but he wouldn't answer my question directly. He said he would take care of me financially and continue to put his paycheck into our bank account twice a month. We were only going to live apart for a few months. Other than that, he had no plans.

"First, I was stunned. Then I cried. John, our oldest child, came into the room, and we asked him to leave. We told him we were having a private conversation. He could tell that we were both very upset. John quietly went back to his room, and then Jim went upstairs and started packing his clothes. He was very methodical and organized and seemed to have a careful plan of what he was taking. He asked if he could take some of the furniture and gave me a list of the things he wanted from the various rooms in the house and garage. He said he would have a truck come by on Sunday to pick up his belongings, and then he left. He came back on Sunday just as he planned and moved out. The children and I sat at the kitchen table and watched him leave—it was so surreal. We were all crying."

GET ORGANIZED AS SOON AS POSSIBLE

I listened to Sean carefully, sympathized with her, and told her I empathized with what she was going through. Then, to get her mind on to practical matters, I asked her to get a copy of her last three years' income tax returns, current year-end brokerage statements, an employee benefits summary, a recent pay stub, and a joint financial statement, because those files would be important. I explained to her that a financial statement would have been required when she and her husband financed or refinanced their house. Also, I cautioned her that if she couldn't locate the information, we needed to find out why. Would Jim have taken it with him? Could it be in his office or stored electronically on the computer? The importance of having financial data early on in a divorce can't be overemphasized. Later, you'll understand why.

I tell clients such as Sean that they should see a financial planner who understands the divorce process as soon as possible when divorce looms. A Certified Divorce Financial Analyst™ (CDFA™) is licensed and trained to provide financial support services to clients, attorneys, and mediators. These financial professionals will help you to:

- Identify, collect, and organize the financial information you and your attorney will need.
- Create pre- and postdivorce budgets.
- Determine the amounts of temporary *maintenance* and child support you realistically need.
- Create a plan to obtain the assets you are rightfully owed.
- Analyze various settlement options.
- Establish a postdivorce financial plan.

You can visit *www.institutedfa.com* to find a qualified financial planner in your area. If you cannot find a local planner with that designation, you may want to use the Financial Planning Association's search tool at *www.fpanet.org/plannersearch/plannersearch.cfm*. From there you can find advisors with the CERTIFIED FINANCIAL PLANNER™ (CFP®) designation.

A financial planner can help you acquire and organize the information you and your attorney will need to be better prepared to cope with the intimidating legal process ahead. The attorney's job is to advise you on such matters as:

- Who should file and when.
- How you will get money for yourself and your children.

- When to issue temporary *restraining orders* on various bank savings and checking accounts.
- How to address other legal aspects of dissolving the marriage.

In Sean's case, no one had filed for divorce, and Jim had told his wife that he hadn't planned to file at the point of their separation. That may or may not have been his intention. Although Sean was shocked at her husband's surprisingly abrupt departure, his actions were not uncommon. In some cases, the departing spouse has been carefully developing a plan designed to hide his intentions. Shock is a powerful weapon in manipulating an unsuspecting partner. In other cases, women overlook or underestimate the signs of impending trouble, naïvely hoping things will improve.

> **In my twenty-five years of experience dealing with divorce cases, I have come to live by the motto Trust, but verify.**

If divorce is a possibility, get organized as soon as possible. Get the facts while the spirit of cooperation and guilt is on your side. Your life will never be the same. You cannot go back to the way it was, as if there never was an erosion of trust. Even if Sean and Jim eventually get back together, their lives as a couple will have changed irrevocably.

THE CORPORATE WIFE

I'll never forget the first woman who came to me about her divorce. Her name was Susan, and she was forty-five years old. One of the first things she told me was that her divorce was going to be amicable. She and her husband had been married for more than twenty-five years, and they had three grown children, all college graduates. Her husband, Tom, was president of a large and successful corporation, and he had become involved with his secretary. Up until Susan had found out about the affair, their marriage had seemed happy and traditional. She had stayed home to raise the children, traveled as his companion when his company sent him around the world, and entertained his business clients and work associates in their beautiful and spacious home. When their children had moved out and started lives of their own, Susan thought it was finally time for them to become a couple again.

She was wrong.

Her story was not an unusual one. During the years that followed, I would hear stories like Susan's time and time again.

Susan did not want a divorce, but she couldn't live with "the other woman" in the picture. Tom, she said, was torn. He did not want to lose his wife, but he was not willing to give up his girlfriend. Since neither wanted a long legal battle, big attorney fees, restraining orders, and the bitterness of a legal squabble, they went to an attorney friend and attempted to negotiate their own property settlement. **Property settlement** is the term used for that portion of the divorce decree that specifies which party receives what assets, including furniture, stocks, insurance policies, and cars, and which party must assume what liabilities, including credit card debt, policy premiums, and loan payments.

During the next year, they were able to negotiate what they both considered a fair settlement. One of the issues for Susan was her earning ability. She had stayed home during the marriage and had been the primary parent raising the couple's three children. During the marriage, Tom had done a great deal of traveling, and she had spent a lot of time volunteering at their children's schools, driving the children to and from various activities, and helping them with homework. Both parents had placed a strong value on her activities during the child-rearing years. But now what? The children were out of the home.

Susan did work fifteen hours a week as a part-time marketing representative for a friend, earning $10,000 a year. As the top executive in his company, Tom earned more than $350,000 annually, in addition to **stock options,** a generous profit-sharing plan, an expense account, a car, and an international travel allowance. There was no doubt that Susan's life was going to change dramatically once she was divorced, since she would no longer be the partner who shared in her husband's corporate benefits.

Susan was plagued by fears, doubts, and insecurities about the transition from being married to being single, with good reason. Not only was she losing her financial support, but her emotional support as well. Many women become emotionally paralyzed during this time. Though they understand that they must bring in some kind of income, the last thing these women can think about is what kind of a career they should pursue. They can barely force themselves out of bed in the morning and make their way through the day.

For the husband, on the other hand, very little changes. He still goes to the same job every day, occupied with a career that normally requires his full concentration. He suffers very little long-term career and financial upheaval. Even so, neither party escapes without some emotional and financial scars and pain.

Susan came to me after she and Tom had been separated for six months. Although Tom was physically out of the house, he had continued to deposit half of his paycheck into their joint account. However, Susan had been informed that Tom was going to start reducing her allowance, or "maintenance" as he called the deposits, by 30 percent starting the next month, because he believed she didn't need as much as she had been getting.

Since Susan and Tom had worked out the details of their separation together, no court order or legal separation restricted Tom's decision. This meant that Tom was free to do whatever he wanted with his earnings—regardless of Susan's wishes or needs. This left Susan at a distinct disadvantage.

Clearly, Susan would need to increase her income to compensate for the reduction in her allowance. She made an appointment to see a career counselor. Although she'd never had a full-time job outside of the home, she felt that she had enjoyed a successful career—that of a corporate executive spouse, managing many business and social functions for her husband and for his company over the years. Now that the marriage had ended, she felt uncertain as to where she could apply her skills in the workplace. She also lacked motivation and drive.

Susan found herself facing some sobering statistics about the financial status of those who divorce:

- Women's economic well-being drops an average of 36 percent following a divorce, while men experience an increase of 28 percent.[1]
- When compared to continuously married men and women, individuals who have not remarried following a divorce have been shown to experience a 66 percent lower level of personal wealth.[2]

The career advisor helping Susan was excited to learn she had someone working with her on her finances. Susan had an attorney—a friend of the family—but she was unable to relate the property settlement numbers being discussed to her life. She needed to create a practical financial plan for her postdivorce life, but the reality of being on her own had not sunk in. She had married Tom after he graduated from college and had never really lived alone. Now, as she and Tom divided up the property, she had to anticipate what life would be like after divorce. For example, she wondered whether she should keep the 4,000-square-foot home. It seemed an attractive option, as it was a nice house and she was emotionally attached to it. But why would she maintain such a large home now that no children were living there, and with no income to support its upkeep? Tom believed she should get the house, along with most of the furniture, while he would get some of the cash from their bank accounts and most of the profit-sharing plan. But Tom didn't need the house. He had purchased a townhouse and lived there with his girlfriend when he was not traveling for his company.

Everyone seemed to have a plan but Susan. Together, we changed that. Working as a team, Susan's attorney, her career counselor, and I helped her create a strategy and execute it. As a result, Susan did receive a fair and equitable settlement. She eventually found a satisfactory job and is happy with her postdivorce life. Choosing the right professional team was Susan's first step toward a win-win solution.

The Wife as Alpha Earner

Sarah is an *alpha earner*,[3] a term that now popularly describes a woman who makes more than her husband. As a radiologist, Sarah earned $300,000 a year. Her husband, Jeff, worked at the telephone company, earning $100,000 a year. They had three children ages twelve, ten, and seven. After their second child was born, Jeff and Sarah hired a nanny to help take care of the children.

Jeff had survived two mergers during the three years he worked following the birth of their youngest child, and he was finding his job less and less satisfying. Given the expense of a nanny and other help for the three children as well as Jeff's increasing job dissatisfaction, Sarah and Jeff agreed he would become a stay-at-home father. He had an interest in graphic arts and planned to take a one-year community college course in this area of study and then open his own business, which he could run from the house. They tried that arrangement for four years.

Jeff became dissatisfied with his role as "Mr. Mom" and found little satisfaction in working only part time at a job he enjoyed. He is now asking for a divorce after their twenty-four-year marriage and wants joint custody of the children, maintenance for five years, and half their assets. Sarah is angry, bitter about the years she has spent away from the family earning the primary income, and resentful of any maintenance to be paid to Jeff. He got the opportunity to change careers, follow his passion, and be the primary caretaker of their children. She wants to work part time and be a stay-at-home mother. The mediator and both attorneys are telling her that this is not a practical solution. As a result, Sarah is feeling trapped in her career out of financial necessity and resentful of not having the opportunity to pursue her own desires as a mother. As with most divorces, this case required compromises by both parties. Using a team of impartial experts was a critical factor in resolving the issues because of the emotions involved.

What Is the First Step?

These women's stories are specific, yet typical examples and may resonate with your own situation. What should you do first? Your own situation dictates the best answer. When faced with a spouse's demand for divorce, you may first need to see an attorney in order to respond properly. Even in such a circumstance, you need to begin financial preparations immediately. If you have any questions about how to address these critical issues, see a qualified financial planner as soon as possible. If your most demanding issues are emotional, and you cannot start being financially practical, take care of yourself. That may mean talking with a therapist, a family counselor, a cleric, or a close personal friend. What is important is that you take a positive, self-affirming step rather than go into hiding. As that maxim goes, "A journey of a thousand miles begins with the first step."

Take that step now.

2

The Five Emotional Stages of Divorce

It always comes back to the same necessity:
go deep enough and there is bedrock of truth, however hard.

—MAY SARTON (AMERICAN POET AND AUTHOR, 1912–95)

According to a survey of 208 leading divorce lawyers in thirty-six states, most women facing divorce do not know how much money their family has or even how much their husbands earn. Fifty-two percent of the attorneys in that survey said that most of their women clients do not have a clear picture of family assets or income.[1]

> During the last twenty-five years, I have worked on more than 3,000 divorces. Dozens of lawyers with whom I've worked report that a significant number of the wives who consult them in divorce actions are fundamentally ignorant about money matters in the family.

Many women have never even examined the federal income tax form their husband places in front of them for signature. The women in these situations may have knowledge of a savings account and a couple of investments, but they have only the faintest notion of the overall finances of the family. This is especially common when a family business is involved. Often the woman works actively in the business in the early stages, then shifts her focus from business to family, raising the children.

> The attitude you have about yourself and the divorce process can affect the outcome and the economic benefits you can obtain for

> yourself and your children. The right attitude can make a tremen-
> dous difference in a divorced woman's future.

Women, by their very nature, typically enter into marriage with the view of a long-term partnership that involves sharing emotions, money, child-raising, and retirement. Most women I meet are in emotional trauma over their divorces. Many feel guilty and allow their feelings to affect their judgment. Often, they have been replaced by another woman, many times a younger one. The sense of betrayal, loss, and anger can temporarily lower the woman's self-esteem and throw her into a deep depression and emotional distress. **Financial decisions based on feelings of unworthiness can be disastrous.**

During this time, the woman is still struggling to fulfill her role as the "supermom," always in control and taking charge of the details of everyone's daily life. Her own needs are not being met and probably have not been met for some time in the marriage. Now she feels rejected, isolated, and often immobilized.

THE EMOTIONAL STAGES OF DIVORCE

In divorce, there is always the leaver and the leftee. Both positions carry substantial emotional and financial baggage. Remember, when you or your spouse files for a divorce, you are on the *legal* journey to dissolution, but acknowledging the *emotional* stages of divorce is extremely important. You must remember that you are not alone, although at times it may feel as if you are. You can pass through the stages to a safe and secure single life if you make yourself aware in advance of the difficulties you will face.

> When it comes to divorce, remember: knowledge is power, and ig-
> norance is not bliss.

If you went into your marriage viewing it as a partnership, you will assume that both spouses make substantially equal—although not necessarily identical—contributions to the relationship. If so, you would expect to receive fairly equal financial benefits from the marriage. You should not be left in a much lower position after the marriage ends. To achieve financial fairness, you need to be able to navigate the emotional stages in divorce.

A MAZE OF EMOTIONS: DEPRESSION, ANGER, AND LACK OF CONTROL

Janice came into my office for an initial consultation, referred by a friend who had used our services. Less than six months before, Janice had been secure in her marriage to a high-income-producing professional. Her upper-middle-class lifestyle represented the ultimate in comfort—a home in the suburbs, new cars, extended annual vacations, annual expense-paid company trips, and an active social calendar. Now she found herself in the midst of a messy divorce.

The trauma and stress of the past few months showed on her face. She had accumulated sizeable legal fees and incurred a level of consumer debt she had never experienced before. She was attempting to establish a personal *income stream*, while struggling to maintain their previous financial lifestyle for herself and her children. She had to cope with decisions involving child custody, the division of property, and parenting issues. She was a woman in the throes of dealing with the classic contemporary divorce—unprepared, traumatized, and with insufficient resources. She had no idea how to find her way out of this maze to create a life for herself and her children, particularly since she felt so depressed, inadequate, and out of control. Without realizing it, Janice was struggling through the inevitable emotional stages of divorce.

FIVE EMOTIONAL STAGES OF DIVORCE
1. Pre-Divorce
2. Decision
3. Final Acceptance
4. Mourning
5. Re-Equilibrium

Recognizing the emotional stages of divorce will give you the wisdom to see yourself through each stage without making financial decisions harmful to your future.

There are five emotional stages of divorce, and each one reflects the advancing process of disengagement. Understanding what you're going through gives you more control and a deeper appreciation of the changes you'll be making in your life.

1. PRE-DIVORCE

This period is characterized by escalating marital dissatisfaction, often felt more acutely by one party than the other. Marital intimacy declines, and you may fight openly, see a marriage counselor or minister, visit an attorney, and physically separate into two households. This is a time of denial and uncertainty. You don't want to acknowledge the possibility of divorce, and you are reluctant to see an attorney or a financial planner to address the economics of a divorce. You fear that seeing a professional might be the first step in actualizing the divorce. In a word, you are traumatized.

Maybe you know, consciously or unconsciously, that your husband is having an affair. I believe most women intuitively know when this is going on. Should you see an attorney and financial planner during this stage? Absolutely! Protect yourself. If your husband is a businessman and you have any inkling he might pursue a divorce himself, you can be assured that he has looked at the financial and business aspects of divorce. If you don't do the same, you will be at a disadvantage.

It is important to see an attorney early to discuss your legal position and to clarify both community and separate assets. Using resources readily available at the local library, Internet sites on divorce, and your attorney, you can obtain answers to such critical questions as:

- How are assets typically divided in the state where you live? For example, are they based on the length of your marriage, property value, income, children, and/or special circumstances?
- How do you protect yourself in the legal process of dissolution and the development of parenting plans?
- What provisions for housing, temporary maintenance, career development, and insurance coverage are available?
- How long will a divorce take?
- How much should you expect it to cost?

The wife who sees divorce on the horizon must stabilize herself enough emotionally to gather the financial facts about her marriage.

When the husband leaves the home, the financial information often leaves with him. As a result, the wife may spend hundreds or thousands of dollars in attorney's fees to gather the missing information.

Know your finances, review the income tax return before you sign it, and ask questions. An experienced financial planner with expertise in the area of divorce can be very helpful in this preliminary stage of the divorce.

What You Need to Know

In many of my divorce cases, other than managing the household budget, the woman had not taken an active role in handling the finances. The husband made the financial decisions and did most of the planning as the family provider. If you know little about your family's money situation, it becomes vital at this point for you to gather information and take other important financial steps. You must:

- Copy and understand income tax returns and investment reports.
- Review current pay stubs with deductions, bonuses, and expense reimbursements.
- Establish a credit history in your own name.
- Order a copy of your joint credit report.
- Research and verify the ownership of all assets (for example, stocks, *bonds,* and annuities) and how they are registered.
- Review life, medical, and disability insurance policies.
- Understand employee benefits summaries, mortgage terms on the family home, and vacation and rental properties.
- Clarify the terms of pension and profit-sharing plans.

Take it slowly during the predivorce period. You are only organizing the facts. The role of a financial planner such as myself is to give you the tools you'll need to get organized, and a practical understanding of how your net worth and income could be affected in a divorce. A qualified financial planner experienced in divorce planning can help you to get focused.

Dealing with Divorce

Women will deal with this first stage in a number of ways:

Denial

Jane was forty pounds overweight and she felt that losing some weight would make her husband become more interested in her. She lost the pounds with six months of exercise and a healthy diet, but the marital situation didn't change much. As a result, Jane became depressed, and during the next few months not only regained the weight she had lost, but added twenty-five more pounds. She felt even worse about herself. She and her husband did not seem to be connecting, and neither of them spoke directly about making a change. This was the silent time. Jane did not want to find out about the family finances, and she withdrew, insulating herself from their money situation and from her husband—a classic case of denial.

Focused and Energized

Jennifer, on the other hand, became focused. She reviewed the wills and other legal papers, photocopied important documents, and took courses to learn about computers, budgeting, and finances. She moved from a time of inertia into action. Her husband liked seeing her become involved. They began going to marriage counseling and started to take time for each other. Jennifer took a degenerating situation and, with action, persistence, and her husband's cooperation, was able to turn that situation around. Jennifer and her husband are still married.

Inaction

When Natalie got involved in the family finances, her husband became angry. Didn't she trust him? Didn't she think he was doing a good job? Money management wasn't her role in the marriage. She should spend more time with the children. She had never been good with numbers and would only "mess things up" if she got involved. He wanted control of the finances, so she backed off, retreating into her role as the trusting, financially passive wife, dreaming that everything would be fine, and that they would live happily ever after. Six months later, her husband filed for a divorce. He also took all the financial data with him. Natalie spent $15,000 with her attorney to re-create their financial condition, gathering bank statements, tax returns, and credit-card receipts. When Natalie came to me, she told me what had happened. Getting organized benefits you at any time in life.

Taking no action can also be a decision.

2. DECISION

The decision period is a time when a woman with divorce on her mind is living in an emotional minefield. Firmly focused on ending the marriage, you will experience a sense of relief, sadness, anger, or even exhilaration. This can be an extremely volatile time. Emotional swings include hope of reconciliation, denial, feelings of betrayal, and immobilization from the fear of loneliness, anger, and concern over finances. You might resort to compensatory behaviors such as overspending and running up credit card balances. Chronic depression is sometimes capable of triggering suicidal tendencies.

If you have reached this stage and have not yet seen a financial planner, do so. The planner can assist you in several ways, including preparing the *financial affidavit* you will need and providing a record-keeping system to track all expenses and income. Attorneys will often hand you a package of forms to fill out, bewildering questions to answer, and data to gather. Overwhelmed, you might easily agree to let the attorney do it, and you will pay dearly for the service. A financial planner can help you organize this information in a methodical and meaningful way so that it can effectively be used by the attorney to establish historical spending patterns for the family. These patterns are essential to convince a judge or mediator of your need for temporary spousal maintenance and to determine your proposed postdivorce budget.

The decision period is one of the most important times in the divorce process for you to become involved and to take charge.

Work with an attorney to get the terms of your separation established properly from the beginning. Have your facts in order. Be organized.

Judges have a hard time denying your motion for temporary support if you can provide them with detailed information about your income and your expenses. It helps your credibility to have an outside specialist such as a CDFA® work with you to organize and audit this information. Financial information is also valuable for your husband to have at the onset of the divorce. He probably has no idea how all the money he puts into the account each month is really spent. This is the time for you to be honest about how much money is involved in running the family.

A qualified financial planner knows about budgets and cash-control systems. This is a specialized area of financial planning. He or she can help you get organized for the next phase of data-gathering on the valuation of assets, pension plans, and tax issues. If you are constantly worrying about money, your decisions may be clouded.

Your divorce could easily be the biggest financial decision of your life. You can do a lot of this organizing of information yourself and save money for the later stages of your divorce process.

During the decision period, I encourage you to see a therapist. If you are an economically disadvantaged homemaker or changing careers, I recommend you visit a career advisor. (See appendix A for a sample career report.) During this time, you will be confronted by a lot of information and decision-making regarding parenting plans, budgeting, schooling, and career choices. It is easy to become overwhelmed and immobilized. If you can afford to hire a team of professionals to assist you in your divorce process, I guarantee you will be more content with your settlement and find it easier to accept your compromises. If you cannot afford these services, do some research. Join a self-help group such as Divorce Lifeline, go to the library, and search the Internet. You will find Web sites and publications listed in the resources section of this book to help you in your research.

Remember, the Clock Is Ticking

Don't call your attorney ten times a day for small things. Every time he consults with you on the phone, every time he communicates with you by e-mail, his clock is running, and you will be charged for every minute he spends on your case. Instead, make a list of the questions you want to ask. When he gives you an answer, feed it back to him with the statement, "Now, do I understand you to say . . ." Keep a notebook of all phone calls, e-mails, meeting notes, lists of documents exchanged, organized by date. This chronological journal will become invaluable as you move through your dissolution process.

Later in the book, I talk about interviewing the attorney, what questions to ask, and how to get started. Now is the time to consider when to see an attorney and the level of urgency in your situation. Everyone's circumstances are different, but I will describe two common experiences.

Matt and Julie have been married for thirty-two years and have three grown children. She is a schoolteacher, and he is an engineering manager at a local aeronautics firm. During the last few years of their marriage, they have grown apart. Julie has become more active in politics, bicycle riding, hiking, and traveling. She has met someone else who shares many of the same interests, and has decided she wants a divorce. Matt is very depressed, the children are angry, but Julie is committed to creating a lifestyle with the freedom to pursue her own interests. Still, she does not want an adversarial divorce and is willing to go slowly.

They have agreed to separate, with Julie moving into a two-bedroom condo for six months. Julie will take furniture and personal belongings from their house to furnish the condo. During that time, they will continue to deposit their payroll checks into the same joint checking account, and Matt will pay the household bills, including the rent on Julie's condo. Each will take $2,000 for personal spending money from the joint account each month and set up separate checking accounts for their personal expenses. They have agreed that any debt they incur during this time will be considered separate debts.

Both Matt and Julie have agreed to take a time-out in their marriage. Neither party will file for divorce. I would expect that one or both of them will do some research about divorce, the process, legal separation, **community property, separate property,** and many other issues. In this case, there is no rush to meet with the attorneys. Matt and Julie aren't facing any significant legal or financial issues at this time—their issues are mainly emotional and personal. Time apart is what they need to evaluate how to go forward with dignity and mutual respect.

Ken, fifty-seven, and Carolyn, forty-eight, have been married for fifteen years. Carolyn met Ken just as Ken's first marriage was ending. Ken has built a career in pharmaceutical sales and travels 70 percent of the time. Carolyn gave up her career in hotel management first to help raise Ken's children from his previous marriage—now college graduates and out on their own—as well as to be a stay-at-home mother raising their own two young children.

Carolyn suspects Ken is having an affair. When confronted, he denies any outside relationship. Carolyn gives him the benefit of the doubt. One day, while going through his briefcase, she finds a love letter from Gloria. When Carolyn shows him the letter, Ken tells her their marriage is over. The situation escalates into a screaming match until Carolyn, angry and hurt, tells Ken to get out.

Ken packs his bags and leaves, finding a three-bedroom condo for himself. He immediately begins spending money to furnish his new home using their savings. Carolyn has always paid the household bills from their joint checking account. Within a few weeks, she sees checks and credit card statements for new furniture, kitchen appliances, bedding, and other household goods. When she questions him, he tells her this divorce will be different. He is not going to lose his children and his money. She can go get a job. In a matter of two days, Ken has opened a separate checking account and is depositing his employment check into that account. He tells Carolyn he will pay the mortgage and the utilities bills at the house and give her a check for $2,000 per month as an allowance to pay her other bills. He has taken all of their financial and tax records out of the house and changed his mailing address. Ken is making it clear to Carolyn that he is going to control his divorce through money.

Carolyn needs to see an attorney immediately to protect herself financially. The attorney can tell her what her rights are from the beginning—how she can access cash for temporary support in the form of maintenance and child support and how quickly she can expect to receive the money. If there is a need for a restraining order, it can be put into place at the time of filing for divorce. It is clear that Ken is going to try to control Carolyn and her lifestyle by putting constraints on how she spends money and limiting her access to it. He could remove her name from credit cards, close credit accounts, and move swiftly to "teach her a lesson."

Controlling a spouse by using money with threats, isolation, embarrassment when she can't pay her bills, and bounced checks are all ways women are held "economically captive" in marriages. If there are issues regarding domestic abuse, child custody, anger, or the safety of any or all of the family members in the divorce process, it is often acted out around money issues as well.

In the end, no one knows your husband better than you do. Stop for a moment and think about your situation. Take a deep breath and sit quietly for an hour and think about your best course of action. Stop arguing and get focused. Consider how your husband has dealt with money and other control issues in your marriage. Once you are calm, write down a plan of action for yourself. Outline your emotional and financial concerns—start with the daily, then monthly issues for you and your children. Don't worry about the big financial issues right now—who will get what, who will stay in the house, for example. Think very short-term at this stage.

If money is on the move or you have no access to money or the relationship turns threatening or abusive, call the attorney *right away*. Otherwise, take a little time.

3. Final Acceptance

When you recognize the inevitability of the divorce, you have reached a milestone. A property settlement is about to be accepted, a counteroffer is being considered, or a court date is near. Intense emotions are buffeting you again. You are being asked to make decisions, compromises that will permanently affect the nature of your new lifestyle.

This is a time when you may find yourself changing your mind, vacillating in your decisions, getting angry, or going into hiding. What you need is your second wind to cross the finish line. This is where all that early organizing pays off. If you have been doing your homework and working with your therapist, financial planner, and attorney, your hard work and training will begin to pay off. This does not mean that this is an easy time for you. It's just that things are coming together, as they should.

You'll be leaning on your financial planner, whose role it is to help you accept responsibility for the outcome of your divorce by means of your active involvement in understanding and selecting a settlement strategy. **An effective strategy must integrate the division of assets, debts, and future income as well as incorporate your career and parenting plans.**

If you don't settle, an experienced divorce financial planner can provide expert witness testimony for you in court. This stage is a particularly active time in the divorce process, and it represents the culmination of everyone's efforts. The goal is a negotiated settlement, which means a compromise. If either party cannot agree to settle, then everyone needs to prepare for court. Typically, this increases such costs as additional attorney's fees, expert testimony fees, and court costs. Depending on the assets involved and areas of disagreement, additional costs may arise from the use of forensic accountants to ferret out hidden accounts, business valuators, tax consultants, or other specialists. You will need to discuss your situation with a qualified financial planner and your attorney to determine these needs and estimate their costs. Most of the services are billed to you on an hourly basis. Some may be shared between you and your ex-spouse.

4. Mourning

Typified by a sense of failure, loneliness, depression, and low self-esteem, this is the period when you feel weary after having fought hard in the settlement negotiations, in child custody debates, and in finalizing parenting plans. The reality of the divorce has set in—emotionally and financially. You will be particularly vulnerable during this stage. Up to this time we have talked about what-if scenarios. Now we are talking about reality— what is. You will have a new legal status, be filing your income tax return alone, creating your own individual financial statement, having your own credit, and becoming sole owner of investment and retirement assets.

A financial planner will help you to set up the post-divorce budget and a cash-control monitoring system. A cash-control system is simply the method you will use to balance income and expenses in conjunction with your budget. (See chapters 6 and 7 for pointers on creating a budget and a cash-control system.) You probably didn't get everything you asked for on the terms you requested. Since you may be disappointed and disheartened, you should continue seeing your therapist as you work on emotional rebuilding. Your financial planner will be advising you on how to:

- Create a specific strategy to pay off the legal costs of your divorce
- Transfer assets
- Monitor career, education, and job exploration activities
- Prepare preliminary income tax projections for quarterly payments to the Internal Revenue Service
- Review appropriate investment decisions

5. Re-Equilibrium

This last emotional stage in the divorce process occurs when you accept your new life as a single person and let go of the anger you have for your spouse. You find yourself living your plans—personal and financial—and accepting responsibility for yourself.

You cannot expect to arrive at this last stage overnight. For some of my clients, this last stage is never fully reached. It takes time to heal at all levels, emotionally and financially. If there are children involved, I recommend postdivorce family counseling for the ex-spouse and children. Your legal documents don't begin to address the many questions and situations that are bound to arise in the postdivorce lifestyle. You can dramatically ease the tension and transfer period for your children by having a few joint sessions with a trained therapist who can work with all of you. Give yourself time to heal and adjust.

Before closing this chapter on the emotional stages of divorce, I want to share some questions many of my clients have posed when first faced with divorce. Each question-and-answer addresses an emotional aspect that is just as important as the legal or "technical" components involved in the divorce process. As you read through them, perhaps you will find answers to your own issues. Understanding these emotional factors will help you to deal more effectively with the other aspects of the issues.

MOST OFTEN ASKED QUESTIONS ABOUT DIVORCE

The following questions are typical of those my clients ask when they confront divorce. Many of the considerations in this chapter may never have occurred to you. If you are like most women who have reluctantly decided to end their marriage, you hope to bring it to a conclusion with the least amount of dissension. You want to get your fair share and start over. But it's not that simple, as you will see in later chapters.

1. Do I need an attorney?

A divorce is a civil action to terminate marriage, and the process is called *dissolution of marriage*.[2] Only one spouse needs to file (apply for the divorce), or you can both file as copetitioners. If you file, you are the petitioner or the plaintiff. If you are served (presented with a legal notice of intent to divorce) by your spouse, you are the respondent or defendant.

You can get divorced without an attorney,[3] but I would not recommend this unless the marriage has been a brief one and each of you has a career, few assets to worry about, and no children. As Danny DeVito said in the movie *The War of the Roses*:

> **"What's the moral? Maybe the moral is that a civilized divorce is a contradiction in terms."**

Are there really friendly divorces in which lawyers are not needed? The answer is, sometimes. Keep in mind, divorce is probably the biggest financial decision you are going to face. Simple missteps in filing a required form or failing to provide adequate documentation can derail the most sincere effort and throw your case out of court. I will discuss **mediation, collaborative law, arbitration,** and self-directed divorce as alternatives to the lawyer-managed process in the courts in chapter 3.

2. What if my spouse will not give me a divorce?

Don't you believe it. The judge grants a divorce, not your spouse. The divorce can be contested, and if so, you will have a hearing set with a judge in which each of you testify and then the judge decides how to finalize the dissolution. If the divorce is not contested, you can be divorced in ninety days in many states. I encourage you to go to the local library, bookstore, or state government Web site and gather information about divorce in your state. Also, visit a divorce court proceeding in your area for the experience and firsthand information, and perhaps observe your attorney in the courtroom before making a final selection decision.

3. Can I expect to get half of everything we own?

One of the most common misconceptions held by women when they enter divorce proceedings is that justice will prevail. They think it will be simple to end the relationship, and that money can make them whole. They think if they are divorcing a man with whom they have built up a comfortable net worth and there has been a growing income, it will naturally be divided equally, and each party will go on his or her way to a new life.

This is not necessarily so. Although **no-fault divorce**[4] exists, this is not the same as no-hassle divorce. With the enactment of no-fault laws, couples are now allowed to get a divorce for "irreconcilable differences." The purpose of these laws was to reduce the pain, indignity, and the perceived injustice of divorce. Moreover, I believe it has allowed the law to view marriage as an economic partnership. As such, the major issues center on who gets which assets. We are now working under laws that adhere to **equitable distribution** of assets. Prior to no-fault, women were getting support until remarriage or death. Today, support is provided for a stated number of years, and many women never collect it. The courts often do not help them, and if they do help, the financial cost to the woman may be greater than the support payments.

Women are also losing their children. Increasingly, men are seeking custody. Sometimes this is a clever ploy in the divorce process to use the offspring as leverage against the wife. Children can be viewed as weapons and become financial assets in the negotiations. On the other hand, many divorcing parents choose to have joint custody of their children, providing loving parents from separate households. The child-custody issue and the parenting plan is becoming the cultural atomic bomb of the twenty-first century.

4. We disagree on some items, but we do not want to go to court. How can we settle outside of court?

There are several ways to settle a divorce outside of court, and they are briefly: arbitration, negotiation, and mediation. I discuss each of these methods in chapter 3.

5. We plan to live apart for a while. Do we need a formal *separation agreement?*

Beware of living apart as a trial basis for divorce and not creating a separation agreement. The courts do look at how long the parties have lived apart and the scope of their reconciliation attempts when calculating spousal maintenance. **With an informal arrangement, neither party has a contractual basis for defending against unilateral changes in support payments, asset sales or transfers, debt management, or parenting arrangements.**

You should know that a separation agreement is a contract between a husband and a wife in which they agree to resolve such matters as property division, debts, custody, and support when they separate from each other. It is best to have an attorney draw up this agreement. You can agree to the division of property, and it can be binding on both parties in the event a divorce is the outcome of the separation. Income becomes separate property when two people are separated. If you are afraid that assets and income are disappearing and you don't trust your spouse, you would be better served to prepare for that at the beginning. A separation agreement will protect you from too many surprises later. You can work on the reconciliation, but don't allow your share of the marital assets to dissipate.

Each divorce is unique and needs to have its own financial plan. What works for one situation may or may not work in the next. Often couples separate and initially share income equally. Then the person providing the money usually starts to decrease the amount being passed to the other party. This can play havoc with a budget. You need to be able to depend on payments that have been based on a budget that the two of you worked out when you decided to separate. If the income stream is changed dramatically, you must be prepared to see an attorney and make a claim for more temporary spousal maintenance. There is no guarantee that you will ever get all that you request. Chapter 7, which is devoted to the budget process, will help you anticipate your needs realistically. In it you'll find information on determining historical spending, getting the funds requested for temporary spousal maintenance, and the postdivorce budget.

I definitely recommend the budget process whether your separation is formal or informal. Be prepared. You may not have enough time to respond if your husband suddenly decides to file. Also, historical personal spending in the marriage, whether it is more or less than what should be allowed in the separation, is fair game for either side to use as the standard that should be applied during separation and postdivorce.

6. We agreed that I would give up my career while the children were in school. My role was first as a wife and mother. My husband's role was to earn the money for our family. What now?

This statement expresses the marital philosophy that has dominated our culture for decades. For many couples this statement represents the basic foundation of the family partnership that was set up by the couple at the time of their marriage and during the planning of their family. Unfortunately, this arrangement is not well supported in our society, either with the payment of maintenance or alimony to the nonearning spouse or in the collection of child support.

Maintenance is viewed as temporary support in most parts of the country and is used to rehabilitate the nonworking spouse so she can enter the job market and earn a living. Courts may also view maintenance as compensatory. In such cases it is allocated on the basis of compensating the nonworking spouse for relinquishing her potential career pay in favor of performing domestic work for the family. Some states base maintenance on the economic lifestyle the couple enjoyed while married, others determine maintenance based on the length of marriage, and there are large variances in between. I will talk more about maintenance later, particularly in chapter 8. Find out what your state provides in the way of maintenance definitions to see what you might expect.

Unless your marriage is long term, meaning thirty years or more, and you are in your late fifties or have health problems, the chances of long-term maintenance through the court system are slim. A three- to ten-year maintenance schedule is much more likely. It will terminate at death or remarriage of the receiving spouse, the money allocated is likely to be modified if the financial circumstances change for the paying party, and the amount often decreases over the span of the short maintenance period.

Earnings Disparity

Creating a win-win settlement with the couple that has a disparity of earnings is one of the most difficult dissolution cases of all. Chapter 8 and appendix A focus on this type of case, and I will provide you with some creative ways to handle the disparity of earnings issue in a complete sample case study. Let me give you a brief example of the problems involved.

John, forty-seven, and Jane, forty-five, have been married for eighteen years and have three children ages eight, fourteen, and seventeen. John is a successful physician earning upwards of $450,000 per year. Jane was a nurse when she met John, who was in medical school at the time. She worked as a nurse for the first three years of their marriage and helped John through medical school by earning the family income. When they decided to have a family, John and Jane, who had both been raised in traditional families, felt the mother should stay home with the children. Jane did volunteer work at the school and church and maintained the home for the family—an arrangement that suited both John and Jane.

Over the years John worked long hours to become a partner in his clinic as well as one of the owners of his office. Now firmly established in his medical practice, John has grown apart from Jane. He wants a divorce, but is committed to staying involved with his children.

The couple has built a substantial retirement fund of $350,000, owns a home valued at $800,000, and has investment assets of $125,000. Their $550,000 mortgage is their primary liability, with house payments of $2,800 per month.

John wants Jane to go back to work and earn money to support herself after the divorce. John also wants shared custody of the children and plans to spend more time with them. He doesn't see any reason why Jane cannot go back to work and contribute to her support. Jane is devastated and is having a difficult time dealing with the emotional and financial realities of her divorce, while wanting to continue as the primary caretaker of the children.

On the advice of her attorney and financial planner, Jane sees a career counselor over the next few months and decides she would like to pursue a career as a medical librarian. This will mean another three years of schooling. With no experience, Jane can expect a starting salary in the $40,000 to $50,000 range. She is concerned about attending school full time at her age while keeping the home going and raising their children. A live-in nanny to help with the child care and housekeeping responsibilities is a good idea, but will cost her $1,800 per month.

Who will pay for all of these expenses? John, reluctantly. And then there is college funding for their oldest child. He is planning to attend a school in the East where the tuition and dormitory costs are estimated to be $60,000 per year. Currently $25,000 has been put aside toward college expenses for their son in a special fund.

By now you should be getting the picture. We have two adults and three children who were consumers, with the surplus after family expenses going to pay for the purchase of an office building, an expensive mortgage, and a free-spending lifestyle for everybody. Two households will not be able to live in the same style as the single unit did. Both John and Jane want continued expensive vacations, club memberships, regular dining out at expensive restaurants, and designer clothing for all.

In many states, the separation period can last up to one year after filing before a scheduled court date arrives or the mediation is complete with a final divorce decree. A postdivorce budget takes into account college funding for Jane and the couple's son, and a monthly salary and benefits for the nanny. Meanwhile, John has rented a three-bedroom condominium so that he will have a home for the children when they visit him. He is considering asking for at least one of the children to live with him, making his home the child's primary residence.

Men also often experience a short-term decrease in their standard of living after divorce, but it is usually one-half to one-third of the loss experienced by women and tends to be shorter-lived. This demonstrates the skewed arithmetic of the typical divorce that results in unfair property division. Undoubtedly, it will happen with John and Jane.

7. If he wants out, why can't he pay for it?

The intent of new laws enacted during the past twenty-five years has been to make divorce fairer for women. The no-fault laws, now on the books in every state, were designed to allow either spouse to sue for divorce without showing cause, which, for example, could be adultery, abuse, or mental cruelty. They were meant to take the public shame and blame out of splitting up and to provide a safe escape from an unhappy marriage. Yet, for many women, no-fault filing has been expensive. It has done away with the concept of the "injured party." Historically, if the injured person was the wife, she would be compensated with property or money. No-fault also removed an important bargaining chip for the woman—the basis upon which she would agree to give the husband a divorce in exchange for a fair settlement.

We are now in the era of "equitable distribution laws." This means, as I said earlier, that marriage is viewed as an economic partnership. The idea is that contributions have been made to the partnership inside and outside the marriage and that assets should be divided equitably to account for these contributions, no matter whose name is on a deed or investment account.

The experts will tell you that the concept of "equitable" is indeed a slippery one that leaves too much to interpretation by judges and attorneys. **The way property is registered legally can be crucial to a partner in a marriage.** There are nine community property states: Arizona, California, Idaho, Louisiana, Nevada, New Mexico, Texas, Washington, and Wisconsin. If you commingle your assets in these states, they are deemed to be community property and can be divided fifty-fifty. Even if you have kept the registration separate, the property can be shared or your community assets can be allocated disproportionately so that there is an equitable distribution of property. Judges have wide discretion in dividing assets and setting maintenance or alimony schedules.

The sooner the nonearning spouse gathers the relevant financial data and creates an income strategy as part of her financial plan, the sooner she can assume control of her life. Too many times I see women who put their heads in the sand. They think that justice will prevail and that they can count on maintenance because, after all, it's only fair.

8. What about keeping the family residence?

I devote a substantial section of chapter 11 to this decision-making process. There are income tax issues and home-maintenance costs to think about, mortgage payments and condominium dues, and the possibility of a soft real estate market affecting resale value. There are many factors to consider before either partner decides to keep the house. It may prove to be better if the original home is sold and two new homes are purchased.

9. Won't I automatically get custody of the children, since I have devoted much of my adult life to being a mom?

So, you say to yourself, "Naturally, I will get the kids." There are never any guarantees that this will happen. More and more often, fathers are asking for joint custody, often hiring a nanny to help care for the children when they are with him. This means less money to the ex-spouse for child support. At the same time it means you have time to pursue outside work and further education—in other words, develop a career plan. Often the replacement nanny could be earning more than the ex-spouse does in her first postdivorce job. The courts are getting more involved in determining what arrangements are in the best interests of the children as they relate to child custody, support, and visitation arrangements. In many states the divorcing parties are required to file a temporary parenting plan with the *petition* for divorce as well as an order for temporary child support. A permanent order is filed with the final decree. The child support needs to be reviewed periodically to adjust for rising costs and a change of circumstances. A number of states have standard guidelines to use in determining the amount of child support required from each parent to maintain the care of dependent children. Talk to your attorney or financial advisor to find out how child support is determined in your state.

10. How can I create a win-win divorce?

I see clients all the time who tell me they want a friendly divorce, with no attorneys. They will do their own divorce with a do-it-yourself kit, or they will seek a mediator and no attorneys. **Beware of trying to handle the entire divorce by yourself.** The laws are ever-changing and complicated. I will say it again: divorce could be the most important financial transaction of your lifetime. Don't trust the process to someone lacking the knowledge to give good advice, including yourself. Even when using a mediator, take your nonbinding agreement to an outside family law attorney to be reviewed before you sign the document.

If you and your spouse decide on a do-it-yourself strategy, you can find many Internet sites that sell kits advertised as compliant with your state's laws. There are also a number of software programs available to help you create legal documents and calculate asset values. These aids are only as good as the information you input and are not sophisticated enough to address every situation. I recommend you review the results with a qualified financial planner and attorney before signing the final agreement.

11. How can I make sure I get the crystal and china we received at our wedding as a gift? It is mine, mine, mine.

Thousands of dollars can be spent on dividing up the personal belongings. Some people get everything in the house appraised, or they draw numbers and alternate choosing an item, keeping track of the cost. In some cases, one will go out and buy new furniture to set up a new home, justifying the cost from community assets, and leaving the other spouse with the old. Try to be reasonable. This is an area of contention involving both sentiment and practicality, and people often torture and harass each other.

Paying an attorney $300 to $400 an hour to divide up your stuff can become very expensive. Tell your grievances to your psychiatrist, not your attorney. Give the attorney your list of requests, but not expensive hours of explanations. Hire an appraiser to give you a value on antiques and other personal belongings. Equitable divorce requires compromise— separate the materialistic from the sentimental.

12. I married for life. What about our marriage contract?

"I have fulfilled my role as a wife and mother. He was supposed to take care of me financially." I hear statements like this all of the time. "At least 50 percent of the assets and half of his income should be mine for life. We made a commitment. He wants out, but financially I deserve half of his income for my life." Well, it doesn't work like that. Marriage is not viewed as a life sentence, and there are no guarantees. Several factors are taken into account when dividing the assets and the income, including the size of the estate, the duration of the marriage, earnings and the disparity of earnings, separate and community assets, and the age and health of the parties. You can eliminate the word "should" from your vocabulary when divorce starts. (Distribution of assets is taken up in subsequent chapters, and an example is provided in appendix A.)

The sooner the family is realistic about finances and the new lifestyle, the better life will become. Sit down with your children and discuss budgets, work responsibilities, visitation with the other spouse, and other issues.

13. I don't want a major court battle and conflict. Can't we be reasonable?

Statistically, fewer than 5 percent of divorces are actually settled in the courtroom by a judge. Most are settled in negotiations prior to a court battle. That doesn't mean you won't be in front of the judge for various motions along the way, to set a child support and maintenance schedule or to interpret areas of dispute, for example. Many women dislike conflict and will do whatever they can to avoid it. They may hire an attorney to do their dirty work or just become passive, expecting the "right" thing to happen in their case. Many men, on the other hand, look at divorce as a business transaction. They want to get to the bottom line quickly and get the divorce over with. If they do get emotional, they still want the divorce over quickly and inexpensively. They are resistant to high legal fees and get angry if the wife can't trust them about the finances and the final settlement. As you can see, this is a dangerous scenario, and there is a delicate balance to be maintained between the parties.

Divorce does not need to be a wholly negative experience. While it generally is not a positive act, people who are divorcing want to believe in a positive outcome. Certainly the person initiating the divorce action feels this way. It makes a big difference whether you are negative or positive about your future when it comes to dealing with the emotional aspects of divorce. Often, a psychologist can help you cope with the emotional turmoil divorce unleashes.

You are separating yourself from your spouse, legally. I must make this warning to women: **If you believe your husband will be generous because he is feeling guilty, forget it. Guilt, or the G word, will only take you so far.** After that, you are in a business transaction, and men can and do separate business from their emotions. That is what the business world requires, whether you are male or female.

This chapter has been designed to make you aware of what you are facing—some of the questions, decisions, considerations, strategies, self-protections, safeguards, and personal planning you have to undertake to emerge from a divorce, if not a big winner, at least with a fair share of the assets you and your spouse have accumulated during your marriage.

This book is intended to give you all the information you will need to prepare for divorce. If it accomplishes nothing else but to serve as a warning that you—the woman, the person who avoids conflict, the one who believes in fairness—must remove your rose-colored glasses and fend for yourself if you are going to get what you deserve, then I will have accomplished my objective.

Remember, the system does not protect you. Your own sharpened sense of survival and your diligence will.

Start to get organized. Research and read everything you can find about dissolution in your state. Find the divorce process that makes the most sense for you, and as always, *Trust, but verify!*

3

How to Choose the Divorce Process That Best Suits You

The meeting of two personalities is like the contact of two chemical substances: if there is any reaction, both are transformed.

—C. G. JUNG

Women typically go into marriage with the view of entering a long-term partnership of sharing emotions, money, child-raising, and retirement. Most women I get to know are beset by emotional trauma over their divorces. While fighting to regain a positive self-image, a divorcing woman often feels pressured to keep up the "supermom" role, must handle problems by herself without the help of her spouse, and often has to contend with a husband who's suddenly become hostile. She feels like she's sliding on thin ice, aware she's headed for disaster, but helpless to change her direction.

Women who have built their own careers and are the primary wage earner for the family frequently become angry about their spouses' lack of significant earnings. If there are children at home, these women are often torn between not having enough time with the family and the pressures of work. I see more and more women in my practice who are divorcing and leaving behind a "displaced husband." Similar to the "displaced homemaker" female counterpart, this is a man who, having abandoned a career to care for the children, must now reenter the job market with outdated or inadequate skills. The issue of disparity of earnings is not gender-driven. More dual-career couples are getting out of first marriages and going into second marriages. Men and women are on the move.

In divorce there is always the sense of the one who leaves and the one who stays behind. The woman who stays behind is usually more disoriented than a husband who has left. She's the one who is reminded of the failure of her marriage by the all-too-familiar physical surroundings. Every picture on the wall, each candid photo, his discarded pair of golf shoes, the basketball hoop over the garage door that somehow never got straightened, or the ragged sweater he insisted on wearing, are searing reminders of ruined hopes and broken promises for an enduring future. Her expectation of permanency is shattered by divorce.

I've already described the emotional stages of divorce in chapter 2. It is important for both you and your spouse to acknowledge those stages, so that you will be better prepared to manage your new life. Once you come to terms with the emotional issues—at least enough to look outward and ask, "What next?"—it's time to consider what process will best meet your needs in the divorce.

Let's look at Janice, whom I introduced in chapter 2. She has to decide which method of divorce is best for her. I will describe the advantages and disadvantages of each method a little later in this chapter.

How did Janice finally get out of her maze and create a life for herself and the children when she felt so lousy, depressed, inadequate, and out of control? The answer to that question involves the information presented in the balance of this chapter. Janice had to go through the process of learning the steps and making choices that fit her own situation.

I had to review some divorce terminology with Janice first: equitable distribution, separate and community property, mediation, collaborative law, arbitration, *litigation,* and *pro se divorce.* I pointed out to her that the state in which a divorcing person lives may make a difference in divorce strategy. She needed to know the laws and statutes in her state as well as those in other states where she may have lived with her husband.

As I advised Janice to do, you should go to the library, bookstore, local support group, or on the Internet to find out what it means to get a divorce in the state where you live. You can learn the terminology, the process, the time frame, and what to expect from the court system. Using the information from these resources, you can create an overall framework for your own process. By learning about your state's laws, you can become your attorney's most important paralegal. This can save hundreds of dollars in legal fees, you will be more informed about the choices you have, and you will have more personal control over your divorce.

Divorce laws are documented in each state's published laws, usually in a section called Dissolution of Marriage Statutes, or some similar title. Many states now provide free access to local laws on their legislatures' Web sites. Some state-specific factors you need to learn about are:

- *Waiting period.* What is the minimum residency in the state required of either spouse to be eligible to file for divorce?
- *Cooling-off period.* What is the required time between filing (the complaint date) and the date of divorce?
- **Fault.** If your state is not exclusively a no-fault jurisdiction, what are the accepted types of fault—abandonment or abuse, for example? You should know what role fault plays in property division, child custody and support payments, alimony or maintenance. If there are guidelines for determining maintenance, do they vary by county, judge, court jurisdiction, or geographic area?
- **Mediation.** Is this process used? If it is required, what are the requirements? If you are going to use this technique, what are the qualifications required of divorce mediators? Get a list of qualified mediators in your area and find out how many cases they have handled and what attorneys they have worked with.
- **Arbitration.** If you are considering arbitration, look for the same information listed above for mediation.
- **Collaborative Law.** Follow the same guidelines as in mediation.

Most statutes will cite the law on a topic and then provide short summary descriptions of cases that have come down from appellate courts to interpret that law. Reviewing the statutes is a good way to get an idea of how the law is applied in your state. For instance, a divorce statute may list factors the judge considers when dividing property in a divorce. The statute does not say that the same factors must be considered and weighted the same way when spouses divide property themselves, versus mediation, or collaborative law. The judge provides a fallback position if the spouses cannot agree. For example, the statutes define marital and separate property. The spouses may agree to define these terms the same way the statutes do, but they are also free to define them in their own way, subject to the judge's approving the settlement. This often happens when the couple uses a mediator or collaborative law. In these settings, you get to own your own compromises that you tailor to meet your individual needs.

DIFFERENCES BETWEEN STATES ARE IMPORTANT

Divorce laws differ from state to state. There are a number of resources I recommend that you utilize to gain a better understanding of your state's divorce laws and procedures:

- State and local bar associations.
- Women's law centers (these are often associated with a college).

- Divorce cases at your local courthouse, where you can sit in as an observer. Court schedules are often published in newspapers, or call the office of the Clerk of the Court. Plan to be there three to five days.
- Local public libraries and university law libraries.
- Books on divorce and family law. Go to *www.amazon.com* and do a search using key words like divorce, family law, dissolution, and the name of your state.
- Internet Web sites focused on divorce. Two popular research sites are *www.westlaw.com* and *www.lexisnexis.com*. These are subscription-based sites, but there are a number of free sites as well.

You will find a list of sites in resources at the back of this book.

WHICH METHOD IS BEST FOR YOUR SITUATION?

To help you decide on what method best suits your needs, here is a summary of the different processes, and some examples of how they work.

Mediation

This is a voluntary and confidential process in which an impartial third-party trained mediator helps disputing parties reach a mutually agreeable settlement. It can be an ideal process for custody issues, because it is less contentious than court proceedings. Mediation can be conducted by one professional acting in the guiding role, and the mediator may be an attorney, financial planner, CPA, psychologist, or social worker. In some divorce mediations, there are two professionals acting as comediators. You will often see a counselor working with an attorney to help the parties negotiate their property settlement as well as create a mutually acceptable parenting plan.

Mediators' qualifications vary widely. The method of conflict resolution may also vary. The following scenarios illustrate two common examples of mediation.

Scenario One

The mediator will have the wife and her attorney in one room and the husband and his attorney in another room, and the mediator will shuttle back and forth trying to reach an agreement between the parties. The mediator will probably be a retired judge or an experienced family law attorney. The mediation can be scheduled for an entire day. The goal is to negotiate until a settlement is reached. This agreement will be binding if read into the record.

With this method, it is typical that each client will have his/her own experts who will provide support for his/her position. The attorney is the client's advocate. The *discovery* work will have been done and valuations of all assets established, but there could be a disagreement between the two sides. Income tax implications have been analyzed, and a division of assets and income is being proposed by each side. In this method of mediation, the pressure is very intense and focused on the attempt to come up with a settlement by the end of the day. You need to be organized, know your position, and be rested for the marathon ahead. This can be a very effective method for reaching an agreement if you are prepared and ready to make some informed compromises—compromises that you can own.

Each attorney will submit a brief to the mediator one week before the meeting. Upon reaching an agreement, you can each read the other side's proposal. I think of it as a "trial run" for court. Nothing presented in mediation can be used by the other side in court unless it is already in the form of an *interrogatory* or *deposition*.

Scenario Two

Other times a mediator will meet with you and your spouse at the same time for a series of meetings, bringing in experts on an as-needed basis. You and your spouse will share the costs of these experts. This type of mediation works well if you are a strong negotiator and you know and understand the facts of your financial life and family lifestyle. This type of mediation does not work well when there are issues of domestic abuse or drug or alcohol problems.

If your spouse has been planning the divorce, be cautious. You may be told this process will be less costly. **Do not be rushed into this type of mediation** until you are organized, have gathered your facts, and have an attorney and financial planner as backup to help you prepare for each mediation session with questions and documentation. There should be a set agenda for each meeting. The parenting plan, temporary spousal budgets, housing issues, disclosure of all assets, liabilities, analysis of pension plans and retirement accounts, and college funding are all examples of issues that might be put on the agenda. With each session, you build toward a settlement.

When you get to the financial issues, try not to make final decisions on each item until you can see the economic impact of the whole settlement.

If your husband has managed the money and is a controller, he may want you to go to mediation with just the two of you without your lawyers from the start. In this type of mediation, the mediator is a neutral party and not your advocate. The mediator may or may not be an attorney experienced in family law. In addition, too many times these mediators are not trained in financial matters and are relying on the two of you for this verification.

Do not allow yourself to be blackmailed into this approach "for the sake of the children" when you don't have the knowledge or expertise to negotiate effectively for yourself. Do not go into this type of mediation until you have done your own research—on the process, the costs, the mediator, and the type of mediation. Interview more than one mediator. Talk to at least two references who have successfully used their services to completion.

The mediator is not there to verify the reliability or accuracy of the financial information provided. Financial planners can be useful in both types of mediation by designing financial models for all parties to help arrive at an equitable division of property and income. Always have a potential settlement reviewed by an attorney before signing any paperwork. Make sure your financial planner looks at the total proposal and gives you input on what post divorce life will look like for you and your spouse. He or she will help you optimize the best tax, cash flow, and asset distribution for each of you before you sign any agreement. This will help you to accept and understand your financial compromises—and there will be compromises.

The biggest problem I see with this type of mediation is the lack of verification of the financial data. Your spouse wants you to trust that all the information presented is accurate and complete. Too many times I have seen the wife negotiating away assets to protect custody of the children, only to discover that the parenting plan can be changed and the mediated settlement cannot. For mediation to work, there needs to be an equalization of emotional and financial power.

If you cannot do this for yourself, facilitated by the mediator, you may need help to present your proposal. You may not know what you don't know until it is too late. Issues like the division of the pension or Social Security benefits, disclosure of all assets, and the potential tax liability on receiving certain assets are areas in which a lack of sophistication can cause postdivorce difficulties for women.

The mediation is private, but privacy may not be what you need to get a fair settlement. If you cannot come to an agreement, you can litigate. The cost of mediation is usually between $150 and $400 per hour. There will be costs to create the agreement and additional costs if there is a conflict when drafting the dissolution agreement. Such conflicts could be arbitrated by the mediator and will result in additional fees. It can take months before the final agreement is drafted and filed with the court.

Mediation is only as good as the professionals you hire and the level of cooperation between you and your spouse. In a contentious divorce, the only alternative may be to go to court and let a judge make the final decisions. I do recommend that you try to do at least one mediation before going to *trial*. At the very least, you will have insight into your spouse's position when you finally go to court. Keep in mind that what is presented and discussed in mediation is not necessarily what will be argued in the court in front of the judge. You cannot disclose where your negotiations fell through in the mediation in court. Your attorney will present evidence in a controlled, structured environment. This is not the place for free conversation, but an environment in which you answer questions when asked. The judge will make the final, binding decision.

You must have a mediator with the skills and tools to get stalled negotiations back on track. The mediation setting can turn into a forum for both parties to vent their anger, frustration, guilt, fear, sadness, and sense of loss. These feelings need to be acknowledged. The skilled mediator will help the husband and wife focus on an effective resolution and channel their energies towards a negotiated and comprehensive settlement. The job of the mediator for women is to address their fears and to help them understand the financial aspects of their pending single lifestyle. A skilled mediator will focus the parties on the conclusion of the mediated settlement rather than on divisive issues that delay cooperation.

Mediation is an intense time of negotiation between the divorcing parties. A major advantage of mediation is that there are no witnesses, evidence, or a public trial. The husband and wife are in complete control of their process. For women who have primarily been caretakers, this can be intimidating. If this is the case, the mediator needs to be certain the less knowledgeable spouse seeks legal and financial help so that she understands the economic implications of the proposed settlement.

As an experienced financial planner, I would enter the negotiations at this point. Typically, the attorney or one of the parties will be meeting with me to determine the economic impact of the future settlement. We will guide the woman to understand and focus on her new lifestyle.

If mediation is the choice you make to dissolve your marriage, it is important that you bring to the negotiating table all of the "lost assets" (that is, the financial advantages you had access to in the marriage) that need to be weighed for reimbursement to you in the settlement. One of these is the "lost opportunity" cost of your marriage.

Arbitration

In an arbitrated dissolution, couples choose a third party who acts as a judge and makes decisions about contested issues in the case. You may have agreed on many of the issues in your divorce and only need help on a few items. I think it is always best to have your parenting plan completed before you arbitrate, mediate, or litigate so the children are not being used as a financial asset in the negotiations. The process of arbitration is generally faster, less costly, and more private than court proceedings. You can expect to pay $200 to $450 per hour for the arbitrator, and the sessions can be held over several weeks or completed during an all-day session.

The decisions reached in arbitration are generally binding and hard to appeal. Few states allow binding arbitration on child custody or support. This process allows spouses to choose a neutral third party who makes decisions on such sticky issues as who gets the summer house, who gets the yacht club membership, or who will pay for the children's private education. Arbitration is usually a last resort.

The American Academy of Matrimonial Attorneys has been developing a model law for divorce arbitration that different states can adopt. It is particularly popular in North Carolina and Michigan, which have enacted statutes in recent years specifying how arbitration can be used in family law disputes.

Another benefit is privacy. Clients do not have to file financial disclosures or sensitive affidavits in court, where the media and public has access to them. This method is being used more often with high-profile divorces.

When Jack Welch, former CEO of General Electric, and his second wife, Jane Beasley, were divorced, she brought to the courtroom a detailed list of executive corporate perks Jack enjoyed with his position and those that he took into retirement. This information was just what the media needed to create a corporate scandal. The SEC investigated GE when this information became public. Going to court and making the records public is becoming a new negotiating tool for corporate wives as they try and get a fair settlement.

Collaborative Law

"Collaborative law" is the name given to the cooperative approach between attorneys, clients, and professionals providing support services. All work together to resolve the problems resulting from the breakdown of the relationship. Each person retains a trained collaborative lawyer to advise and assist in negotiating an agreement on all issues. All negotiations take place in a settlement meeting that both clients and both attorneys attend. The lawyers and shared experts cannot go to court or threaten to go to court. They normally sign a formal agreement to that effect. Spouses also sign a contract with their lawyers agreeing not to litigate. Settlement is the only agenda. It works only if mutual respect is given and received.

No one has more power than anyone else. One person may have more knowledge, which is shared during meetings in order to create constructive solutions.

If the couple cannot reach an agreement, they must find new lawyers and experts and start the process again. This can be costly. If you are an economically disadvantaged spouse, it may prove difficult to find the resources to start over. Go to *www.collaborativefamilylawassociation.com* to get answers to frequently asked questions about collaborative law. If you have a controlling husband, do not be manipulated into choosing this process for your divorce.

Pro se Divorce

This is the method in which you choose not to use an attorney. Most people who go through a divorce have lawyers, but pro se divorce is a growing trend. Some studies have suggested as many as 50 percent of the parties in divorce proceedings do not hire an attorney. "Starter marriages," marriages that begin and end before the parties are age thirty and where there are no children, may contribute to this figure. (I will discuss these in more detail in chapter 4.)

If there are assets, make sure you understand the income tax implications when transferring those with a low *cost basis.* Such assets appear to be more valuable than they really are because the taxes due at time of sale substantially reduce the value you will actually receive. You will also want to understand the difference between marital and separate assets and the legal significance of each. Know about retirement assets and other employee benefits, like stock options. There are many different types of retirement plans, and I have seen spouses trade a house for a pension plan without understanding the financial aspects of this exchange. Finally, be aware of joint credit card debt. Get a credit report before finalizing the divorce so you are sure of all the liabilities.

Pro se divorce usually costs $1,500 to $2,500 per spouse. The couple negotiates the property settlement and other details, and the court approves the agreement in a short, simple hearing. Both parties must agree that neither spouse is at fault.

Internet Divorce

This is a popular term, but it is really a misnomer—no one actually gets divorced over the Internet. Web sites are sources of forms and software that can be used in preparing your own divorce, but you won't find a judge handing out final decrees online. This method can take very little time and could cost as little as $50 to $250 per spouse. The difficulty comes when the legal paperwork is not properly prepared and processed in court.

The American Bar Association wants to ensure that these dot-com services are not engaging in the unauthorized practice of law. This type of service does not work if spouses disagree on any substantive issues. Attorneys make their money in the divorce area on contested issues. The trend with these services is to speed up the divorce process and make it easier. In my experience, when there are assets and financial issues to be sorted out, you want to slow down the process, not speed it up.

Using the Same Attorney

This is not a separate method from those listed earlier, but a variation on the theme. It is usually attempted by couples trying to minimize legal costs and/or capitalize on familiarity with a longtime family attorney. I don't recommend this variation for two reasons. First, the attorney has an inherent conflict of interest. Second, by sharing an attorney, you and your spouse both lose your personal advocates.

In summary, arbitration leaves the final decision in the dispute to the arbitrator. You agree beforehand to a binding decision. The arbitrator's decision is public. Mediators or collaborative law professionals suggest solutions and their suggestions are confidential. The power is reserved to the parties.

In a litigated divorce, the marriage partners have a judge hear the case in court and his decision is binding and final. I have found the courtroom procedure to be cold and impersonal. You speak when spoken to and give answers to specific questions when required. You pay to have your day in court and it can be a costly process. All the preparations made by your attorney, including depositions of the divorcing parties and their experts, can really run up the bill. Ask your attorney what going to court might represent in dollars—it could be $60,000 to $100,000 on average for each person, or much higher if it is a high-net-worth divorce. Maybe that is why more than 95 percent of divorces are settled out of court.

No matter which process you choose, get good, sound, comprehensive financial and tax advice before signing your final agreement. If you cannot achieve a fair settlement through mediation, collaborative law, or arbitration, then the litigated divorce may be your only option. You always need to be prepared to go to court when working with your attorney and experts, but you probably will not have to use this last resort to achieve the dissolution.

FREQUENTLY ASKED QUESTIONS ABOUT HIRING AN ATTORNEY

A do-it-yourself divorce is as dangerous as walking through a red light at a busy traffic intersection, hoping you can dodge the cars and trucks that come hurtling at you! If you have any property, children (who are considered assets), and a desire to emerge from divorce with something more than an empty pocketbook, hire an attorney.

I have developed the following questions from my consultations with hundreds of women facing divorce.

1. What kind of an attorney do I want to hire?

Most important, you want an experienced domestic relations lawyer. Look around to find a good personality fit and one you can afford. Don't be afraid to ask about the cost of legal fees. Be wary of paying below the norm and finding a bargain lawyer in the matrimonial field. Often, deals come from inexperienced lawyers, who try to make up in determination and persuasion what they lack in experience. I will talk about how to interview potential attorneys in question three on p. 44.

If your case is likely to involve lengthy negotiations and a complicated property settlement or if it might go to trial, you should never take a chance on someone who is not recognized in the family law field. Look at the attorney your spouse has hired. Make sure you have someone who can work with him. If there are issues of abuse or child custody, be sure your attorney has experience in this type of case. Many established attorneys will not take this type of case. You are going to be spending a lot of time with your attorney. Make sure that your working styles are compatible. As I mentioned earlier, see your attorney in action in court on motions or in a trial. Meet the paralegal—you may spend a lot of time together.

2. Where do I look for the attorney?

Ask your friends who have gone through a divorce if they have a recommendation. The pastor at your church may also be helpful in finding an attorney. Contact the bar association in your state. Ask for a listing of those attorneys in the state bar association who live in your area and are members of the family law section.

Call the local bar association listed in the white pages of your phone book and ask if there is a lawyer referral service for domestic relations lawyers. You can also try to find a Women's Law Center, which are becoming increasingly popular, particularly in metropolitan areas.

Go to the library resource section and find the *Martindale-Hubble Legal Directory*. This huge volume lists lawyers by city along with information on the specialties of each lawyer's firm. You can also go online to *www.martindale.com* to conduct a search. Read the biographies. Also, make sure the attorney you pick is active in organizations for family law lawyers such as the family law section of the American Bar Association. By far, your best bet is an attorney recommended by a woman who has gone through the divorce process and is still happy enough with the attorney to recommend him.

3. What are some tips on looking for an attorney?

Do not use an attorney who is a family friend or business associate of your spouse. Don't set yourself up for a problem that might arise with divided loyalties. This third party could be brought in at the end of the negotiations to give perspective, but be very cautions if you do this. You could lose a friend and be unduly influenced in an emotionally unstable time of your life.

Do interview at least three attorneys before making your final decision. Some family law offices accept free initial appointments to discuss the basics of a potential case, but many of the more prominent attorneys require some payment even for an initial consultation. When calling to make an appointment, explain you have not yet selected an attorney and would like to discuss your situation prior to choosing one. Be sure to clarify whether you will be charged a fee before setting the appointment. You will be looking for a good personality fit, evaluating costs, and discussing the payment of a *retainer* fee. The retainer fee a lawyer initially charges is for taking on your case and rarely represents the entire fee. Typically, the attorney will work on an hourly basis, billing against the retainer on a monthly basis. The retainer fee "reserves" your lawyer's time to pursue your case.

Do make a commitment between the two of you. Make sure you have an attorney who will work with you rather than for you. This is the team concept in which you cooperate to do your own paralegal work.

Find out whether your attorney is willing to have you work with a financial planner during your divorce. If she has worked with a financial planner in the past, find out whom she would recommend. Or tell her with whom you are working and watch for her reaction. Some attorneys don't want to have anyone "interfering." If you hear that, consider it a red flag. The financial planner is the one professional on your team who is concerned with and focused on your future postdivorce lifestyle—and the financial realities you will face. The rest of the team is gone once the divorce is final.

4. What kind of questions should I ask my attorney in the initial interview?

I recommend the following questions:

- Will you charge me on a retainer, hourly basis, or will you sign a contract for a set fee?
- What kind of expenses should I anticipate and who will pay for them?
- What kind of experts do you think I will need and do you have any recommendations?
- How soon can I start receiving temporary maintenance and child support?
- What is a realistic time frame for our working relationship and for this divorce to be final?
- How can I get money out of our joint accounts to pay for some of these costs?
- Have you ever worked with the opposing attorney?
- How many divorce cases did you handle last year?
- How many of your cases went to trial? How long did the trials last?
- What portion of your law practice is devoted to family law?
- How much of the work do you do personally and how much is handled by your assistant?
- What is the billing rate for your assistant and staff time? Can I meet your staff?
- Do you use experts often and, if so, in what capacity? Who pays for these services?
- Do you work with financial planners as part of your professional team?
- Do you work in mediation or arbitration cases?
- Can I expect any attorney fees or expert witness fees to be paid by my spouse?
- What kind of temporary maintenance do you think I can get with our income levels?
- How detailed is your request for temporary maintenance? Do you usually get what you request?
- What can I expect in child support?
- Can you recommend some books I should read regarding getting a divorce?
- Do you have any articles or information that can be helpful in my case?
- Do you recommend a therapist whom I might see? How do you work with the therapist?

- What are the strengths and weaknesses of my case at this time?
- How do I protect myself and children during this time?
- Should I try and get a job now or change jobs? Do I need to see a career advisor?
- My spouse has taken all the financial information. What do I do? How can we get it from him?
- When do you have your next trial or hearing scheduled? I would like to see how you work in the courtroom.
- Based on what I have shown you about our situation, where do you think I can go to get money to pay your fees?

Remember, when you hire an attorney to represent you in your divorce, you are depending upon him to get the most for you from the divorce process. The attorney you want must be smart and have your ultimate benefit as his primary goal, rather than the dollars you represent.

CHECKLIST FOR THE INITIAL MEETING WITH YOUR ATTORNEY

You will be expected to provide some of the information in the following list in your initial meeting with the attorney, known as an "informational interview." If you are on an informational interview I suggest you take a copy of your last year's income tax return, a pay stub, and a list of assets and liabilities. The remainder of the financial information would be provided once you have hired the attorney to represent you.

- Date of marriage, names, ages, and dates of birth for you, your spouse, and children.
- When and where you were married and where you have lived during your married life.
- A history of all of your employments.
- A recent income tax return and W-2.
- A summary balance sheet including assets and liabilities. (Even if this is incomplete, it will be helpful.)
- Chronology of marriage in writing.
- Identify separate and community assets if you can.
- Why are you getting a divorce? Describe your reasons briefly.
- Separate, prenuptial, or community property agreements.
- Social Security earnings record, for you and your spouse.
- Most recent pay stub.
- Employee benefits summaries.
- Medical history (if relevant) for you and other family members.

Janice's Decision: Mediation

Once Janice understood that she had to rely on herself for good advice, she read about divorce in her state, hired an attorney, authorized her to find a professional mediator, and with her husband's reluctant cooperation, managed legally to end her marriage with a fair settlement. Both Janice and her husband had separate legal representation apart from the mediator. During and after her divorce, Janice also worked with a financial planner, career advisor, accountant, and therapist.

Janice's transition from a married spouse to a divorced woman illustrates how you can take control of your own divorce process, rather than feel like a victim.

4

The Financial Implications of Contemporary Relationships

You gain strength, courage and confidence by every experience in which you really stop to look fear in the face. You are able to say to yourself, "I've lived through this horror. I can take the next thing that comes along." You must do the thing you think you cannot do.

—ELEANOR ROOSEVELT

Maintaining a long-term relationship in today's world is increasingly complicated. Many women marrying in the twenty-first century have a good chance to participate in a wide range of roles: corporate wife, trophy wife, alpha earner, second (or third) wife, dual-career couple, starter marriage, cohabitation, covenant marriage, or social contract.

When I began working with divorcing clients twenty-five years ago, most women I saw were nonworking "housewives," who were financially dependent on their husbands' income. The media's fascination with the plight of the 1960s and 1970s version of the corporate wife had largely died off. *Fortune* magazine had not yet coined the term *trophy wife*. Families with both spouses working were still not the norm, though their numbers were increasing. Living together without being married was considered risky and not well-accepted. No one had heard of starter marriages or alpha earners. Although there was a concern about the divorce rate, little had been done to change the laws. Covenant marriages were almost unknown.

Today, fewer than half of my clients can be characterized as displaced homemakers. Though every divorce is unique, there are significant similarities among the roles these women portray. Because of these commonalities, this chapter is organized to illustrate important financial issues facing women in each role.

Before we look at these issues, I want to give you an important background, using some interesting statistics. (The data in the following table are for 2002, except where noted otherwise.) These numbers were compiled on *Divorce Magazine's* Web site at *www.divorcemag.com*.

COMPARATIVE STATISTICS ON MARRIAGE AND DIVORCE[1]

Percentage of population that is married:
   59 percent (down from 62 percent in 1990 and 72 percent in 1970)
Median age at first marriage:
   Males: 26.9
   Females: 25.3
Median age at first divorce:
   Males: 30.5
   Females: 29
Median age at second marriage:
   Males: 34
   Females: 32
Median age at second divorce:
   Males: 39.3
   Females: 37
Median duration of first marriages that end in divorce:
   Males: 7.8
   Females: 7.9
Median duration of second marriages that end in divorce:
   Males: 7.3 Years
   Females: 6.8 Years
Median number of years people wait to remarry after their first divorce:
   Males: 3.3 Years
   Females: 3.1 Years

Percentage of married people who reach their fifth, tenth, and fifteenth anniversaries:

Fifth: 82 percent

Tenth: 65 percent

Fifteenth: 52 percent

Percentage of married people who reach their twenty-fifth, thirty-fifth, and fiftieth anniversaries (also reflects increased death rate in older people):

Twenty-fifth: 33 percent

Thirty-fifth: 20 percent

Fiftieth: 5 percent

Number of unmarried couples living together:

5.5 million

Percentage of unmarried couples living together that are male-female unions:

89 percent

Married women earning at least $5,000 a year more than their husbands:

8.408 million (14.9 percent of all married women)

Unmarried women earning at least $5,000 a year more than their partners:

821,000 (21.5 percent of unmarried couples)

Married men earning at least $5,000 a year more than their wives:

33.228 million (58.8 percent of all married men)

Unmarried men earning at least $5,000 a year more than their partners:

2.099 million (54.9 percent of unmarried couples)

Married couples in which only the husband is employed:

12.642 million (22.4 percent)

Married couples in which only the wife is employed:

3.855 million (6.8 percent)

Married couples in which both partners are employed:

30.212 million (53.5 percent)

Unmarried couples in which only the male is employed:
    695,000 (18.2 percent)
Unmarried couples in which only the female is employed:
    410,000 (10.7 percent)
Unmarried couples in which both partners are employed:
    2.484 million (65 percent).

WHY WE GET DIVORCED

Life is fast-paced for today's families. Male and female relationships are constantly being stimulated, interrupted, and agitated with instant messaging, cell phones, beepers, voice mail and e-mail. TV, movies, magazines, and radio bombard all of us with the "ideal" of constant happiness, excitement, and companionship. Internet romances are becoming common and having an affair in the workplace has gotten easier and more acceptable. Married couples are faced with fewer socially imposed barriers to terminating their relationships.

Men and women are getting divorced for many reasons. With no-fault divorce cases, the term *irreconcilable differences* covers a host of causes. This general term can mask uncomfortable realities we would rather not be publicly known. Some of the reasons for divorce I have seen include:

Extramarital affairs
Emotional and physical abuse
Family strains (financial, health, in-laws)
Midlife crisis
Addictions—alcoholism, gambling, drugs
Workaholism
Sex changes and shifts in sexual preference
Children (behavior, death, mixed families with stepchildren)
Boredom and conflicting personal goals
Lack of sexual compatibility
Religious conflicts
Desire for sole custody of children

In the following section, I want to explore the characteristics and financial implications of typical relationships I deal with in divorce cases. I have used the stories of real people, even when I include nonclients such as the Wendts, Welchs, and Goldmans. In reading these cases, you can identify the issues that relate to your own situation. (In later chapters I will return to these legal issues and provide pointers on how to deal with them.)

CONTEMPORARY RELATIONSHIPS[2]

The Corporate Wife

Increasingly, the courts are recognizing that couples who build up wealth and increase their lifestyle, do so jointly over their married lives, even if only one spouse has been the main financial contributor. A divorce financial analysis today should carefully consider career assets in arriving at an equitable settlement. Take a family in which the husband is the sole wage earner. Many times, the wife put the husband through school or helped him become established in his profession. She abandoned or postponed her own education in the process. Together they have made the decision to spend the time and energy to build his career with the expectation that she will share in the fruits of her investment through her husband's enhanced earning power. Over time, he has built up career assets that are part of what he earns, even though they may not be paid directly to him. What are these less-than-obvious assets, and what are they worth? Let's look at two examples.

Lorna Wendt and Vira Goldman

The 1998 divorce of Lorna and Gary Wendt featured a highly publicized battle over career assets, landing them on the cover of *Fortune* magazine.

The Wendts, who married after both graduated from the University of Wisconsin, began with a net worth of $2,500. She gave up her career as a music teacher after her husband graduated from Harvard Business School. At the time of their divorce after thirty-two years of marriage, Gary had risen to CEO of GE Capital.

Lorna Wendt willingly took on her role as a corporate wife, doing what women of her time did when married to an upwardly mobile, corporate man. She stayed home, cooked, cleaned, moved from city to city while, as Lorna has said, ". . . raising productive children who would become productive adults as Gary wanted." In other words, the children were a feather in his cap. Lorna attended corporate and charity functions and entertained business clients as needed.

When they divorced, Gary declared their **marital estate** to be worth $21 million and offered her $8 million as her share. She argued that the estate was worth $100 million and she wanted half—$50 million. Her position was that his future pension benefits and stock options had been earned during their marriage. She said that her contribution as the home-maker and wife of the CEO enabled him to rise through the ranks to the top of his organization. To make their case, Lorna's attorney introduced the "Ph.T. degree"—"Putting Hubby Through"—as evidence at the divorce proceedings.

The Wendt case broke through the long-held legal belief that a spouse deserved enough to maintain her lifestyle and nothing more. In this landmark decision, the judge awarded her $20 million. It was less than the $50 million for which she asked, but far more than the $8 million her husband had initially offered. She also received $250,000 per year in alimony for the rest of her life, and 50 percent of the marital assets as determined in court. These marital assets included the traditional real estate, cash, and vested stock interests, but also the as-yet unvested or exercisable stock options and unvested pensions. The judge gave her only a small award of any future assets.

Vira Goldman was married for thirty-three years to Robert Goldman, CEO of Congress Financial Corporation—his second marriage and her first. Like Lorna Wendt, Vira believed she had worked hard in her marriage and had done her job well. She even gave her husband weekly haircuts.

Vira, like Lorna Wendt, believed she had contributed equally to the success of her marriage. When it came time to terminate the relationship after more than thirty years of marriage, both were being told they were not equal partners when it came to divorce.

Vira Goldman did not agree and went to court to fight for an equitable property settlement. In 1998 she got one of the largest settlements in the history of the New York courts—half the marital assets, which included $44 million of *restricted stock* of Congress Financial Corporation that the company was forced to buy back.

Gary Wendt and Robert Goldman appealed the decisions by the judges. There were many arguments over what constituted marital assets, equitable distribution, and what happens when a partnership ends.

Lorna Wendt and Vira Goldman were pioneers in helping reshape the way marriage is now viewed by judges, moving from the position of "enough is enough" to the concept of "equitable partnership." It is true these divorces were high-profile divorces with large assets, but they set the stage for other women. Because of these two women and their divorce cases, more women are choosing to fight rather than settle for less than their fair share. More significantly, by refusing to settle out of court, which was the usual path taken in these types of divorces, Lorna Wendt and Vira Goldman helped to remove the stigma once associated with women who

refused to accept an inequitable settlement and wouldn't leave quietly after decades of marriage.

Jane Beasley Welch

Jack Welch was married to Jane Beasley for thirteen years. They had a
prenuptial agreement and a highly contentious divorce. He was admired
by many for his twenty-year term running General Electric, where he was
called "neutron Jack" for firing thousands of GE employees, restructuring,
keeping costs down, and creating profits for shareholders. GE liked Jack's
skills so much that they gave him millions of dollars in retirement benefits
and perks to keep him around as long as they could. These perks included
sports tickets, exclusive use of a Manhattan apartment worth $11 million,
unlimited personal use of GE's corporate jets, a chauffeured limousine, a
leased Mercedes, bodyguards, and security systems for his several homes,
office space, financial services, and much more. Jane enjoyed the life these
perks provided and knew the cost to replace them in her postdivorce life.
She wanted her share of this retirement benefits package.

When Jack fell in love with another woman and wanted a divorce, the
duration specified in the prenuptial agreement Jack had asked Jane to sign
had expired. Prenuptial agreements often include clauses stipulating a
spouse will receive limited assets if the couple divorces before a certain date
or event. Such clauses become unenforceable (as in, expire) after the specified date. Jane was not willing to accept Jack's settlement offer and was prepared to go to court to present her case in public, with no sealed files.

Jack and Jane Welch had their first encounter in court over temporary
support. She asked for much more than he wanted to pay. She came into
court with documents detailing the financial value of the lifetime perks she
and her husband were receiving from GE. Her attorney used an economist
as her expert witness to value the perks. The economist spent five hours on
the witness stand. She had organized the sources of expenses and income,
and categorized the information with footnotes and color-coding, clearly
illustrating the disparities between the two parties' predivorce, temporary,
and postdivorce lifestyles. The judge gave Jane substantial temporary support. The final property settlement was upwards of $180 million.

In my own practice, I am often hired as a financial expert to analyze
and project the spending patterns of my divorcing clients. Their lifestyle is
examined under a microscope to show historical spending, the amount of
money needed for temporary support, and the proposed amount for the
postdivorce lifestyle. This kind of work can be critical to a fair share settlement, whether the client has many assets or very few.

I have worked in a number of high-profile, high-asset cases in which a group of advisors were hired to consult with the wife and her attorneys, creating a professional team to structure the buyout of one partner from another in a business partnership.

One of these cases involved more than $60 million in real estate holdings. The couple were prominent citizens in a Southern city. When the husband became involved with his secretary, he wanted a divorce so that he could remarry. Both spouses had been active in all levels of charitable and art functions, especially the wife, who had no intention of losing her lifestyle and position in the community.

The woman knew of her husband's well-earned reputation for being a tough negotiator. What he didn't know was that his ex was a "steel magnolia" in disguise.

He offered her $200,000 per year for living expenses, and said he would pay 100 percent of the educational costs for two of their children, who were still attending expensive private schools in the Northeast. I established that she had been spending more than $2,000,000 per year during the three years prior to their separation, documenting every expense through credit card statements, bank records, and cash transactions. Ironically for the husband, it was his secretary who provided the necessary information during this time because she had been paying the bills.

Tracking the wife's expenses was a major undertaking for my staff. The notebooks, color-coded spreadsheets, and footnotes we created were instrumental in settling this case on the courtroom steps hours before going to trial. The wife did not back down—with the help of her professional team, she was able to get what she felt was a fair share of their marital assets and a substantial maintenance award.

The Trophy Wife

We all know the trophy wife stereotype, often referred to as a "bimbo" or "arm candy." Her main job is to look sexy, be sexy, and make the husband feel sexy. If successful, she would get your husband, his money, and your money.

The new trophy wife ironically is the result of the rise of feminism and increased female participation in the workplace. She is still much younger than her husband, slim, beautiful, and accomplished. Today she must be intelligent. She probably has a career and is successful, but not as successful as he is. A big part of her job is to look good, make him look good, and rebuild his social life. Typically, the trophy wife is a second wife, and there is a prenuptial agreement. This second wife is often replaced with a third version in a few years—one with the same prerequisites. There may be children in each of the marriages.

Donald Trump is the quintessential trophy wife collector. He filed for divorce shortly before the expiration of his five-year prenuptial agreement with Marla Maples, and then remarried.

I should note here that the media has recently become enamored with yet another trophy wife stereotype. This version of the trophy wife is not viewed as arm candy. Rather she is a strong, self-possessed professional, armed with a potent educational background, lots of ambition, substantial income, and good looks to boot. In other words, she is a likely candidate to be an alpha earner. Contemporary men seem to be increasingly attracted to these characteristics. Some observers see this as a major shift in male values. I believe it is creating a whole new category of divorce—I'll call it the alpha-alpha dissolution group. It is populated by mutually ambitious, high-income couples desiring a mate worthy of their own skills, accomplishments, and successes. Children are secondary to career, and any significant change in one spouse's stature places intense strain on the relationship. But let's return to the original version, with a different case history.

A Tarnished Trophy

Marlene was forty-six when I met her. She was eight months into her divorce process and had become an emotional wreck. Twelve years earlier, she had married James, now fifty-nine, the president and CEO of a major software company. He had three grown children from a previous marriage, and an eleven-year-old with Marlene. Marlene had been a flight attendant, but gave up her career to be able to travel with James and raise their daughter, Sarah, even though she'd had a full-time nanny when Sarah was young. Sarah was now in boarding school.

Marlene was very active in the community—the arts, charities, and civic boards. She and James were a visible couple. Marlene loved the spotlight, but life with James had been difficult over the past five years. He had a temper, and Marlene felt controlled by him. She felt pressured, constantly trying to be the "perfect wife with the perfect body." Unfortunately, a casual drinking habit had escalated into a serious problem for her during the marriage, and alcoholism became an issue. She had also visited a therapist. He hired the best attorney in town, and the battle began.

First, he put Marlene on a budget, something she'd never had to contend with before. She'd had no money of her own in the marriage. The money Marlene spent had always been put on credit cards, and James had paid all the bills. She did not write checks and had no idea how much was in their checking account. Private corporate jets and cars had become her world. James made it very clear he was not going to continue to finance this lifestyle. Everyone accepted this but Marlene.

She continued to spend money—and overspend. She remained active in the usual social and charitable organizations, attending functions as if nothing had changed. It soon became obvious that she was not as welcome as when she had attended these events with her husband. She slowly began to realize that it was James—with his money and his prestige—who had the influence. The loyalties and friendships she thought she had were evaporating. Her drinking increased, and the resulting negative behavior caused more isolation and depression.

Marlene's financial and emotional world was collapsing. She insisted upon going to court to get a "fair settlement." Marlene worked with three different attorneys during her divorce process. There were extensions and missed deadlines. Her problems with alcohol increased. I was asked to analyze the historical spending for the couple for the year prior to divorce. James fought releasing the records, but finally we were able to create a financial affidavit. We then did the same for the first ten months of separation, and what we found was shocking. James was paying all house expenses, the cost of their daughter's private boarding school, for Marlene's health care, and insurances for all of them. He gave Marlene $15,000 per month for discretionary expenses, and she had an advance of $100,000 for legal fees and experts. Marlene had accumulated a consumer debt of $250,000 during the ten months since James had filed for divorce.

Some would think she was smart—she clearly knew how to get money and spend money, but the truth was that Marlene was out of control. I knew it, her attorney knew it, but Marlene didn't want to know it and wouldn't accept anyone's advice that she needed to stop spending.

It is not unusual to see uncontrolled spending during the separation period in the divorce process. This often happens because the woman is trying to maintain her status, indulge in "retail therapy," or buy the affection of the children if she is concerned that her husband is trying to take them from her. The first few months can be very irrational and emotional. Seeing a therapist and financial planner early in the divorce process to set up emotional safeguards and cash-control systems can help reduce the stress and minimize the damage.

Marlene and James finally did divorce, and James got custody of Sarah. Marlene went into treatment a year after the divorce, after having gone through most of her property settlement. She had four years of maintenance left and would then be on her own. The last I heard, Marlene had moved to be near her family.

The Alpha Earner

An alpha earner is a wife who earns at least 60 percent or more of the household income for the family. She has the dominant career. The study

I cited in chapter 1 reported that 11 percent of current marriages have an alpha earner. The husband is often a stay-at-home dad taking care of the family responsibilities and working part time in a lower-paying job.

This trend is likely to continue. Gender-based value systems are dynamic. What worked for our grandparents doesn't necessarily work for us or for our children. Young women today would be well-advised to invest in their own career development and to maintain their skills. It is clear from looking at the statistics that women are likely to be single or divorced for significant periods of time in their lives.

The alpha earner can have the same challenges as the upwardly mobile male in the corporate world. She may need a "corporate husband" at home if there are children. If the marriage ends in divorce, this stay-at-home dad easily translates into the "economically disadvantaged spouse." Here is a true-to-life example from my own client files.

Scott and Julie met in South America on a three-week hiking tour. Julie lived on the East Coast, where she worked as a leading bioresearcher in the medical field with an up-and-coming company. She had been hired immediately out of Harvard Medical School, from which she graduated at the top of her class. Scott lived on the West Coast. Bright and articulate, he was a poet, philosopher, thinker, and writing teacher at a local community college. They corresponded by e-mail and met as often as they could for two years. Then Scott agreed to move to Maryland to live with Julie. After living together for three years, they married when they were both thirty-seven.

Although they wanted to have at least two children, Julie couldn't get pregnant right away. Their first child was born when she was forty-one years old, the second child when she was forty-three. She took a three-month leave of absence from work when each child was born. Money had never been an issue with them. They were comfortable. They owned their own home and had retirement savings. Travel was their biggest expense.

Julie worked long hours and was now earning more than $250,000 a year with stock options and excellent benefits. Scott published a few poems and managed an independent bookstore.

They hired a nanny to help with the children two days a week, and Scott took care of them three days a week. After their second son was born, they decided it would make more sense for Scott to obtain a graduate degree in writing. He could then pursue a teaching position when the children were older. Scott left the bookstore and went back to school to get his master's in creative writing and English, taking courses in the evenings and on weekends. The children were in day care part time. The plan was that they would start regular school about the same time that Scott would be able to take a full-time teaching position. All seemed to be going as planned.

The second child was fussy and irritable and not as easy to take care of as the first. This kept both parents awake at night and stressed out during the day. They had a high-maintenance child in the family, even though there did not seem to be any physical problems. The strain on their relationship continued until Scott and Julie became more and more distant. Scott missed his solitary life. He loved his children, but found he really didn't want to be a full-time stay-at-home dad. Julie liked her work but wanted more time with her children. She resented the long hours at her job and the total responsibility for earning the family's money. Their ten-year marriage ended in divorce.

Julie became an angry alpha earner who did not want to share her future upward financial mobility with Scott. Scott felt trapped on the East Coast because of his children and lack of career, but he had come to like the life their income had provided. When it came to the divorce, he wanted his fair share of the property and future earnings to establish a fresh start. He received a disproportionate (60 percent) division of the marital assets, and five years of maintenance in the settlement. Julie didn't see why Scott couldn't just get a "real" job as she had, earn some money, and quit draining "her" resources.

Women have the same challenges as men in the workplace when it comes to divorce. Alpha earners resist dividing their future earnings the same way as men do. If the alpha earner has been married to a "trophy husband," she will want to have the same tight prenuptial agreement that a man would have negotiated.

A second version of the angry alpha earner is the one who is left by her husband for another woman, and then asked to pay substantial maintenance, share 50 percent of the assets, and give up custody of the children. This is particularly distasteful if she has had to be the "superwoman" both in the home and at the office.

When husbands are in primary caretaker roles, these families are challenged to make sure dad doesn't become the family "employee." Attitudes about ownership, responsibility, and rights are significantly affected by how marital roles are determined. Did dad become Mr. Mom by choice or by downsizing at his company and a forced job change? I often see divorce as the eventual outcome when the woman becomes an alpha earner out of economic necessity. Men and women approach their marital and vocational roles differently. Unless a significant change in "who does what" is carefully planned and based on mutual choice, the risk of dissolution is high. In such a setting, solid financial planning can help reduce the strain.

Starter Marriages

A starter marriage is usually considered to be one that begins and ends before the spouses are thirty years of age, and one where there are no children. The term was popularized by the journalist Pamela Paul in her 2002 book, *The Starter Marriage and the Future of Matrimony*. Her definition of a starter marriage was, "first-time marriages that last five years or less and do not yield children." Paul believes these marriages end primarily because the partners are fresh out of school, often still living with their respective parents, and see marriage as a way to move out on their own, or both are on fast-track careers, are successful and ambitious, and see marriage as a way to enhance their status.

Many of these couples do not consult financial planners for their divorces. The partners have accumulated few assets about which they could disagree in such a brief time. Even when they have enjoyed high incomes, much of the money has been spent on maintaining an expensive lifestyle. Many of these couples are loath to engage in the extended, contentious court battles characterized by their parents' generation.

Since most of these couples are very computer-savvy, they are comfortable using online do-it-yourself kits and packaged software to conclude their marriages. They take back what they came into the marriage with, divide any community assets between themselves, file the appropriate forms, and quietly end the relationship. That is not to say the process is painless or even fair. In many cases, reviewing asset allocation decisions with a qualified financial advisor can provide a more equitable division of property and avoid future complications.

Second Marriages

Increasingly, one or both of the spouses I see have been married before. Second marriages occur at all ages, so I see blended families with multiple sets of stepchildren, stay-at-home mothers and fathers, remarried widows and widowers, retired and semiretired spouses, and numerous other combinations. Many of these cases involve a dual-career household where stepchildren come and go on a predetermined visitation schedule.

Money, a major source of conflict in many marriages, can be particularly problematic in second marriages. This is often demonstrated in the different money-management styles of the spouses. If they didn't discuss money issues in their first marriage, setting short-and long-term goals and priorities, reviewing expenses on a regular basis, creating and monitoring a budget, then it is unlikely an individual will do this in his second marriage.

We each have our own money-management style. We learn it from our parents, relatives, and friends. In chapter 12 I will give you a resource to use to learn more about your personal money-management style. It is also a great tool to share with a prospective spouse or significant other in establishing a financially compatible relationship.

When a first marriage ends, it is common to hear complaints about how one person or the other was "taken to the cleaners" in the divorce—usually by an ex-spouse, the ex-spouse's attorney, or even by the judge. If you are in your second marriage and getting a divorce, I would ask you to explain how you handled the money during your marriage. I would want you to show me the sources of all income coming into the household and what expenses were paid with that money. In my experience, most people in second marriages start out having a joint account into which each contributes funds. Some common household expenses are paid from this account, such as food, utilities, and vacations. The mortgage would be paid from this account if the house was owned jointly. If the house was maintained as a separate asset, the spouse who wanted it to be kept as a separate asset would fund the mortgage. The other spouse would contribute money toward the utilities or the use of the home. That spouse would not be a signer on the mortgage nor sign on a new equity line of credit to pay down debt or to do a remodel. These last two activities can become big problems in the area of commingling funds when there is a divorce.

If your husband has maintenance and child support payments to an ex-spouse, he will typically pay this out of his separate account. If you have child support coming in from an ex-spouse, you will deposit the funds into your separate account to pay for your child's expenses. This is where the problems begin. The two of you might have differing parenting styles. Perhaps one of you is much more generous than the other parent about what is spent on the child and those extracurricular activities. For example, your husband is at work, and your stepchild needs new shoes for soccer practice and some school supplies. Do you pay for these expenses and get reimbursed? What about spontaneous expenses that come up? Do these come out of the joint expenses? Are you exchanging receipts every week? Maybe you are detail-minded and your husband is not, or it is the other way around. It is easy to see how the resentment can build. Children are masters at manipulating parents who are not consistent and vigilant in maintaining the money system created for the family.

So you decide to get a joint credit card to make your daily life easier. You start by paying the balance off each month, then one thing leads to another and the balance balloons. If and when you get divorced, suddenly you are stuck paying off "*his* credit card debt." Or perhaps your ex-husband files for bankruptcy and the credit card he was supposed to pay off comes back for you to pay.

Unraveling the finances when a second marriage ends in divorce can be costly. I recommend that my clients about to enter a second marriage come in for financial planning on the management of money prior to getting married. This means more than creating a prenuptial agreement. It means creating a cash-control system for the family—yours, mine, and ours—so you don't make the same money mistakes a second time around. If there is a divorce, we can easily track what has happened with the money. Too often these systems are not maintained or the two systems are so different that the parties cannot coexist. When you look at the divorce statistics with second marriages, there is reason to pause and do some careful financial planning.

Usually in a second marriage where there are children, a prenuptial agreement is drawn up. These agreements will identify separate assets, but too often do not address the cash-control system they will use in the blended family. I like to create a detailed system that includes a list of accounts, sources of income, budgets, discretionary expenses, allowances, and procedures for funding shortfalls, settling disputes, tracking expenses, and holding family meetings. This family system starts with the husband and wife, and then flows to the children and stepchildren. This financial blueprint will reduce family conflicts. If there is a divorce, you will have a paper trail of the joint finances. If either of you is faced with demands for increased child support from an ex-spouse, you have financial records to justify your response.

I will talk more about second marriages in a later chapter when I discuss prenuptial agreements.

Dual-Career Couples

The dual-career couple is becoming more common. The Census Bureau figures for 2003 show that one-third of men and nearly one-quarter of women between the ages of thirty and thirty-four have never been married, nearly four times the rate in 1970. Americans are no longer in a hurry to get married.

When dual-career couples do get married, their biggest challenge comes when they decide to have a family. There is a lot of discussion each year about family-friendly corporations, but in reality, this is often only lip service. It is very difficult to integrate two fast-track careers and raise kids at the same time without huge sacrifices.

For many couples, finding affordable, quality child-care services is a major ordeal. In 1998, shortly after President Clinton's proposals to improve child care, Harris Interactive reported that 51 percent of their survey respondents said finding affordable care was either "extremely difficult" or "very difficult." Forty-four percent of those surveyed also indicated it was similarly difficult to find high-quality care for their children. Furthermore, 43 percent said the lack of acceptable care had prevented them from taking a job they wanted. According to a February 2006 poll by the National Association of Child Care Resource and Referral Agencies (NACCRRA) 11.6 million children under age five are in some type of child-care arrangement every week, and 53 percent of children between the ages of five and fourteen are in similar care environments. The report goes on to say that more than 1 million children between the ages of nine and eleven whose mothers work are alone at home after school. So where are all the "nannies" we hear about? This report suggests they are in very short supply. Of the 2.3 million caregivers they identified, less than 300,000 were paid nonrelatives (the classic nanny). It is obvious that most dual-career couples do not employ a nanny; there simply are not enough to go around.

These couples start out loving each other, love their children, and want the marriage to work. One day, they sit down and carefully calculate which parent has the best paycheck potential for a designated period of time, and that is the person who will continue to work outside the home. The assumption is the-stay-at-home spouse will return to the workplace in a few short years and that he or she will be able to resume earning a high salary right away. The spouse who stays in the job market is assuming the spouse at home is maintaining his or her skill level in "some way."

The stay-at-home spouse will be the primary caretaker for the children until the children start school full time. This spouse will do some part-time work, or try to work from home, or job-share, but if the strain is too much, may decide to be a full-time parent. The spouse who is working outside the home may or may not like this compromise over time. Resentment can build from either side.

Spencer and Maria were thirty-five when they met. Both had successful careers—she as an architect and he as a graphic artist for a large corporation. They lived together for four years then decided to get married. They wanted children and had twins a few years later, followed by another child when Maria was forty-four years old. They had a nanny living with them for two years, but with the birth of the third child, the nanny no longer fit their family values.

By this time, Maria had become a partner in her firm and earned $215,000 a year plus a share of the profits. Spencer was competent at his job and regularly received perks and bonuses for his outstanding work. Periodically he had considered going out on his own and starting his own business.

After taking a two-week family vacation to Hawaii and talking about their goals, Spencer and Maria decided to let the nanny go and take back their family life. Spencer would leave his corporation and open a business in the home. The twins would start preschool in the fall and the youngest child would go to day care. Spencer would do freelance work at home each day from 8 A.M. to 2 P.M. and in the evenings when Maria would take over the family responsibilities. They would continue to use baby-sitters to help with the children, employ a cleaning service, and simplify the gardening required at their home. If they were prudent in their spending, they could afford to lose Spencer's salary and give him a year to start replacing his income with outside work.

A good plan—but it was not so easily implemented. It took Spencer four years before he was able to generate any meaningful business income. During that time, he bought equipment to use in his business and set up a beautiful office at home. He did enjoy the children, but found himself being distracted and short-tempered when interrupted. Marketing was difficult for him, and he missed the interaction with other adults.

Many evenings when Maria came home from work to find that Spencer hadn't completed her list of tasks, she couldn't understand why. She was working longer hours, trying to keep her billing hours up and earnings high. Their house was expensive to maintain, and setting up Spencer's business had been more costly than they had anticipated. Their conversations had disintegrated into "when could he expect to bring in some money for the household?" Raising three young children was proving to be time-consuming as well as financially draining. Spencer was responsible for the children after school, prepared the evening meals, and did the grocery shopping and laundry. Somehow he had become a stay-at-home dad instead of a successful graphic artist.

One day, ten years into their marriage, Spencer told Maria that he wanted to live apart for a while. He needed time away. She was hurt, frightened, and then angry. He had a commission that would give him enough money to support himself in an apartment for six months. He would take his office furniture and specialized graphic art equipment and a few pieces of furniture and continue to help out with the children when he could.

This continued for four months. Maria then decided she wanted a legal separation. Spencer agreed to the separation, but after six months told her he would convert the legal separation to a divorce as soon as he was legally able to do so.

I worked with Spencer and Maria for several weeks in a collaborative law setting with each of their attorneys. First we created a temporary parenting plan, then worked out a temporary budget. Next, we valued the assets and determined that they should sell the house. They agreed to take the equity from the sale and buy two houses of less value in the same neighborhood so they could share custody of the children and the parenting responsibilities. Maria paid Spencer maintenance for four years, and he paid her child support. They split their retirement assets equally and shared the limited investment assets on a fifty-fifty basis. Maria had to stop contributing the full amount possible into her 401(k) plan at work. They both agreed to contribute to Roth IRAs for the four years Spencer would be receiving maintenance. They shared custody of the children.

Living Together, Then Marriage, Then Divorce

Data from the Census Bureau's Current Population Survey released at the end of November 2004 shows the age at which someone typically marries for the first time rose from 20.8 for women and 23.2 for men in 1970 to 25.3 and 27.1, respectively, in that year. For many couples, careers and education are the clear focus before settling down and beginning families. The number of unmarried couples who live together in the United States increased by 72 percent, according to the 2000 census.

However, researchers now say that married couples who lived together before marriage are 50 percent more likely to get divorced. They tend to have a "renter's agreement" philosophy that makes them less committed to sticking together through hard times. Their financial challenges often come to a head if the disparity of earnings gets greater over time and one person cannot keep up with the other person, or doesn't want to spend money the same way.

If one spouse spends significantly more than the other for personal items this disproportionate spending can have profound effects on an individual's sense of value in a relationship. A wife who sees her husband cater preferentially to his own desires is likely to become concerned about her future financial security. Divorces involving these issues are often emotional and the subsequent settlements can be complicated and drawn-out.

Covenant Marriages

Covenant marriages bar divorce except under extreme circumstances such as adultery, abandonment, or "cruel and barbarous treatment" to quote Arkansas law. If you agree to marry in Arkansas under the covenant marriage law, you agree to obtain and are required to have marriage counseling before taking your martial vows or divorcing. The cooling-off period for ending this type of marriage is two and a half years.

In 2001 Arkansas became the third state to adopt the covenant marriage law, following Arizona in 1999, and Louisiana in 1997. The intent behind establishing this type of marriage was to counter what some social observers believe is a decrease in moral values and marital ethics arising from the now universally available no-fault divorce laws.

I have not worked with any divorcing women who have a covenant marriage, but I have consulted in marriages where there have been strong connections to fundamentalist religions. In either situation, the pressures to preserve the marriage can have unintended consequences, particularly when abuse is involved.

Martha married Jim when she was thirty-nine and he was forty-five, her first marriage and his second. They had two children ages fourteen and sixteen. She gave up her career as a technical writer when her first child was born, because Jim wanted her to be home with the children. He had a ten-year-old daughter from his first marriage whom Martha helped care for under the parenting plan established by his divorce. Jim did not have a good relationship with his first wife. He spoke angrily about her, if he mentioned her name. It was as if she no longer existed.

Jim worked in a job at a technology company that required he travel one week a month. He was very controlling in the home about how Martha and the children spent their time. They attended church two evenings a week and one day on the weekend. TV was not allowed in the home, and Martha was allowed to socialize only with women from the church. Jim also chose her reading and clothing. The children were home-schooled from the time they were in third grade. The older son took courses at the community college in the "running start" program. The younger daughter was starting to resist this rigid lifestyle, wanting to go to the mall with friends and have unscheduled free time.

Martha was lonely and isolated. She was not allowed to see her family, because Jim believed they were a bad influence on her, and there was only an occasional phone call. Martha worked at the church in the youth program with the youth pastor. They talked often and laughed, something Martha never did with her own husband. Over time the two became close, then one day, the closeness led to physical contact.

The youth pastor was also married with two children. He and Martha felt guilt and prayed for guidance. They asked for forgiveness from the pastor of the church, but he decided to announce the adultery to the entire congregation. The two were separated from the community, and no one was to talk with them for thirty days, after which they were to make a public apology to the congregation.

The persecution at home was even greater. Jim took away Martha's credit cards, money, driver's license, and identification, and locked her in the house. She was never left alone.

After several days of this, a neighbor noticed Martha walking in the backyard looking very distressed. She called 911 after talking with Martha in her dazed state of mind. Martha was taken to a shelter.

She filed for a divorce and began working with a therapist. It was very difficult getting any financial data from Jim. He had notes showing property as his and other postnuptial agreements, all signed by Martha. He finally gave her an allowance during the first three months after she left of $1,000 a month for living expenses—and then only under duress.

Meanwhile, he was writing her e-mails suggesting reconciliation. After a year, she was able to rebuild a fragile relationship with her daughter, but her son would have no contact with her. Martha eventually received maintenance for four years to become retrained, 55 percent of the marital assets, and 50 percent of the retirement assets. Unfortunately, Jim was able to preserve his claim of separate property for many of the assets—Martha wanted her freedom more than a fight. Jim paid off a school loan of $40,000 for his daughter from his first marriage with community funds while Martha was being held in the house as a "prisoner"—just one of his many fast predivorce financial transactions.

Although Jim did not physically abuse his wife, he consistently used guilt as a weapon to control her and justify his actions. Martha's sense of self-worth was shattered, and she spent many hours in therapy struggling to regain it.

Emotional and Physical Abuse

I have seen instances of emotional and physical abuse in all types of marriages, initiated by both husbands and wives. The abuse impacts how money is handled in the marriage and can be a significant factor in the divorce.

If the woman has been in a marriage where there is emotional abuse concerning money, I will work with her, the attorney, and the therapist to illustrate the relationship of the money to the wife's behavior in the marriage. The psychologist is the expert who diagnoses the woman's mental condition and emotional state. I connect the emotional state to the wife's actions involving money during the marriage. The wife's dysfunction will come out in one form or another. If the wife lives in an abusive relationship for a long period of time, her self-worth can be very low at the time of divorce. The husband often portrays his wife as unfit, mentally disturbed, incompetent, a poor manager, an overspender, an alcoholic, or a depressive personality.

Working with the client's other professional advisors, I will create an integrated postdivorce financial plan for the woman, evaluating the need for maintenance and a career plan if these are deemed to be appropriate by the team. I will also work with the woman on her finances with regard to historical spending, the temporary budget, and eventually the postdivorce budget. This will give me a good sense of how the woman deals with money issues. Each of the experts will submit a report supporting the final settlement recommendation.

I have often been asked to review a psychologist's report describing a woman's mental and emotional condition and discuss how this condition has been acted out in the handling of finances during the marriage when the husband is recognized to be emotionally abusive. I will then give specific examples of the woman's behavior with money during the marriage. Geraldine and Phillip are a good example.

Geraldine had built a career in middle management at the phone company before marrying a very successful businessman. She took early retirement to become Phillip's second wife at the age of fifty-two. Prior to marrying, the couple dated for two years. During this intensely romantic period, Phillip showered Geraldine with gifts, took her on numerous trips, and involved her in entertaining and community social activities. Following such a display of affection and support, Geraldine did not question Phillip's insistence that she sign a prenuptial agreement limiting her recourse if there was a divorce. After all, he did have substantial separate assets.

In the first month of marriage, Phillip set the rules. Geraldine's job would be to keep up the house, entertain when necessary, and become active in the community as a volunteer. She used the joint credit card for everything, including the household budget, so he could review all purchases. She never used a checking account. She was also to be on call when he wanted her and stay out of his way when he didn't want her around. He gave her a weekly schedule. He chose everything in her life, from what she wore to parties to what she could read. She soon found herself with a man who controlled her.

When she first came to see me, I asked her why she hadn't left Phillip earlier. She said at first his behavior was subtle and done with good humor and affection. But as time went on, coldness, anger, and punishment emerged when she didn't follow the rules. She was in shock. They saw his friends, not her friends or family any longer. She became increasingly isolated. Again, I asked her why she didn't leave. Geraldine finally admitted, "I was ashamed, embarrassed, and very afraid of what he would do to me."

Her torment went on for five years until she finally told Phillip she wanted a divorce. He flew into a rage, and she became a prisoner in her own beautiful home, guarded by Phillip's personal security staff. It got so bad that one day she broke into a jar of quarters in their bedroom thinking she would get enough cash to escape. Her attempt was thwarted. Finally, her sister came to the house and managed to take Geraldine away. This successful career woman was an emotional and physical wreck. It took years before she felt safe living in a nearby city. Her divorce was an ugly courtroom battle.

LESSONS LEARNED

Here are a few pointers some my clients in the previous scenarios have shared with me.

- Mediate if at all possible, but don't be afraid of a public divorce. The old social stigma of divorce has lessened considerably.
- A divorce involving highly visible individuals, public officials, or very substantial assets may require public relations management.
- Career assets have value. Don't underestimate corporate perks and management benefits.
- Who signed the confidentiality agreement? If it wasn't you, your ex's business will want to protect the privacy of any "off-the-record" financial benefits enjoyed by executives and managers. You are not bound by that agreement.
- Know your ex-spouse's money personality as well as your own.
- Document your family money-management practices—who controls what and how.
- Create historical financial and social calendars for your marriage years. They verify your participation and contribution to the relationship.
- Evaluate your situation carefully and choose a team of qualified experts that best suits your needs.
- Remember, crying is healthy—use it to acknowledge and release your feelings. Turn that emotion into resolve. Don't talk—strategize!

5

Living with Change Does Not Mean Dealing with an Enemy

Trust, but verify.

—Ronald Reagan

No Fraternization!

You have been living apart from your husband for the past six months, trying to determine your next step. He has taken an apartment and you have stayed in the home with your two teenaged children. You and your children are trying to get on with your lives under an emotional cloud. You and your husband share the money that comes into the house from a joint account upon which both of you write checks. Now he has informed you that he wants a divorce. He wants out and says he is going to start the filing process. What do you do? Do you stop seeing each other, hire an attorney, wait for the papers to be served, cry, talk to your friends, go to church, what?

I know there are numerous thoughts going through your head at the start of the dissolution process. The truth is that the ending of your marriage likely has been coming for quite some time, and you chose not to see the signs or believed you could change the events. After all, as a woman, you probably subconsciously believed in the fairy-tale ending so prevalent in books and movies—that of living happily ever after.

The time right after the shock of his announcement of divorce is a good time to have a "cooling-off period" and to not see each other for a while. I've learned that women need time to gather their wits emotionally, while men typically want to divide the estate and dispense with the business aspects of their married life quickly. Both of these requirements will eventually be met during the divorce process.

You have to get used to the idea that divorce means separation—emotional, physical, and financial. It does not mean that you are no longer going to be parents to your children. Since feelings of hurt and injustice run high, it is important for you to find a method of communication with your estranged partner that does not require you to meet face-to-face or have direct voice contact. You can choose to exchange messages on answering machines, leave notes, or communicate by e-mail. Keep your messages factual and unemotional. Remember that these types of communication leave a trail, one that attorneys for both sides can access. Do not make your children the delivery service. That puts them in the middle, a place that is neither fair nor safe for them.

Get some distance during the divorce preliminaries. Spend the time getting yourself organized. The "Don't Fraternize" rule may be difficult to put into motion, because it's human nature to want to justify yourself to the person who has offended you. If you need to let off steam, do it with a friend, not your ex-partner-to-be.

DON'T TALK TO HIM ABOUT THE DIVORCE CASE ON YOUR OWN

Many women I've met let divorce overwhelm them. Don't fall into this trap! Take the time to get comfortable with the financial issues of your marriage and don't allow yourself to be badgered by your ex-to-be. Your strategy should be to listen to your spouse's comments and gather the facts, figures, and documents you will need. Encourage your husband to provide this information without a struggle arising between your attorneys. Point out to him in a note that cooperation will save you both money.

The initial petition for divorce often has such inflammatory clauses written into the boilerplate as "freezing of assets in a joint account" and "comprehensive and all-inclusive restraining orders." These phrases are there to protect you. Your husband is probably going to be upset if your attorney puts this type of wording into your legal response to his petition. He may think your attorney is encouraging you to be adversarial. Your husband wants you to be cooperative, to trust him. The byword for you to memorize is, Trust, but verify! Believe his actions and not his words. Trust your intuition. Listen to your inner voice and protect yourself legally.

As an aid to your intuition, review in your mind how your husband handled himself in business transactions in the past.

- Was he detail-minded?
- Did he want to win at all costs, play hardball in negotiations, use intimidation?
- Did he act like a controller?

Now think of how he acted in your personal relationship.

- Did he treat you as an equal partner in your financial affairs?
- Did he have you sign the income tax return at the very last minute without explanation, or did he make sure you thoroughly understood the facts and figures?
- Did he work with you on a written budget for the family?
- Did he encourage you to work outside the home?
- Did he use your religious beliefs to keep you subservient?

Think about the answers to these questions. Then ask yourself, is he suddenly going to change now, when there is a lot at stake?

Make up a list of your husband's strengths. How does he deal with people in business and in friendships?

Make the same list for yourself.

Next, write down how you think your spouse viewed you during your marriage. For example, did he think you were a spendthrift, a time-waster, a good mother, listener, or companion, physically fit, a good money manager? Is his opinion of you going to change suddenly? Is he going to try to use some of your weaknesses against you?

Start keeping a personal journal. Write down your feelings instead of keeping them pent up inside. Eventually, you will begin to see some behavior patterns unfolding. You will have an opportunity to change and refine habits during this period of self-examination. Also, keep a financial record of all of the expenditures for yourself and your children. Maintain a calendar showing when the children are with you and with him. Both of these journals can be very helpful for your attorney and financial planner when looking at monthly budgets, historical spending, and parenting plans.

This is a time of temporary arrangements and court orders. Until the final decree is issued, nothing is permanent. Whether the case takes ninety days or three years, the stage between the beginning and the end of the case is a time when the financial and emotional life of the family must go on. There are children to feed, mortgages to pay, and insurance premiums to deal with. It is usually during this period that divorcing couples reach a settlement about how to manage their lives while they are waiting for the divorce to be finalized. If they cannot agree on how they are going to share income during the time of separation—who is paying which bills, the source of the money to pay them, and who pays child support and how much—they will go to a judge and have a *temporary orders trial*.

A common *temporary order* is one that directs one spouse to pay support to the other until the divorce trial begins or a settlement is reached. The person seeking the support needs to show why it is needed and must usually file a formal financial affidavit with the court. I devote all of chapter 6 to this topic, showing you how to prepare this document. It is critical to prepare the affidavit properly at the very beginning and base it on facts to substantiate your request for support. Take enough time to fully document your financial needs—it is difficult to get the amount of support increased, and usually costly if there is a disagreement. The judge is going to look at one party's ability to pay and the other spouse's need for support. No one will get everything he wants. Most states will require each party to prepare a sworn statement, a financial affidavit, detailing both spouses' living expenses and income.

You will also file a temporary parenting plan that will outline how you plan to share the responsibilities of raising your children, including visitation schedules and monetary support. Every state has guidelines you can use to establish child support. Remember, there is only so much money to go around. You, your spouse, and your children face compromises.

If you are going to talk about the divorce with your husband, have an agenda. If you can't talk or communicate effectively about financial matters—most divorcing couples need help in this area—suggest to him that you meet with a qualified financial planner specializing in divorce who can help you to understand all of the issues you are facing. If you are working with a mediator or using collaborative law, keep such discussions for those meetings. Your husband is no longer your trusted advisor and partner. You need to equalize the power. Suggest a settlement conference with your attorneys and financial planner if you believe it will facilitate a timely and fair property settlement.

The traditional approach to dissolution has each of you duplicating the process of reporting the same financial information to your own attorneys. You can keep the costs down if you cooperatively prepare one summary and share it with both attorneys. A second approach is for each party to share independent reports with his own attorneys, and the attorneys then exchange requests for the other spouse's information. This may involve the use of formal depositions, during which the attorney questions the other spouse with a court reporter recording the answers. If one spouse refuses to provide the requested information, the opposing attorney will get a court order requiring that data be submitted. This increases the cost of the process considerably.

Too many times I see the woman attempting to negotiate with her husband or allowing him to provide countless proposals or having countless telephone conversations when she doesn't understand the full economic impact of what is being discussed. The divorcing woman needs an attorney to handle the legal aspects of her case and to quarterback her professional team. If your husband argues against this help, pause and take a hard look at what is going on in your case.

Don't Let Him Come Between You and Your Lawyer

Once you have hired an attorney with whom you are comfortable, use your lawyer to help you organize your financial information. If you have an attorney who is not responsive to you and with whom you are not communicating, then write a letter explaining your frustrations. If this doesn't work, and your lawyer continues to ignore your requirements, you may need to get a new attorney.

Your entire financial life is going to come under scrutiny as an overall strategy is determined for dividing assets, sharing income and retirement benefits, claiming personal belongings, and devising a parenting plan. These financial concerns are just the beginning. You can share information either cooperatively or by force, by means of subpoenas. Some attorneys prefer a confrontational approach and this adversarial method can lead to higher costs. It is best to choose an attorney who complements your style rather than one who is like you. In other words, if you tend to be passive, pick someone who is more aggressive. If your spouse is not confrontational, use an attorney whose style will not antagonize your husband into becoming adversarial. You and your attorney are going to be working very closely together, and you need to have mutual respect and trust.

I remember a case I worked on two years ago. Edward and Joanne were in their early forties. He was a physician, and she had been a nurse until their children were born ten years earlier, when she gave up her career to be a stay-at-home mom. This couple had built up significant savings; they had 60 percent equity in their home and more than $400,000 in retirement assets.

Joanne wanted out of the marriage for reasons of emotional incompatibility as well as Edward's long working hours, which resulted in little family time. She decided she did not want the house and moved into a rental home a few blocks from the family residence so the children could be close to both parents and stay in the same school district.

I cautioned Joanne about leaving her home at this point, because it could reduce the support she might otherwise justify, resulting in a reduced standard of living for her and the children. She was adamant about leaving. She thought she and her husband had reached a joint financial decision about dividing their furniture, purchasing new furniture, and handling the costs of her move by dipping into their savings. They had agreed on a base amount for her living expenses for the first month, and then they were supposed to sit down and revise the numbers. She did all of this in good faith. Before they could meet to discuss the numbers, Edward filed a divorce petition with the aid of a well-known adversarial attorney.

There were restraining orders, a bid for custody of the children, and a claim that Joanne was an unfit mother. Edward hired a part-time housekeeper to compete with Joanne's being home with the children after school. His strategy was that the cost of his "hired wife" would reduce the amount he had to pay his spouse for alimony and child support. Court evaluators were appointed to make recommendations on the parenting plan. Joanne had to hire separate financial experts to have Edward's medical practice evaluated for its assets and goodwill. In general, "goodwill" is any business asset that is not included in the tangible assets of a company. It can include an estimated value of the brand loyalty of customers, or the firm's reputation in the marketplace. Originally, they had agreed to hire the same business valuation firm, so now the costs for hiring third-party experts had escalated.

Edward changed his position, not wanting to sell the house to make funds available for each of them to purchase two new residences. He hired a detective to follow Joanne, even though this was a no-fault divorce. Edward's actions were hostile and aimed at preserving the major share of the property for himself. He was furious with Joanne's attorney for consistently checkmating his attorney's actions.

Joanne had to work her way through demands from his attorney harassing her every move, including unnecessary requests to review how she spent her temporary maintenance and child support. Often, the controlling husband will hire an attorney whom he can control, micromanaging the letters and information submitted to his wife and her attorney.

In the end, Joanne received custody of the children and a flexible parenting plan. She moved to another area of the city and purchased a new home after Edward refinanced their residence to provide her with a down payment. Edward was required to pay alimony for four years on a declining scale while she upgraded her nursing skills to become a nurse practitioner. His retirement assets were divided, and he signed a ***promissory note*** secured by the house to buy out her interest in the medical practice over the next five years. She will receive 22 percent of his average earnings for the next four years. If his earnings are above this historical average, these dollars will be shared as follows: 15 percent of the gross to the wife and 10 percent of the net to the children for the maintenance period.

If you are in this type of divorce, you have no choice than to check-mate your husband's actions methodically. It will cost you money, but re-member, historically men have controlled women through money, and the strategy is designed to wear you down, reduce your self-esteem, and heighten your sense of guilt and failure so that you will settle for less. Such strategies make it critical for you to do your own homework and save your-self money by doing some of the necessary paralegal work. Save your at-torney's time for what you cannot do. Become your own paralegal for as much of the administrative work as you can.

To keep your costs under control, ask questions, have an agenda when you meet with your attorney and experts, and ask what you can do to con-serve your money. Be sure your experts talk and share information by fax, phone calls, e-mail, or copying letters to one another as needed. Ask for a monthly bill and call your attorney only when you have something impor-tant to say.

You should learn about the attorney your spouse has hired. Find out what you can about him. Ask your own attorney about his adversary; ask your other experts as well. You might want to view your husband's attorney in action in the courtroom on another case. Do your research. Be pre-pared. Prepare a defense with your lawyer and do not allow yourself to be bullied.

Divorce is a time of highly charged emotions. Often you will feel as though the process is making you crazy, so it is important to stay as objec-tive and focused as possible. Take care of your mental health. Use trusted friends, religious advisors, or a therapist to help you stay on track.

Watch Out for Late-Night Telephone Calls

Keep a diary of all your husband's phone calls. If they are harassing in na-ture, tell him you are recording the conversations. If he writes notes to you offering helpful hints on how you should live your life, organize your time, how to dress, what to say to others, whom to trust, where to go to church—keep the correspondence filed chronologically. When the divorce is final and you are ready for your paper cleaning, you'll have something to burn.

The late-night phone calls from your husband can be tearful, angry, sad, or an attempt to reconcile. They may be humorous, guilt-ridden, or all of the above. Remember, both of you will go through the emotional stages of divorce I described earlier. You can keep moving through these emotional stages or get stuck. Refresh yourself on these stages, so you can identify the changes happening to you and mark your progress by them.

WHAT NOT TO TALK ABOUT

When you and your husband talk, it's important that you don't give away information that may allow him to take advantage of you. Here are some "don'ts" to remember. Don't talk about:

- What you don't understand.
- What you have heard through the grapevine or rumor mill.
- Your proposed financial settlement.
- Your plans to move away from the area.
- Your health problems.
- Your sex life.
- How you spend your free time.
- How much money you are saving or spending.
- Your detailed vacation plans.
- Early-stage career plans.

Women often talk too much and give away their position on a financial strategy, child custody issues, and other aspects of the divorce.

I suggest you rent the movie *Kramer vs. Kramer* with Dustin Hoffman and Meryl Streep and also *The War of the Roses* with Michael Douglas, Kathleen Turner, and Danny DeVito. Both of these movies paint a realistic picture of how good intentions in the divorce process often disintegrate into bitter enmity.

DEALING WITH YOUR HUSBAND

For many people, death is easier to deal with than divorce. You will still see each other occasionally. If there are children and common friendships, I encourage you to try to work out a way of dealing with each other. To help you deal with your ex or ex-to-be, I've compiled a list of things to do and not to do.

Things to Do

- Stick to the facts and details.
- Take a deep breath before you speak.
- Have a joint mediation session to handle disputes.
- Call 911 if you feel threatened.
- If you feel strong, look him right in the eye when you speak and stare him down.

Things Not to Do

- Don't wander or invite commentary on "what was."
- Don't look at your husband during the deposition or at the trial if you feel intimidated by his aggressiveness.
- Don't argue with your husband or threaten. Keep to the facts. If you don't want to talk, leave the situation until you feel you can deal with him.
- Don't get into what he has or has not done.
- Don't quiz the kids about his actions, his new girlfriend, how he spends his money, and don't try to turn your children into spies when you can't communicate with him. If you put your children in the middle, they will be angry with both of you.

If your husband won't communicate with you, you can't make him. Just remember, he can't avoid you forever. He'll be forced under the legal system to deal with you through your attorney.

Anna was quite proud that she had no relationship with her soon-to-be ex-husband. She had decided what she wanted from her divorce. She had written her own property settlement proposal and had convinced her children not to speak to their father. She even told everyone at their church about his departure and his infidelity. She insisted on referring to his new girlfriend as his "floozy."

Anna had created her own vision of her divorce, denying the reality of her situation. Her expectations for the property settlement and her alimony request were unrealistic. She was controlling, inflexible, and unwilling to consider any point of view other than her own. I listened to her for an hour and a half and then sent her on her way. I was unable to break through her naïve, ironclad position. She had no attorney and intended to handle her own settlement. I asked her to do some reading about the emotional and financial aspects of settling a divorce after a long-term marriage—thirty-eight years in her case.

She came back to see me one year later after having to go to court to get her settlement, which was quite different from what she had proposed. She was bitter about the legal system and angry with her ex-husband, with her children for living with their father, and with anyone else who had crossed her path. I advised her to see another advisor for her postdivorce planning, as I did not work with clients who insisted on living out the victim role. I'm delighted to see recovering victims, however, and help them with their new life.

I do not recommend a "her against him" mentality. I suggest an attitude that creates a win-win settlement, emotionally and financially. This will take time and cooperation. It is not realistic for most divorcing couples to remain trusted friends after a divorce. It seldom happens. Be willing to settle for mutual respect from a distance.

It is asking a lot to expect you to like each other. If you have been through a court battle, child custody conflict, or have been the recipient of nasty letters, the best you can hope for are controlled conversations and contacts, dealing with the facts and leaving out the emotions. Achieving this is not easy, and it takes time. If there are no children, there may be no need to see each other ever again.

Most divorcing couples have friends in common, similar hobbies, the same church, or children who will bring them into contact with each other. When there are young children, I recommend that the parents attend postdivorce counseling sessions with the children to create a safe haven for them. The divorced couple needs to understand the parenting agreement and all the things that are not written into it. How do they share information about school or social activities? What do they do in a crisis or emergency? These are things that should be settled by agreement. Let the children know how much you care for them in a mediated session with a qualified therapist. Plan on four sessions during a three-month period. If there are new stepparents, get them involved.

This chapter has focused on the behavior-management aspects of divorce. I have found coming to grips with this side of the process is often one of the most difficult challenges a woman faces. If you can master these issues early on, the legal side of divorce will be much easier to weather.

6

What Determines the Cost of the Divorce?

The cost of a thing is the amount of what I call life which is required to be exchanged for it, immediately or in the long run.

—HENRY DAVID THOREAU

One of the questions I am often asked is what determines the cost of a divorce. My answer is simple—for the most part, you do. Estimating how much your divorce will cost is not a simple calculation. Every divorce is unique in terms of financial considerations and emotional issues. Using a variety of resources can be very expensive. In this chapter I point out what drives the cost of divorce by walking through the legal process in a logical, step-by-step way. The examples I use are from actual client cases and illustrate effective ways of containing costs as well as what can happen if you are not prepared.

USING MULTIPLE EXPERTS

Most attorneys and qualified experts charge by the hour for their services. You have to pay a retainer to each of them. Depending on the complexity of your divorce, the list of experts you'll need varies. Experts can include an attorney, family or business accountant, a qualified financial planner with expertise in divorce, business valuation expert, an appraiser for both personal property and real estate, a career specialist if there is an economically disadvantaged spouse or other potential career issues involved in the divorce, a psychologist, medical doctor, employee benefits specialist, or actuary if there are pension plans to be valued.

Adding to the list of professionals are trust officers, social workers if there is a child custody dispute, schoolteachers and administrators—the list can go on and on. The more experts, the more money you can expect to spend. Each divorce requires an individualized strategy. You may be asking, "Why do I need all of these experts?" When attorneys apply the team strategy to the divorce process, they are better able to understand your needs and build a more thorough case. You become a team member and are accountable for the outcome as well. You want as much participation as possible in planning your postdivorce life, and you will get better results if your attorney treats you as an equal partner in the divorce process.

The traditional approach to divorce settlement, which I believe no longer fits the needs of modern couples, is characterized by the attorney, assuming he or she has all of the knowledge and expertise to handle the case. Divorcing clients often have complicated financial, career planning, and mental health needs that attorneys are not trained to assess. The attorney only deals with the legal aspects of the case, leaving the client potentially underserved. In the worst cases, disadvantaged spouses are left to sort out their emotional, financial, and career needs on their own, with no assistance from qualified professionals.

Traditionally, the attorney defers to the client, asking what he or she wants in the settlement, without considering if those goals are realistic. In some cases, the attorney doesn't know what outcome the client wants or expects. Often the attorney refers the clients to experts for counseling and there is no follow-up to learn what issues the clients face. Worse yet are situations in which attorneys do not make sure the client made the recommended appointment or sought out the expert.

With the team approach, the attorney seeks outside consultants in the financial, educational, and mental health areas, business and pension evaluations, taxation, and others to create a more comprehensive, integrated dissolution agreement. The lawyer acts as the point person or team leader to make sure you meet with each of the consultants before, during, and after the divorce. During your meetings, each professional works with you to assess your current situation and to establish common goals. Together you establish a strategy for the divorce.

WORKING WITH A TEAM

Let me give you an example of how to use a professional team, and the related costs. Several of the experts with whom you will be working are going to need copies of your income tax returns. You can make these copies at a discount copy center and place them in organized folders for your experts, or you can have your attorney copy them and have them sent to the expert. In the first case it will cost you $5 at most and in the second case $150 or more. Keep a written log of who has received what paperwork and the date it was delivered.

What about creating a budget? Are you going to code and organize your checks and deposits, or are you going to have an expert's paralegal do this laborious work? You can save a considerable amount of money by doing a lot of the delivery work among your experts.

A fax machine is also a good investment in your divorce case, as is a recorder on your telephone so that you can document conversations. Have an e-mail account for sharing general information. You will want to have the ability to record any nasty-grams or threats that may be coming from your estranged spouse.

Learn the buzzwords and procedures for what is ahead of you so that you can ask intelligent questions and have a better understanding of what to expect. Have you ever read a divorce decree, property *settlement agreement*, financial affidavit, or a parenting plan? Do you know what to expect at a deposition hearing? Are you really aware of what a restraining order can and cannot do? Do you have any idea what legal rights you have during separation? What would happen if either you or your spouse should die during the divorce process? Invest the time and effort to become prepared. After all, it is your money.

The good attorneys want you to be educated, helpful, and not naïve. Handling divorce can be stressful for all parties concerned, including the professionals. Even if you are organized and do all of the things I outline in this book, there are many instances in which our legal system creates a money-spending monster that gobbles up your capital. Let me give you an example.

UNCOOPERATIVE SPOUSES

Ellie, fifty-three, and her husband Richard, fifty-eight, were married for twenty-five years. He is an attorney in the real estate mortgage business; she is a university professor. Together they have a child in college, and he has two older sons from his prior marriage. Richard has lived out of the country for much of the past ten years. Prior to the divorce, they owned their home, a beach house, a small rental property, some antiques, several cars, and less than $200,000 in retirement funds. The total estate was valued at about $4 million.

Richard is a wheeler-dealer with a strong ego. He decided to represent himself in court. Although he is an expert in real estate law, he does not know family law. Ellie hired a prominent attorney to represent her. Richard was found in contempt of court several times during the year of their divorce, because of his attitude and flamboyant style. Judges are somewhat intimidated by him. They are cautious, because he is a lawyer representing himself, and they could easily make mistakes that could extend the case on appeal for years.

Richard's blatant disregard for the normal dissolution process resulted in his ignoring subpoenas, canceling depositions, not getting his experts listed on time, and more. Time and time again Ellie and her lawyer went back to court trying to enforce a previously established ruling that her husband chose to ignore. In each instance, the judge awarded her $300 for court costs, but she had to pay her attorney $1,000 or more. Expenses were building just to enforce what had already been agreed to in an earlier session.

Finally, the court date was set. The property settlement was one of the most convoluted decisions I have seen in years. No alimony was awarded. A fifty-five–forty-five split of the assets was ordered. A small allowance was given for Ellie's court costs, even though she had provided all of the information, did all of the data-gathering and discovery, and fought an uphill battle against Richard's deplorable legal antics. They were divorced, but now needed to sell the house and rental property and split the proceeds.

He was required to make the mortgage payments and she had to pay the utilities until the property sold. It was agreed the house should be put up for sale immediately. They went back to court five times for clarification of issues, including with whom the property should be listed, how to determine the sale price, and what constituted fix-up costs. Richard won a decision to have his inexperienced son, who has a real estate license, list the house. The next time they appeared in court, Richard argued that only the son could show the house and no other realtor could represent the house unless through him. There went the benefit of using a multiple listing service.

Richard then began working on a deal with a group of offshore buyers and attempted to cut out all of the existing real estate agents from the transaction. Ellie, meanwhile, was paying all of the utility costs for the home. The proceeds from the rental property were placed in a trust fund from which real estate taxes and insurance were paid. The court set up an intricate formula for recovering the housing and other expenses that was probably unfair to Ellie, as she has paid more than $4,000 out-of-pocket—money we believe should have been coming out of the joint rental account.

Should she have gone into court at $350 per hour, plus preparation time, to clarify what should have been established by the judge at the beginning of the process? You are probably getting the picture. Facing a combative, quarrelsome ex-husband, Ellie still has another round of legal courtroom drama to endure involving the sale of the house and who will pay the closing costs.

The divorce has been final for two years. Richard finally did purchase the house from Ellie. His new live-in loaned him the money, and my client received a cash settlement for her interest in the home. But that was not the end of the nightmare. Now Richard is appealing the divorce settlement and the purchase of the residence from his spouse. He is arguing that the sale should have been a normal sale between a buyer and seller and not incident to divorce. If this viewpoint were accepted, it would cause my client to have a substantial gain on the sale of the residence, and she would have a significant income-tax liability. She received the vacation home in the property settlement although she was never interested in having the home. She negotiated the sale in good faith. A real estate attorney, Richard continues to represent himself in the appeal of the case, while my client continues paying a new set of attorneys to handle her response.

My client keeps asking if it will ever end. Probably not for another year or so. Stay tuned!

COMPLICATIONS WITH CHILDREN

Prolonged expenses can be generated when there is a dispute over child custody. Since fathers have become more involved in raising their children, joint custody has become more popular and works for many couples. I support cooperative efforts in the raising of children, but I think the plan has to be practical and take the children's emotional well-being into account.

Some of the parenting plans I have seen require the children to be transported back and forth between parents two times a week, as they try to attend school and keep up with their extracurricular activities. In this situation, the family might consider a joint nanny or housekeeper. Instead, what often happens is that the spouse with the higher earning power— usually the husband—hires a nanny, while the wife attempts to go to school, raise the children, and possibly even work part time. Yet child support is based on the amount of time a parent has the children. If the wife works part time, money that would have gone to her is now going to the nanny. If one of the spouses is on a business trip, should the other parent have the children instead of the nanny? How do you resolve these conflicts after divorce? Is it mediation or back to court for enforcement?

If you are dealing with someone who is unreasonable, it is very difficult to get on with your life. There are legal and financial issues at every turn that you must handle. As one wife said to me when I suggested she consider giving up her battle for custody, "I couldn't live with myself if I put a price on my children." But sometimes you need to know when to back off—for your own well-being and for that of the children.

I have mentioned that children have become more of a financial asset as well as a source of extensive costs in divorce litigation. Let me elaborate. If you want to intimidate the other party, cause him to become somewhat unhinged emotionally, and get into a nightmare marathon with the courts, just question his suitability to be a parent, or even worse, accuse him of sexual abuse. In the past three years, I have seen many such accusations. All too often the children become pawns in the vindictive battles that ensue. The court gets involved, a variety of court-appointed guardians, psychologists, and social workers are called, the divorce process slows to a crawl, child custody becomes an issue, and the children are allowed to be with the accused parent only in the company of a therapist. It goes on and on. The financial costs are astronomical, and the emotional costs are beyond calculation.

One client of mine has spent more than $50,000 trying to resolve visitation rights with his daughter during the past four years. His ex-wife lives out of state and has made it her career to keep him away from their child.

Aaron was just twenty when he married Melinda, a woman ten years his senior with two daughters. They stayed together for ten years and had a daughter of their own. He is an heir to a sizable estate, and Melinda has consistently demanded part of this inherited money. The parenting plan established in their divorce granted Melinda custody of all three children, and she has been receiving child support in excess of $5,000 a month for several years, plus private school costs. Aaron has also financed the college educations for his two stepdaughters.

Aaron made arrangements to visit his daughter during the Christmas holidays, but Melinda claimed at the last minute that the ten-year-old girl did not want to see him. He has decided to withdraw from trying to see his daughter in an attempt to stop the drama his former wife insists on creating. Visitations will now be set up in Melinda's state of residence by his attorney. As a result, Aaron will incur legal expenses every time he wants to visit his daughter.

A Road Map for Divorce

In my twenty-five years of experience working in the area of divorce, I've found one thing to be clear. Everyone has a fear of the unknown. My clients don't know what to expect, how things work, and what is going to be required or when. To help you navigate this uncertainty, I have

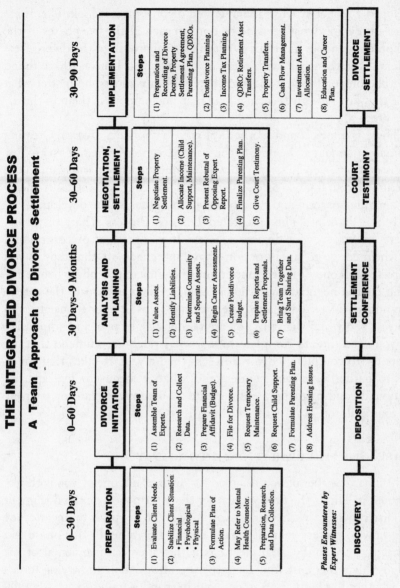

FIGURE 6.1 The Integrated Divorce Process

developed a model of what an integrated divorce process looks like. It includes a time line, what needs to be done in each of the five phases of the legal process, and an illustration of the team approach to the divorce settlement. I use this chart with every divorcing client I meet. I have found this to be one of the best tools to share with my clients, no matter what phase they are in. It gives them a road map and empowers them in the divorce process.

There is a logical and methodical way to approach divorce. Creating the final settlement is the next to the last phase, not the first. If you follow my instructions, step-by-step, you will become an active participant in the structure of your final divorce settlement. If you complete the tasks one by one, a natural, orderly, and comprehensive proposal will be developed.

Take a look at "The Integrated Divorce Process" chart on p. 87. Where are you in your divorce process? If you feel out of control and overwhelmed, go to the initiation phase and check off the steps as you complete each one. It is very important to complete this phase before focusing on the negotiation-settlement stage. You can't create the settlement until you have completed the previous steps. If your spouse tries to rush you, show him the steps you are taking, one by one, and emphasize that you need time to complete your work. I rarely recommend that my clients try to complete a divorce in less than a year. It takes that much time to gather your facts, understand what it means to live apart—emotionally and financially—and create a postdivorce plan for yourself and your children.

Phase One—Preparation: 0 to 30 Days

At this phase neither of you has filed for divorce, but one of you is thinking about it. This is the time you gather the information on the document checklist provided in chapter 3. You may want to speak to an attorney about how to protect yourself legally during this time. In this phase you are having very confidential meetings with a financial planner, attorney, and possibly a therapist. You are gathering information and trying to decide whether to file. If you suspect your husband is going to ask for a divorce, you are trying to get prepared.

A few months ago a client came to see me at the predivorce phase. Cynthia, fifty-six, had been married to Sam, fifty-eight, for more than fifteen years—a second marriage for both. Sam had four children from a previous marriage, all of whom worked in the family business. The couple lived in a lovely home out in the country, and Sam was generous in providing her with a comfortable monthly budget for the household. They traveled together and generally were happy.

Cynthia felt insecure, though. Sam did not talk about the finances with her and she was becoming increasingly concerned about his gambling. She had found receipts showing that his losses were more than $150,000 in the past five years. Sam kept detailed receipts at home and had been audited once by the IRS. Cynthia was concerned for her financial security and had begun to contemplate divorce as a potential solution. She wanted to see a complete picture of their personal finances in order to understand how she would be protected if Sam died before she did.

I helped Cynthia gather documentation on their personal finances. I also prepared a budget establishing how the household funds had been spent and what it would take for her to live if she was divorced or widowed. She found the data-gathering very helpful. She was finding out more and more about their finances and finally was able to get a copy of their most recent income tax return. Cynthia was asked to sign the tax return each year on April 15 at the last minute with no time to review it, which is not unusual in many families.

I recommended that Cynthia see a therapist. After six months of therapy and work with our office and an attorney, she decided not to go

0–30 Days

PREPARATION

Steps
(1) Evaluate Client Needs.
(2) Stabilize Client Situation • Financial • Psychological • Physical
(3) Formulate Plan of Action.
(4) May Refer to Mental Health Counselor.
(5) Preparation, Research, and Data Collection.

FIGURE 6.2 The Preparation Phase

forward with the divorce. We did recommend that they see an estate-planning attorney.

Cynthia showed an interest in her family's personal finances. She learned about her financial security, and what Sam had planned if he predeceases her. Cynthia certainly does not have all of the answers, but she has a better understanding of her legal rights if there is a divorce or death. Sam has agreed to name Cynthia as a beneficiary on his life insurance and as an IRA beneficiary to give her the security she needs, a lifetime residency in their home or a similar condo, and the funds to maintain it through a trust.

Let's look at the first legal phase of divorce and see what tasks are involved in negotiating it.

Step One: Evaluate Client Needs

You are gathering the financial information listed on the document roundup list, doing the research on attorneys and the divorce process that best suits you. This is also when you would take a look at your historical spending. A financial planner is an excellent guide for you during this stage. Also, have a one-hour informational meeting with two or three attorneys. During these sessions your potential team members will analyze your situation and suggest approaches consistent with your individual needs. Listen carefully to their suggestions and determine what is in your own best interests.

Step Two: Stabilize Client Situation (Financial, Emotional, Physical)

Imagine that you are considering sailing alone around the world. You will need to make sure that your financial, emotional, and physical resources are in place to complete the trip. If you have limitations or problems, this is the time to identify them and start planning for how to overcome them.

Experience has taught me that one spouse almost always is planning the divorce before the other spouse. It is logical and natural that this person has been thinking about what his or her postdivorce life would be like. In many cases, there has been significant preplanning.

Whenever you have concerns about the stability of your marriage, look back over the previous one to two years. What has been going on with your finances—a refinance of the house, increased spending for luxury items, unusual clothing expenditures, a sudden or unexplained increase in travel or cell phone expenses, an exercise program that wasn't there previously?

In addition to financial signs, there may be other indications. An increase in the frequency or duration of absences from home, loss of sexual or romantic interest, heightened periods of irritability, anger, or withdrawal can all signal trouble. I am not suggesting that these necessarily mean your spouse is planning a divorce. There can be many reasons for such behavior. I am simply saying it is important to understand the reasons for these changes to avoid being caught off guard. If physical or emotional abuse occurs, get professional help immediately.

Only you will know the signs if your spouse is planning to depart. At least one spouse invariably goes through this phase before the actual filing of the petition for divorce.

If you have been blindsided by a spouse who has been seriously planning a divorce, there is automatically a conflict in the preparation phase. You can feel rushed to catch up during this time. Resist the temptation to leave anything out of your own preparation.

Step Three: Formulate a Plan of Action

The nature of this plan depends on your circumstances as to whether you are going through this phase to protect yourself from your spouse's actions or to initiate the divorce yourself. Whether you take the initial action or your spouse does, the first visible evidence is often when one party moves out of the family home. Such a move should not be undertaken without careful planning. Think through how you want to proceed, be clear about your reasons, and consider how your spouse is likely to respond.

Step Four: Make an Appointment to See a Mental Health Counselor

Most of the clients I meet with have seen a marriage counselor, either jointly or separately. If your spouse won't see a therapist regarding your marriage, find out why, and evaluate what this means to your relationship. Frequently, it is the marriage therapist who actually works with the couple to help them separate. This counseling can provide a safe environment in which to set the separation process into motion, and it may also strengthen the relationship or even prevent the divorce.

Step Five: Begin Preparation, Research, Data Collection

Get all the financial information you possibly can during this time. A photocopier can become your best friend. Ask for passwords for the computer where financial data is stored. Ask for financial information from your spouse. Take a short basic financial course at a community college or look for seminars in your area. Start reading books on marital finances and the raising of children around money and values. All of these are a catalyst for sharing between spouses. If your spouse refuses to tell you how to access such information, questions your need to know it, or otherwise signals he or she doesn't want to share, this could be a red flag. Find a safe place to store your newfound information—not in your briefcase, probably not on your computer. You might want to put this data on a disk that you keep in a safety deposit box with copies of important documents.

Phase Two—Initiation: 0 to 60 Days

In this phase a decision has been reached. Someone is going to file for divorce. It is now time to begin activating the plans you established in phase one. The legal escalator is moving and you must be ready.

0–60 Days

DIVORCE INITIATION
Steps
(1) Assemble Team of Experts.
(2) Research and Collect Data.
(3) Prepare Financial Affidavit (Budget).
(4) File for Divorce.
(5) Request Temporary Maintenance.
(6) Request Child Support.
(7) Formulate Parenting Plan.
(8) Address Housing Issues.

FIGURE 6.3   The Divorce Initiation Phase

Step One: Assemble Team of Experts

Initially, this team will include your attorney and financial planner. Start meeting with a career advisor as soon as you can if it's necessary for your situation. You will need an estimate of the costs of the services each of these professionals to provide when you prepare your financial affidavit. Try to determine what other experts will be needed in your divorce. Ask about retainers, hourly rates, and an estimated total cost for the services you will require. For example, there may be a need to have a valuation of a business, analysis of stock options, tax analysis regarding the sale of a house or assets, or a pension valuation. Not all of these experts need to be hired at this time, but I suggest you get a rough idea of the fees involved so that you, your attorney, and your financial planner can create a funding plan. Remember that some of these expenses may be shared or partially offset by the terms of your final settlement. You can also do much of the preliminary work in this area to reduce your costs.

Step Two: Research and Collect Data

Research and data collection are ongoing activities during the divorce process. You must create a system to organize the information you will accumulate. The heavy data-gathering occurs in the next phase. There will be a lot of paper to organize, so I recommend creating a filing system similar to the one I am about to describe. Too many times I see clients arrive with bags and boxes filled with scraps of paper that are totally disorganized. Either you must organize this material or pay someone else to be your clerk.

Admittedly, this can be an overwhelming task. You will not have all of this information in the initiation phase of the divorce. It is a work in progress. So relax and do the best you can. Just get started.

My clients find it helpful to make copies of the information they need to collect by creating three notebooks—or boxes with labeled folders, depending on the amount of information—one for you, one for the attorney, and one for the financial planner. Organize the information in various colored and labeled folders, keeping information in chronological order. Each time you learn something new or have a phone call, record and note it in the appropriate files. Maintain an easily accessible list of experts with their cards, phone numbers, and e-mail addresses.

One client I worked with kept this information summarized on large index cards, and she kept backup files for each card. The note cards went everywhere with her. Some of my other clients have the information organized on their computers. There is no best way to do this—just use a system that works well for you.

Sample File Folders

- **Family Data.** Include names, addresses, Social Security numbers, dates of birth for you, your spouse, and children, date of marriage, and date of separation.
- **Time Line for Your Married Life.** Include children's births, major events and crises, key dates, moves, and work history. A sample time line is included in appendixes A and B.
- **Case Schedule.** This is the schedule established by the court specifying dates for submission of documents, and court appearances. Your attorney can help you create this.
- **Personal Calendar for the Coming Year.** This should include every date associated with your activities connected to the divorce, including appointments with your team members and any social or familial activities you should document that could relate to your divorce.
- **Correspondence with Attorney (maintained chronologically).** Keep a copy of every letter to or from your attorney.
- **E-mail Correspondence (maintained chronologically).** Keep an up-to-date record of every e-mail you send or receive involving any person involved in your divorce, including your spouse, children, and team members.
- **Temporary Orders.** This file should include copies of all court documents that establish deadlines, procedures, restrictions, or instructions related to your divorce process. Examples of these are restraining orders on your spouse, temporary maintenance, child custody, and visitation.
- **Employee Benefits Summary.** This file contains records showing what benefits you and your spouse are receiving through your employers. Firms usually have a human resources contact who can provide you with these documents.
- **Bonuses, Employee Reimbursements, Expected Promotions.** Keep a copy of all documents showing payment (or anticipated payment) of employment bonuses, reimbursement for expenses such as travel, training, and office supplies, as well as any document indicating a pending promotion or salary action. This should include records for both you and your spouse.
- **Pay Stubs for Past Six Months.** Keep a record of both your and your spouse's pay stubs.
- **Income Tax Returns—Personal and Business.** Be sure these are the final signed returns submitted to the IRS, not just interim worksheets.

- **Budget and Financial Affidavit (as submitted to the court).** Include all your notes—you will need a file for yours and your spouse's.
- **Request for Child Support.** If either attorney has filed a request with the court for one spouse to receive financial assistance as child support, a copy of the document should be kept here.
- **Temporary Parenting Plan.** This should include any document issued by the court or signed by both spouses establishing a plan of care for your children.
- **Request for Temporary Maintenance or Alimony.** Your attorney will submit this request to the court. Be sure to keep copies of all proposals and counterproposals involved, not just the final court-approved version.
- **Interrogatories.** Keep copies of all questions submitted in writing by your attorney or your spouse's attorney that the court requires be answered to provide information either side needs to prepare a case. Failure to respond to an interrogatory can result in a charge of perjury, so it is important to maintain a record of what has been asked for and when.
- **Summary List of Assets.** This is a comprehensive line-item listing of all marital assets, similar to what is found in reallocation of assets figures A.1 and B.2 in appendixes A and B. It includes single-line summary values for all real estate, investments, personal property, and other assets, such as a financial statement. The other asset folders contain the details.
- **Real Estate.** This includes values, mortgages and terms, appraisals, taxes, and insurance.
- **Corporate Perks.** List anything provided by your or your spouse's employer that could be viewed as having monetary value, including travel or housing allowances, domestic services such as maids and chauffeurs, vehicle leases, vacation time-shares, educational reimbursement, access to corporate transportation, financial planning services, and insurance policies.
- **Career Assets.** I recommend you talk to an experienced financial planner to establish what assets may apply in your case. They are often "hidden" in employment contracts or assumed in nonverbal communications. These assets are usually related to the unique knowledge, skills, and business relationships an individual develops over time. If your spouse has a uniquely valued skill in his or her field of expertise, it may be seen as a career asset with quantifiable monetary value in terms of future income potential.
- **Investment Assets.** Include brokerage and savings accounts, investments, and partnerships.

- **Retirement Assets.** Include statements on IRAs, *SIMPLE IRAs*, *SEP*s, 401(k) plans, profit-sharing plans, pensions, annuities.
- **List of Personal Property and Valuations.** List your personal property by room and by item. For gifts, state the source—inheritance, spouse, mother. If there is a special value, get it appraised.
- **Other Assets.** These include educational funding accounts for children, personal property such as art on loan to others, and any asset that doesn't fit into one of the other categories in your files.
- **Prenuptial Agreement.** If either of you signed one, it should be included here.
- **Community Property Agreements.** Any document showing you and your spouse own property subject to community property laws should be included in this file.
- **Insurance Trusts and Family Partnerships.** If you or your spouse established a trust fund or signed a business partnership agreement, file a copy in this folder.
- **Child Custody Evaluations.** Any report filed by a social worker, psychologist, or other professional related to a request for custody of your children should be included.
- **Settlement Proposals.** Both your attorney and your spouse's attorney are likely to submit written proposals specifying terms for agreeing on a division of assets and liabilities in the divorce. Whether they are filed with a court or not, you should keep copies of all such proposals.
- **Issues that Concern You.** Keep a running tally of issues that surface during the divorce for which some follow-up action is required. These may include statements made by your spouse, his attorney, or one of the third-party experts in the case.
- **Children's Visitation Calendar and Weekly Notes.** Document all visitations on a calendar with comments about any problems that arose such as missed or tardy appearances, and behavior issues.
- **List of Questions to Be Answered.** Some clients prefer to keep a separate folder with specific questions they want to ask the attorney or financial planner, rather than group them with the items in the issues of concern folder.

Step Three: Prepare Financial Affidavit

Preparation of the financial affidavit is often the first formal budgeting process and cash-flow management process the divorcing client faces. It is usually required immediately after filing for divorce. For many people, completing this document becomes an overwhelming task. You are asked to enumerate your income and expenses in great detail. To derive total income, wages and all other sources of income have to be listed. You are asked to list your anticipated expenses in several categories provided by the standard financial declaration form. This data-gathering and organizing of the financial information for the divorce takes time.

A financial planner can provide special expertise at this phase. The numbers the client provides in requesting temporary spousal maintenance or alimony will be those upon which she must rely for income for a long time, often up to a year until the divorce is settled or until there is a court decision. This phase of the divorce process is critical for your financial and emotional well-being. The time prior to the final divorce decree will be filled with compromises about the parenting plan, custody of the children, valuation and division of assets, and payment or legal and expert fees. Each of these compromises and decisions will have a money counterpart. No one understands the numbers about your living expenses better than you. It is your money, and there will be a strong need to protect it. The spending habits of each of the divorcing spouses will be under a microscope. There will be accusations and comments about each party's spending habits during the marriage.

I urge you to have an experienced financial planner take a look at the financial affidavit before submitting it to the court. Make sure the advisor you select is experienced and trained to prepare a comprehensive financial affidavit. Your financial planner needs to be an expert in the divorce area— someone who can testify in support of the information on the affidavit, for the temporary order, in a mediation setting, or in a court. Ask whether the financial planner has testified in court before.

If you are the person who is not the primary wage earner, you need to request the appropriate support at this time. Your information must be well-organized and accurate before submitting it to the court. In my experience, it is both expensive and difficult to change a court-awarded support amount that is based on inaccurate or incomplete data in the financial affidavit. Too many times I see attorneys and clients rush to complete this document. It costs less and is more effective to do it right the first time.

The two most common mistakes I see in the historical budget analysis are that the client provides an incomplete summary of the expenses and the information is disorganized. The client leaves expenses out and later on in the divorce process complains that she does not have enough money. If the client is called in for a deposition by her spouse's attorney, she may be unable to explain where her numbers have come from. Judges are very busy. As a result, the more detailed and accurate the information you provide in a hearing, the better results you can expect. A client who has adequate cash flow tends to be much easier to work with than the client who is always worrying about the next dollar she must spend and where it is coming from.

Since many women are too passive during this phase and regret their lack of organization later in the divorce process, it is essential to build the budget comprehensively from the beginning. The process gives the client more control, better perspective, and a sense of organization about her past and her anticipated future.

After preparing the historical budget, I review past spending patterns and calculate the net monthly income available for child support or alimony. There are always issues when the chief breadwinner is one who takes a draw or minimum salary from his business and takes bonuses for a substantial portion of the annual income. Another problem arises with a business owner who uses the business to pay for expenses that supplement the family lifestyle. Normally, spouses agree to share the income derived partially from the business in some acceptable manner. Any new bonuses received post-separation are generally considered to be the separate property of the person earning the money.

I recently worked with a client whose husband moved to a new job in another state over a weekend, notifying her of his plans as he was packing to leave. He thought everything would remain the same at home, and that she would wait for his indefinite return. She filed for divorce one month later when he returned home for a visit. In his absence she was able to review their finances in great detail. More than $30,000 had disappeared from the sale of their residence in the previous year.

She found other irregularities in the spending and deposits in their personal checking accounts during the previous few months. She would never have discovered the missing money if she hadn't inspected the bank statements, cash withdrawals, credit cards, and the brokerage statements. Prior to her investigation, the wife had handled only the household budget.

She had commingled her inheritance and separate funds during the past year with her husband, and his name was on the brokerage account in which her separate funds had been held. When she tried to remove her husband's name, she found she couldn't do so without his signature, and he refused. Immediately, she had a restraining order placed on this account and several others. Money is often in motion before one party files for divorce and this may require the other spouse to initiate protective action to preserve the family assets.

Step Four: File for Divorce

One of you will need to do this. Coordinate with your attorney about the best way to proceed. The person who wants the divorce is usually the one who files. If you are not getting temporary child support and alimony, you may need to file to have the judge issue temporary orders.

Step Five: Request Temporary Maintenance

Complete your financial affidavit, and from this information make a request for temporary maintenance or alimony. Your attorney can make the request to your husband's attorney, or you can make the request in a mediation setting. Make sure you have the backup data and notes to support your request. It always helps if you can identify where the money is coming from for your support. If it is disputed and you cannot come to an agreement, your attorney can make a motion for a temporary order.

Step Six: Request Child Support

Most states will have child support guidelines based on your income. This is a starting place. In chapter 7 I will give you a spreadsheet to create the "Historical Spending Template." (A sample of this analysis is included in appendix A.) The spreadsheet is very effective in determining how income can be divided to pay for the temporary maintenance or alimony and child support awards.

Remember, child support guidelines are just that. There may be special circumstances in your family that justify requesting more than the guidelines indicate. This is particularly true when the income is there to support the request, as evidenced by historical spending for items like private school education, sports, summer camps, and other special activities for the children. Everyone's situation is different.

Step Seven: Formulate Parenting Plan

Keep in mind that this is a temporary plan, not the final determination of custody and visitation. If you cannot agree with your spouse on a plan that is fair to your children, review some samples from your attorney or mediator. Do not get trapped in an emotional tug of war that disrupts your children's lives. It can be easy to use this issue as a weapon if you are feeling vindictive, but doing so can emotionally scar your children and alienate them indefinitely.

Step Eight: Address Housing Issues

Decide who is going to stay in the family home and how the expenses will be paid. If you stay in the home and are unable to do some of the work such as landscaping, plumbing, or other maintenance chores, make sure that you build an allowance for these expenses into your temporary budget for the financial affidavit. Go to the files you created earlier that document values and costs associated with the residence and any other real property. Reviewing these items will help you to determine which spouse should keep the house or whether it should be sold to finance postdivorce residences or perhaps maintained as a source of rental income.

PHASE THREE—ANALYSIS AND PLANNING: 30 DAYS TO 9 MONTHS

You (or your spouse) have filed. Either temporary child support and maintenance has been established or you are both continuing to deposit your checks into the joint account and are each paying for your living expenses from this account. If you can do this without formal orders, all the better. Usually one spouse or the other elects to make a change in this arrangement, particularly if there is a shortage of money or a disagreement on how it is being spent during this period. Keep in mind that you will be asked to account for what you have spent during the time of separation. Keep good records.

In this phase you will be focusing on completing the data-gathering, analyzing the information, and doing some planning. It is usually not a time for major decision-making or making changes. In this phase you are also performing what the legal system calls "discovery." Discovery is a process of gathering information about the nature, scope, and credibility of the opposing party's claim. The procedures used include depositions, written interrogatories, and notices to produce case-related documentation. This phase is vital because your case can be won or lost in the discovery stage.

The theory behind this process is that justice is best served if both sides have access to the same facts and evidence. With a spouse who is sophisticated about financial affairs—and willing and able to manipulate records—discovery can turn into a struggle.

If your spouse works for someone else, be thankful, because tracking down accounts and investments will be easy compared to a self-employed professional or business owner. Manipulation of the financial data may be relatively easy for those who are self-employed, such as doctors, dentists, lawyers, accountants, financial consultants, and independent contractors, or those who run a cash business.

The law gives your lawyer wide discretion to review tax returns, business and personal records, contracts, canceled checks, credit card receipts, and other documents, and to question your spouse, his or your friends, relatives, or business associates about your spouse's financial dealings. Additionally, the law provides your attorney and expert witnesses liberal access to inspect and evaluate the books on any enterprise your spouse owns, controls, or profits from. This is the time for you to verify any errors that were on the temporary financial affidavit that you each completed.

There are two types of discovery: formal and informal.

Formal Discovery

Formal discovery includes such legal procedures as depositions, interrogatories, and requests for production of documents.

- **Depositions.** A deposition is the sworn testimony of a witness taken outside of court in the presence of lawyers for each side. A court reporter is present to record the proceedings, and the testimony must be given under oath. Since it is a sworn statement, a deposition becomes part of the record of the case. If you say one thing in the discovery deposition, and something else in the trial, you will have to explain why your answer changed. The statements from the discovery deposition that are in conflict can be read to the witness at the trial. If the change is substantial and unexplained, the overall testimony of the witness is less believable.

  Depositions are used for many purposes, for example to gather information that the witness may have that would be difficult to obtain in a written exchange of questions (interrogatories), to compel a reluctant witness to share information, or to test the competence and reliability of an expert witness, and generally to get information into the record.

- **Interrogatories.** Interrogatories are written questions submitted to the other party. Since interrogatories are written and do not require the live presence of the attorneys and court reporter, they are used more frequently than depositions. The answers to interrogatories must be written, made under oath (in the form of a statement you sign), and filed within the prescribed period of time. Interrogatories are commonly used to obtain detailed information from such items as an employment contract or pension plan.

- **Request for production of documents.** Requests for production require the spouses and third parties to deliver documents necessary to understand the issues in your case. These documents might include employment contracts, grants of stock or stock options, or other special corporate perks or privileges with monetary value that have not been made public.

- **Expert opinions.** A number of issues that can arise during the divorce process will require expert testimony to support your case. Examples include: an actuary to assess the value of your pension or that of your spouse; a real estate appraiser to establish the value of the family real estate or commercial real estate; a business appraiser to determine the value of a family-owned business or a family-owned partnership; a doctor to assess specific medical conditions that may affect a spouse's ability to work or physically support himself; a career advisor to discuss training needed for a spouse to reenter the job market; a human resource specialist from your spouse's employer to explain stock options; a financial planner to analyze the financial affidavit and to project and explain the long-term financial effects of specific financial settlements being proposed.

    This expert witness testimony can be essential in uncovering hidden assets or key facts in your case that your spouse may have failed to disclose or did not properly present. Make sure your expert witnesses are experienced and recognized by the courts as experts—if they are not and you end up in trial, their testimony may not be allowed. You don't want to find yourself in this position after you've already committed your time and money.

    Most professionals who act as expert witnesses have a schedule of fees that itemizes their charges for court appearances. Some charge by the hour with a minimum time, a few charge a fixed rate for the case. Costs can range from under $200 an hour for a career advisor to more than $400 an hour for specialized forensic accountants and real estate attorneys.

Informal Discovery

Informal discovery can be as simple as one lawyer calling the other lawyer and saying, "Send me everything you have on your case, including financial affidavits, tax returns, check stubs, investment statements, a list of assets, and anything else that I might need to see." The other attorney then sends the information in a timely manner.

In the informal discovery, the information is voluntarily exchanged and the documentation is included. The other attorney is not required to send something that is not requested. An experienced attorney will have a comprehensive list that will request information for your divorce.

In mediation or collaborative law, this exchange of information is voluntary. If you don't have an attorney representing you, then you are the one who must document the accuracy of the information.

30 Days–9 Months

ANALYSIS AND PLANNING
Steps
(1) Value Assets.
(2) Identify Liabilities.
(3) Determine Community and Separate Assets.
(4) Begin Career Assessment.
(5) Create Postdivorce Budget.
(6) Prepare Reports and Settlement Proposals.
(7) Bring Team Together and Start Sharing Data.

FIGURE 6.4   The Analysis and Planning Phase

Step One: Value Assets

The states differ somewhat on marital property laws, but the concepts presented here will help you with some background information.

Equitable Distribution

Most states have adopted a system that gives courts the discretionary power to divide marital property in a fair and equitable manner. Decisions are based on the ages of the spouses, their employment, the length of the marriage, and income. There can be a wide variation in how the law is interpreted. This concept draws from common law and community property law. Property acquired during a marriage is regarded as marital property, regardless of which spouse holds the title, and the court may divide such marital property proportionately.

Common Law

This concept is based on the old English legal system that transfers a wife's *real property* in total to the husband at the moment of marriage. Present-day interpretation of common law recognizes property held in both spouses' names as jointly owned. Property with the title in one name can be sold or given away without the other spouse's consent. A problem arises if a wife does not work outside the home and all the property is held in the husband's name. The court can regard the husband as the sole owner. Only three states, Mississippi, South Carolina, and West Virginia, retain vestiges of common law.

Community Property

Property acquired during the marriage is owned fifty-fifty by both spouses, even if the title is in one name only. The basic premise is that the labors of both parties are recognized as contributing to acquiring marriage assets. To keep a specific property item in separate ownership, it must be kept separate, not commingled with the marital property. Texas, Louisiana, New Mexico, Arizona, California, Nevada, Idaho, Wisconsin, Washington, and Puerto Rico use some form of this law.

Four Ways to Own Property

There are basically four types of property ownership. Each may be treated somewhat differently in a divorce, depending on your state's laws.

- *Joint tenancy.* You both own half, but you cannot will your half to anyone other than your partner, who automatically inherits your portion when you die.
- *Tenancy in common.* You own half, and you can will your portion to whomever you like.
- *Tenancy by entirety.* In separate property states only, this form of ownership works like a joint tenancy, but is reserved for married people exclusively.
- *Community property.* A special form of ownership for married persons in community property states.

Property, especially real estate, is often one of the most contentious areas of divorce. Real estate can be the largest single asset in many marriages. Unfortunately, the laws governing the disposition of property are complex. I have presented only a few basic terms involved in the concept of ownership. You need to understand the laws governing property in your own state, which may require the expertise of a local attorney.

Step Two: Identify Liabilities

Order a copy of your credit report, and you will find a beginning list of liabilities. Also look at a recent mortgage application for financing on your real estate. Find out if you have cosigned any loans, or if money has been borrowed from a 401(k) plan. Get a complete list of all the credit cards you and your spouse use. Call each card issuer to find out the current balances, and check on how they were issued—who the primary account holder is, who the authorized signers are. Be sure to include any cards on which your older children are listed as authorized users.

Step Three: Determine Community and Separate Assets

During this stage of the divorce, you should do research on how you own your property in the state in which you reside. There may be a difference between how you think you own property and how it is actually registered. You may think you have separate property that you received in an inheritance. If you have registered this inheritance in a joint account at a brokerage house or bank, you may have some difficulty holding onto the separate property.

I have a case currently in process where this is an issue. There is a restraining order on an investment account, requiring that both husband and wife need to agree and sign for any cash withdrawals. The wife continues to manage the investments as she has done in the past. The husband is arguing that she gifted her $200,000 inheritance to their community assets when she put his name on the account. The attorneys will give their arguments before the judge, who will determine the ultimate division of this property in the divorce property settlement.

In another case two years ago, the woman had received an inheritance of $100,000. Initially, she kept the funds separate. Then the husband and wife signed a community property agreement as part of their estate plan. This document renamed everything they owned presently, in the past, and in the future to be community property. The case went to trial, and I will never forget the tough questioning my client faced from the husband's attorney in the courtroom.

My client had opened joint brokerage and credit union accounts with her husband several months after receiving her inheritance. She told the judge that her husband had encouraged her to do this, as his credit union had a better interest rate than hers. That particular credit union would not allow her to open an account without his name on the account. The judge ruled that the inheritance had been commingled and would be divided with the remainder of the marital assets. My client was understandably upset by this result.

She felt betrayed by the system, by her estate-planning attorney for recommending the community property agreement, and by the credit union and brokerage house for not sufficiently explaining to her the new account form she had signed and the implications if there was a divorce or death. Most of all, this professional woman blamed herself for not doing her own research. Her husband earned eight times her income as a manufacturing manager. During this marriage, her pattern with him was to give in to his requests for the "sake of the children" and to maintain her married status in the community under a subtle, but all too common, form of "economic bondage."

Financially, he had made some poor investments in limited partnerships during the prior ten years. One investment had cost them more than $100,000 in back taxes, and they had to mortgage their home to pay off the debt.

What Kind of Property Is Divided in a Property Settlement?

There are three kinds of property to be divided: real property, which consists of land and the buildings (improvements) on it; *tangible property* such as cars, jewelry, furniture and antiques; and *intangible personal property*, which includes bank accounts, stocks and bonds, vested pensions, life insurance, annuities, money market accounts, and retirement accounts.

Before you agree to keep one asset over the other, you should create a record of the date it was acquired and its value at that time, the tax basis of the asset, its potential for sale, current market value, and the value at date of separation. Know what your state laws say about property. For example, do you live or have you lived in a community property state? Have you ever signed a separate property or community property agreement?

What Is Separate Property?

- What you bring into the marriage.
- What you inherit during the marriage.
- What you receive during the marriage as a gift.

To keep such property separate, you must not commingle the separate assets into a joint account or sign a community property agreement that specifies everything you have now and in the future is joint property. Assuming you have not signed a community property agreement or commingled the assets, the following are examples of separate property.

Assume your aunt died and left you $50,000. If you put the money into an account with your name only and do not commingle the funds, your inheritance can continue to be viewed as your separate property. When you list interest and dividend income or capital gains on your income tax return, put your initials beside listed separate property income.

Let's say that you received a gift from your grandmother of $10,000, with the check made out only to you. If you put those funds into a separate account, they remain separate. Beware if you are buying a house with your separate assets and then funding the payments with joint income. You will need to trace the contribution of separate funds with written documentation and records. You may be converting part of your separate assets to marital property. See an attorney for an opinion on these matters.

Marital property is any property acquired during the marriage, no matter whose name is on it. In many states, the increase in value of separate property can be deemed to be a marital asset. Again, this should be discussed with your attorney. A financial planner can work with you to trace assets over a long-term marriage and create a spreadsheet with documentation to support your claim. It is up to the person who has the claim of separate property to prove that it is, in fact, separate property.

Careers as a Financial Asset

Career assets can be very important in a traditional marriage in which the wife has stayed home and raised the children, worked part time, or helped the spouse to obtain an education. The spouse, or wife in this instance, is oftentimes called a "displaced homemaker" or the "economically disadvantaged spouse." There are courses at community colleges and career experts who counsel women in this situation. If you are in this category, seek help as soon as possible to determine your rights and a course of action. Long-term alimony is almost impossible to receive out of a mid-term marriage of ten to twenty-five years in most states, so identifying other potential sources of postdivorce income is important.

Career assets can include education or training, the license or degree one has, job experience, seniority, life insurance, health insurance, disability insurance, unemployment benefits, Social Security benefits, paid sick leave, vacation time, present value of defined benefit pension plans, retirement plans, and a network of professional contacts and goodwill in a business.

Step Four: Begin Career Assessment

Start working with a career advisor—either a consultant who specializes in this area and is experienced as an expert witness—or someone recommended by your local university or community college. In appendix A I include a vocational career report to give you a sense of what a competent career advisor can bring to a divorce, and appendix C provides more details about the role of the advisor. The costs for a written report range from $1,500 to $2,500. Make sure you also budget dollars for postdivorce career counseling. Too many times the final legal phase of divorce—implementation—is compromised due to a lack of funds. Make this a part of the plan. Also, seek to have these expenses paid from joint assets.

Step Five: Create Postdivorce Budget

Chapter 7 describes the postdivorce budget in detail. You have prepared your historical spending summary, submitted your temporary financial affidavit, and have records showing how you spent your money during the separation. Using this information and other financial decisions you are making as the basis, you need to prepare your postdivorce budget. This budget will now include: revised housing expenses, medical costs, child-rearing costs, educational costs, and more.

Step Six: Prepare Reports and Settlement Proposals

You have been doing your preparation step-by-step, and you are now ready to start putting the financial issues together with your attorney and financial planner. The various experts have been providing you with the correct information on income, expenses, and asset valuations. Now the "what-if" scenarios can be created. These scenarios will illustrate the effects of different settlement proposals on your postdivorce life. Each of your experts will have prepared detailed reports that need to be integrated into a settlement proposal that meets your specific needs. You will want to be an active participant in this work.

Step Seven: Bring Team Together and Start Sharing Data

It is now time to gather all the experts on your team and combine their contributions into an integrated settlement plan. Your financial planner will play a key role in assisting your attorney in devising a strategy to create a win-win solution for your divorce. There may be numerous meetings and/or written exchanges with the various team members to finalize this strategy. Be patient and stay involved in these sessions. The final decisions are yours to make. This is a critical time for you to maintain control of the process and ensure you understand the consequences of what the team is recommending. The hardest work is behind you, but the process is not complete. Stay vigilant.

PHASE FOUR—NEGOTIATION-SETTLEMENT: 30 TO 60 DAYS

This phase requires a budget for your postdivorce lifestyle and that of your spouse. The income components will be made up of wages, investment income, alimony, child support, income from separate property, and a property settlement note, if applicable. The expenses will be projected based on this future lifestyle. You may be selling a residence and purchasing a more cost-effective home. The monthly costs of maintaining the home, real estate taxes, mortgage costs, and the desire for a smaller space to maintain are usually factors that go into this change in lifestyle. The postdivorce budget will reflect the changes in housing and utility expenses.

Likewise, depending on the parenting plan and the amount of time each parent has with the children, the expenses are shared so that one party does not pay more than his or her share of child support to the custodial parent. In the case of an economically disadvantaged spouse, there could be a need for increased child-care expenses while the parent is attending school and preparing to reenter the job market. As well, you may be prequalifying for a mortgage, looking at an alternative piece of real estate to buy as a residence, and/or fixing up your current residence for resale.

During this phase the property settlement is negotiated, mediated, arbitrated or litigated, or subjected to a combination of these settlement procedures. The outcome from this phase is the final divorce decree, a property settlement agreement, and a permanent parenting plan.

Step One: Negotiate Property Settlement

You have collected and evaluated all the information related to finalizing an acceptable property settlement. Working with your team of advisors you have created a proposal that you believe is equitable to both sides. Now begins the process of trying to get your spouse and his attorney to accept your position. You may have been presented with his proposal first, in which case you have prepared a counteroffer. Rarely is the first proposal the one both parties accept. The process of negotiating a mutually acceptable agreement can be long and arduous. It may involve going to court to settle some disputes. The longer and more contentious this process is, the

30–60 Days

NEGOTIATION, SETTLEMENT

Steps
(1)　Negotiate Property Settlement.
(2)　Allocate Income (Child Support, Maintenance).
(3)　Present Rebuttal of Opposing Expert Report.
(4)　Finalize Parenting Plan.
(5)　Give Court Testimony.

FIGURE 6.5　The Negotiation/Settlement Phase

more expensive it will be. I have seen cases in which the legal costs of such battles erode a substantial portion of the initial property value.

Step Two: Allocate Income (Child Support, Maintenance)

Child support is negotiated and, if applicable, the alimony terms are projected for you and your spouse. The various sources of income have been verified, and both parties have projections of how much is available for what expenses. This information should be analyzed by your financial planner to determine the long-term economic impact of the various proposals.

Step Three: Present Rebuttal of Opposing Expert Report

If your expert has written a report, this is the time it needs to be presented as part of your comprehensive settlement proposal. These reports or summaries can be used in the mediation or settlement conference or in court if the contested issues cannot be resolved.

This is also the time your expert can present a rebuttal of the opposing expert's report. When both parties use experts to establish a position on an issue, each has the opportunity to counter the opposition's stand.

Step Four: Finalize Parenting Plan

Ideally, you and your spouse have finalized this part of your divorce, and you are dealing with the financial aspects of the parenting plan in an integrated, decision-making model. That means you both have a complete picture of the financial, emotional, and physical consequences of the various options available. If you have not come to a mutual agreement, you may have to utilize outside experts to establish a viable plan.

The worst-case scenario arises when you have to resort to step five, give court testimony, and leave the decision in the hands of a judge. You both have the experience of living with the terms of the temporary parenting plan. This should serve as a basis for evaluating what is in the children's best interests and what is emotionally and economically feasible for you and your spouse.

Step Five: Give Court Testimony

If you and your spouse have been unable to come to an agreement, you are on your way to court. A judge will determine the property settlement and other issues. You will be required to explain your position to the court and to verify any claims you have made. Fewer than 5 percent of divorce cases in this country result in a trial, but many more cases involve some appearance in court to resolve issues along the way. If you are forced to go before a judge, your attorney will help prepare you and any other experts you have used. This is when you will know for certain whether you chose the right professional team.

At the end of this phase you are divorced and starting your life as a single person.

The Financial Planner's Role

I work very closely with the attorney and client during the negotiations in phase five. I do short- and long-term cash-flow projections to determine the economic impact of various property settlement proposals. I help the client and attorney structure the property settlement proposal presented to the mediator based on the postdivorce budget and anticipated expenses of the new lifestyle. A career and education plan has been proposed with the costs and time frame determined by the career counselor. I know what current sources of income are available to be shared by the divorcing clients and have a proposal as to how the income and assets can be divided.

Using computer models, I have the ability to show the client and attorney how the property settlement proposals provided by each side financially affect my client. I am able to help all the parties involved in the divorce see the economic impact today and in the future of various property settlement proposals. I am able to provide an integrated and comprehensive analysis of this new lifestyle, including a tax and cash-flow analysis that incorporates income from all sources. These include wages, bonuses, investment income, alimony, child support, settlement notes, pension, Social Security, and IRA distributions. From these I subtract money needed to cover living expenses, college education costs for the spouse and/or children, private school expenses, and income taxes.

From this cash-flow analysis I am able to show where both parties are likely to be five to ten years after the divorce with respect to their net worth. I have prepared yearly estimates of taxes and net cash flows. This analysis demonstrates where there are shortages or a requirement for additional alimony. It may show that there is not sufficient income to provide the alimony requested, and the sale of an asset or a reduction in the standard of living for both parties may be necessary.

The cash-flow spreadsheet is a guide to exactly what you are giving up or getting. A property settlement proposal should not be exclusively analyzed for just one of the parties, but this philosophy is not shared by all attorneys or financial planners. That is why I recommend using an experienced financial planner specializing in divorce planning, who is trained to look at the future income impact for both spouses. Some professionals, particularly accountants and attorneys, prefer not to get into this part of the analysis, because it is necessary to deal with projections and assumptions. I believe that this work is essential to understanding and accepting an equitable property settlement.

In each of my financial models I show clients what their short- and long-term cash flow, income tax, and net worth will look like with alternative property settlement proposals. This gives them effective decision-making models to apply to their postdivorce life. After the divorce, I begin the process of postdivorce planning, including the client's risk tolerance and potential investment strategies. Chapter 12 deals with this phase of the divorce process.

I am often asked to attend the settlement meetings or to be available to revise spreadsheets during the settlement conference. Judges and mediation attorneys call to discuss how a recommendation would change the financial situation for one of the parties. I am also called to discuss the income tax impact of various settlements as they relate not just to one but to both of the divorcing spouses. Samples of some of the models I use are provided in a case study in appendix A.

Here is an example of how I was able to assist a couple with some special circumstances in the negotiated property settlement.

The Value of a Third-Party Perspective

Charles and Marian, both forty-six, had been married for twenty-two years when he filed for divorce. They have three children, ages six, twelve, and sixteen. Marian taught school for the first two years of their marriage, while Charles was starting his career as a dentist. He now earns $450,000 per year and has a dental practice valued at $550,000. They own a residence valued at $700,000 with a $400,000 first mortgage balance and a $100,000 equity line of credit. The retirement assets consist of $425,000 held in Charles's profit-sharing plan, and $18,000 in IRAs in Marian's name. They own two one-year-old automobiles of equal value free and clear. Their personal property is valued at $225,000, including antiques, shop tools, jewelry, and furs. They have $80,000 in a brokerage account of stocks and municipal bonds and $25,000 in savings accounts. Their children attend private schools for which the annual cost is $18,000.

Marian has gone through career counseling and has decided she would like to return to school to update her teaching credentials and to complete her master's degree. After two years of study, she would look for a job. She anticipates her starting salary will be $32,000 per year. Both parents are interested in being involved with the raising of the children during and after the divorce.

Charles has hired a nanny for the children when they are with him—about 40 percent of the time presently. Marian wants to attend school part time and teach part time until the youngest child is in middle school, in about six years. Marian would like to be the custodial parent and is concerned that the children need to have just one home base.

Charles is concerned about national health care proposals being considered by Congress and is predicting a 20 percent reduction in his income. Both parties would like to have the primary residence. Charles has a net income of $20,000 per month after he pays his taxes, his payment to buy into the medical practice, the children's private school tuition, and his annual pension contribution. Before they separated, Charles and Marian were spending $15,000 per month on their living expenses. They have a fifteen-year mortgage and their principal and interest payments are $3,900 per month.

This separation finds both of them feeling strapped for cash. Arguments have already begun as to how the net income should be shared. I have been asked to come up with the historical spending pattern and determine Marian's expenses during the separation. I will help Marian create a realistic budget and cash-control system for the upcoming year. Both Charles and Marian face a lifestyle change. Marian is very emotional and frightened about her financial security. Charles believes Marian does not manage money wisely and is sending Marian $4,000 per month after paying the mortgage and children's tuition.

Marian is struggling to make ends meet. She is preparing to make a motion for temporary support and child support. There are attorney fees, expert witness fees, and other professional fees to pay, including money for the financial planner, accountant, business valuator, career counselor, and the psychologist she and the children are seeing. Custody of the children is becoming an issue and a court evaluator has also been hired to provide a recommendation for primary custody of the children.

The situation is a financial and emotional minefield. Getting through this minefield is much easier when both parties can see the reality of their former spending habits, the new financial shape of things during separation, and the financial portents for the future based on cash flows. Providing this information is what makes divorce planning so effective. By establishing irrefutable, objective financial benchmarks for both parties, such planning eliminates the subjective, contentious basis that often fuels arguments in divorce cases. This often eases the difficult emotional transitions both spouses are experiencing.

Phase Five—Implementation: 30 to 90 Days

Postdivorce planning is the phase in which a financial planner applies your property settlement to your life. For my clients, I create a personal and realistic cash-control system. I also develop a strategy to pay off the legal expenses of the divorce, taking into account cash flow and income tax considerations.

If assets are being transferred between the divorcing spouses, I help to get these assets reregistered. Typically, I give the client form letters to send out for the change of ownership and I explain the procedures. The client can personally take care of many of these transfers and save herself money. If a *Qualified Domestic Relations Order* (*QDRO*) needs to be administered, I help the client select the new custodian for the retirement assets and arrange for the transfer of the assets. QDROs are used to transfer certain marital assets such as pension funds in compliance with federal regulations. The court establishes them at the time a final decree is issued. These assets need to be transferred without a check being sent directly to the client, thereby preventing an immediate income tax liability. I will share a number of specific planning ideas with you in chapter 12.

30–90 Days

IMPLEMENTATION

Steps
(1) Preparation and Recording of Divorce Decree, Property Settlement Agreement, Parenting Plan, QDROs.
(2) Postdivorce Planning.
(3) Income Tax Planning.
(4) QDRO: Retirement Asset Transfers.
(5) Property Transfers.
(6) Cash Flow Management.
(7) Investment Asset Allocation.
(8) Education and Career Plan.

FIGURE 6.6   The Implementation Phase (Postdivorce)

The implementation (postdivorce) phase is a critical and vulnerable time for a woman. As a single person, she will need a financial plan to get her started properly. Postdivorce is also the time to systematically address each of the elements of the financial plan.

I wish I could tell women that their financial worries are over in the postdivorce phase. Too often this is not the case. If your property settlement has been achieved with stress, volatility, lack of cooperation, and costly legal maneuvers, it probably will continue in this vein and enforcement will be your next hurdle.

By now both you and your attorney are ready to have your case over and done with. As a matter of fact, after the divorce, many attorneys all but drop out of the process. There are no trial dates facing them. But sometimes you will have to go back to court for an interpretation or enforcement—more time and money. The struggles encountered up through the negotiation-settlement phase are usually strong indicators of what lies ahead. That is why in this last phase before implementation, you want to be sure that your final property settlement agreement is as detailed as possible, leaving little room for interpretation and protest.

Step One: Preparation and Recording of Divorce Decree, Property Settlement Agreement, Parenting Plan, QDROs

You are now divorced, and this is the paperwork trail implementing the divorce. Your financial planner and attorney will help you complete this step. As a special word of caution, I suggest you review the status of any documents filed in the divorce process that are considered to be public records. Not all legal jurisdictions protect personal information in the same way. Avoid becoming the victim of identity theft by finding out what information about you is available to the general public. Discuss this with your attorney and your financial advisor, preferably before the final divorce decree is issued.

Step Two: Postdivorce Planning

You have worked on several proposals. Now you will deal with the facts of your new life and the real settlement with all of its compromises. Your financial planner will use your real numbers and project your financial life going forward. Based on the final outcome, you will work together to create your postdivorce financial plan. (Chapter 12 is devoted to the key elements of this plan.)

Step Three: Income Tax Planning

You will need to find a CPA to work with who understands how your tax filing status has changed and what will be required for you to start doing an individual income tax return. Your filing status, estimated quarterly income taxes, the deductibility of divorce fees, and retirement distributions are a few of the issues you will need to incorporate into your postdivorce financial plan.

Step Four: QDRO: Retirement Asset Transfers

Your financial planner will help you select qualified trustees for those assets requiring them, and he or she will assist you in setting up the proper accounts to hold the retirement assets transferred to you in the final settlement. Moving assets assigned in the Qualified Domestic Relations Order can be a laborious and time-consuming process. It is important to continue documenting these transfers and to follow up on their timely execution.

Step Five: Property Transfers

Transferring property may seem like a simple step, but it is often complicated by the rules governing how different types of property must be registered. You may need the help of several professionals to ensure that this is done properly. An experienced financial planner can usually help you identify what resources you need. Again, good documentation is essential to completing this step without undue entanglements.

Step Six: Cash Flow Management

This is a critical part of postdivorce planning. Figuring out how to pay for all of the costs of the divorce will need to be addressed. Creating a realistic budget and cash control system for the dollars you receive each month is important to your continued financial well-being. I usually advise my clients to follow the system they created during the divorce process.

It is essential to keep track of any money being spent on the children, since child support may be revised at various times in the future. Document these expenses and the time the children spend with you and your spouse. Keep a financial diary and have a record of the actual visitation between parents. Such records can come to be significant if increases in child support are needed or if your ex-spouse attempts to reduce the agreed-upon amount. Requests for reductions in support payments are common, particularly if the paying party experiences a significant change in income or health.

Step Seven: Investment Asset Allocation

You are now in charge of the money you received in the divorce settlement. Establishing your risk tolerance, investment time horizon, taxation and asset allocation needs, college and retirement funding, insurance requirements, and credit management are now part of your postdivorce financial plan.

Step Eight: Education and Career Plan

Much of what I have dealt with in this phase of divorce has concentrated on financial issues. Even implementing the final parenting plan has significant financial dimensions. The last step in the process also has a monetary side—perhaps the most important of all. Executing the education and career plan successfully is what brings many women the greatest stability, independence, and financial security from a divorce.

If you had an established career and independent income before your divorce, this may be an unnecessary step. Many of the women with whom I have consulted were not so fortunate. Even those who received substantial settlements were sometimes faced with the necessity of augmenting these payments—particularly after the years of alimony or maintenance had passed. If projected net income statements show a time when expenses exceed income, there is often no alternative except getting a job. Whether this is part time or full time, some preparation for earning a living is necessary.

During the analysis and planning phase, you encountered the opportunity to begin assessing your career needs. If you pursued that effectively, you are now ready to get the necessary training and prepare for finding an appropriate vocation. In many cases, women begin the educational preparation before the final decree is issued. When career planning is needed, the sooner you start, the better your financial health.

Figure 6.7 illustrates the relative cost of the different phases of divorce.

Remember, there have always been three primary ways to achieve wealth in our society. You can work for your money, marry and participate in jointly creating wealth, or inherit wealth. Each of these methods of achieving wealth becomes significant when you are getting a divorce and attempting to win a fair and equitable division of assets, liabilities, and

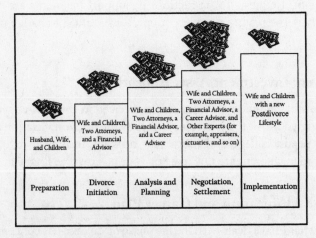

FIGURE 6.7   Relative Cost by Divorce Phase

income. Our courts do not support long-term alimony for women. The only bright light is a trend toward longer terms of alimony if an economic need can be demonstrated.

In some states, alimony (also often called maintenance) can be awarded to "rehabilitate" or it can be deemed "compensatory." In the first case, it is provided to pay for education or training to upgrade the skills of a spouse who has been out of the workforce while raising children or performing domestic duties. As compensation, alimony is granted as payment for a spouse who worked in the home instead of in an office or factory. The amount of alimony or maintenance approved by the court can be affected by which of the two perspectives is applied. Whenever possible, I recommend obtaining cash or assets up-front as an offset against maintenance— a sure thing versus a promise to pay that could be defaulted.

Document Roundup List

Do yourself (and your attorney) an enormous favor and save money by assembling the following items for your first data-gathering appointment. Besides copying account numbers, make copies of the actual statements— it makes tracking and verification easier.

- Federal income tax returns for the last three to five years.
- Copies of W-2 statements for each tax return.
- Last three pay stubs for both spouses that show deductions from gross pay.
- Your current check register and bank statements for the past year.
- The most recent annual statement of pension or retirement benefits furnished for each spouse. Three years would be best.
- Savings passbooks, current and for the previous year.
- Stock brokerage account statements. The current statement and the year-end statement for the past two years.
- Money market fund statements, current and past two years' endings statements.
- Certificates of deposit, treasury bills, and the like.
- A list of the contents of your safety-deposit box.
- A copy of your current will.
- A copy of any community, separate property, or prenuptial agreements.
- Financial statements given to a banking institution in connection with any loan application filed within the last two years.
- Monthly or quarterly bank statements for all checking and savings accounts.

- Credit card statements for the last two years. American Express and many gold cards now offer an annual recap of spending for members.
- The history of the purchase of your current home: closing documents, a list of improvements, current mortgage information, Form 2119 from your income tax return if you deferred the gain from a prior home into the current home. (Form 2119—Sale of the Primary Residence—would have been filed with your income tax return in the year in which you sold the prior home and purchased your current home.)
- Warranty deeds, contracts, title insurance, and other documents establishing ownership to real estate and your residence.
- Title certificates and registration statements for boats, cars, recreational vehicles, and trucks.
- Property and casualty insurance premiums for all of your homeowner and auto insurance broken down by the item being insured. Also get information on any personal umbrella liability insurance you might have. Find the name and phone number of your insurance agent.
- Get copies of any life or disability insurance policies on each member of the family. What are the premiums for each policy? When are they due, and how are they paid? Do the same for health insurance and long-term nursing care policies. Verify beneficiaries. Is there a life insurance trust?
- If a business or businesses are owned, the most recent income tax return, annual profit-and-loss statement, and most current monthly and quarterly profit-and-loss statements. Go back at least three years if possible.
- List all current debts, monthly payments, interest rates, and reasons for the debts.
- Current property tax statements on any real estate owned.
- Each employer's annual statement describing the corporate benefits package including medical or life insurance benefits, balances and loans on 401(k) plans, pension summaries, deferred compensation balances and terms, stock options exercised and nonexercised. (Find out what restrictions there are on any of these stock options as far as ownership, exercising, and taxation.)
- Do you think either of you will have an inheritance coming to you? Is there one in process? Are there any side loans with family members? Provide detailed information.
- Copies of your current wills and estate planning documents.
- Pre- or postnuptial agreement.

- Do your children have funds set aside in trusts for college education? Provide statements, if so. Who provided these funds, where are they located, who is the trustee or custodian on these accounts?
- Has there been any unusual spending or movement of funds you have noticed in the past two years? If so, list what you know and the history surrounding any transactions.
- Is there another person involved in the divorce, a boyfriend or girlfriend? Have community finances been diverted to this person's account? Provide as much of a history as you can.
- Has there been a history of drug, alcohol, or sexual abuse? Do you have documentation and dates of treatment?
- Are you receiving money from other family members to help you financially? If so, please describe.
- How long have you been separated? Are you separated? Do you want to stay in the house for now? Has anyone filed at this time? Does the other party have an attorney?
- What are the current financial arrangements with your children or any relatives? Please describe.
- Are either of you in school? Did either of you get a degree during your marriage? Did you live together before marrying? What separate financial assets did either of you bring into the marriage? Please describe.
- Provide complete K-1 reports on any limited partnerships you may own. This IRS schedule is part of the 1041 tax form. The complete K-1 is not filed with your annual income tax return. Also gather any depreciation schedules that are being used on your current income tax returns.
- What kind of health insurance do you have? Is this coverage connected through an employer? Do either of you have long-term nursing care insurance? Is COBRA coverage available with your spouse's employer?

You will want to make one copy of this information for your records and one for your attorney and financial planner. Be organized. You will pay for your own disorganization. You also want your attorney and experts to be organized and efficient with the massive amount of paperwork that is heading their way. You are attempting to unwind the family marriage and business relationship, and you are doing it during a time of intense emotion. Organization will help you take control.

Remember, once you decide to divorce, you have stepped on that moving escalator. Eventually your ride will come to an end, but you can choose how that happens. You can walk up the escalator methodically, confidently, and step off under your own power, or you can remain immobilized on one step, and simply wait to be "dumped off." If you can take control of your divorce process, one step at a time, you will be better prepared for that final step—the actual divorce.

YOUR DECISIONS TO MAKE

I said at the beginning of this chapter you are largely responsible for determining the cost of your divorce. The reason for that statement should now be clear. We have stepped through the entire divorce process and looked at a number of client experiences along the way. I have identified the sources of costs and suggested ways of controlling them. From choosing the right team of experts to being your own paralegal to keeping your emotions from triggering expensive mistakes, you have decisions to make. Now it is up to you. No matter where you are in those five phases of divorce, you can exert some control over the expenses—the sooner, the better.

7

The Budget Process

Never ask of money spent
Where the spender thinks it went.
Nobody was ever meant
To remember or invent
What he did with every cent.

—ROBERT FROST

In chapter 6 I pointed out the importance of creating three different budgets. The first budget was based on historical spending before the spouses separated. The second budget is used to forecast income and expenses for the period during which the couple will be living apart while waiting for the divorce to be final. The third budget will be used to establish cash controls and a financial plan for life after the divorce is granted. These budgets are critical to providing financial stability for both spouses and for their children. Most of us have used at least a rudimentary budget at some time, but few of us have had to deal with the financial complexities associated with divorce. Given the importance of preparing these documents properly, I am devoting a separate chapter to the topic. In this chapter I'm going to present a case history of a divorced woman and how I helped her create historical, temporary, and postdivorce budgets. This information is a how-to approach for every woman who wishes to conserve her assets in a divorce and create a financial recovery.

Judith was a forty-three-year-old divorcing mother with three children. She did not want the divorce, but her estranged husband, Jake, became emotionally involved with another woman and wanted his freedom.

Judith went to an attorney only after she had been served divorce papers. She had a limited amount of time to respond, but Jake had assured her he would take care of her and the children. It is apparent now that neither of them understood what this meant in either the short or long term. Based on the financial declaration that Judith was required to submit to the courts, she asked for $3,000 per month in alimony and $1,500 in child support. On the surface these amounts seemed to be sufficient. However, when she started reviewing the numbers more carefully and began actually paying the bills, she discovered that there was an inadequate cash flow.

Her attorney had told her to make preliminary estimates to which adjustments could be made later. "Later" has arrived for Judith. She feels a lot of financial pressure and does not want to charge more on her credit cards to finance her divorce.

Judith arrived at my office feeling out of control financially. We had met three times, and each time I heard about how her dwindling savings account was down to nearly nothing, having been depleted to meet the family's current living expenses. When she had presented her proposed temporary budget to the court three months ago on the financial declaration, she admitted she had estimated her projected expenses. Each day she finds expenses she had not anticipated in her budget. She has come to realize the importance of detailed, complete information.

Now Judith is in panic mode. She borrowed money from her parents to make ends meet the previous month but she doesn't want to ask them for more. Her parents live comfortably, but can't support her and the children. Jake doesn't want to talk with her. He feels she is being too emotional, and he won't listen to any of her financial concerns. He thinks she should tighten her belt and get on with her life. Meanwhile, her attorney has asked Judith to gather financial information for a preliminary settlement conference. The children are not handling the divorce well. Their grades have dropped in school, and they do not want to visit their father with his new girlfriend.

Judith's plight is not unusual. In an ideal situation, the client comes to see me predivorce, and we complete the document roundup and gather all the financial records. We complete the budget documentation and the accompanying reports, and we have everything ready for the first hearing on temporary alimony and child support.

If the two parties can agree to the division of income between themselves and their attorney, there is no need for a hearing. If you are in a collaborative law setting or doing mediation from the beginning of your divorce process, make this division of income your first priority. See figure 6.1 regarding the integrated divorce process in chapter 6.

Nine months remain before Judith's trial date. She has 270 days and nights before the finalization of her divorce. My goal is to help her regain her power in the divorce proceedings. We will start with the budgeting process and assist her in preparing a motion for a reconsideration of the financial affidavit.

When we started, Jake was keeping 53 percent of the family's discretionary income. He was taking care of himself, while Judith managed the house and children—a household of three receiving less than half of the net family income. In addition, she paid a career advisor $2,500, a $5,000 retainer to the attorney, $150 an hour for the therapist, and now she would be paying my firm a retainer and an hourly rate for services. None of these expenses were included in the initial financial declaration. I have seen this happen too many times.

You need to start with accurate numbers, and do the process right the first time. Otherwise, you will be fighting a time-consuming and costly uphill battle to get this initial amount of temporary alimony and child support increased. To help you through the budget process, you will need the help of a financial planner. The attorney will probably suggest you use a paralegal, but you need a specialist. From this initial information, you will analyze historical spending, create a temporary budget, and over time, develop your integrated postdivorce budget that will be defined in the financial declaration.

I am going to show you, step-by-step, how to create a detailed, comprehensive budget you can use from the beginning to the end of your divorce process and also in the postdivorce phase. As part of this process, you will have a detailed notebook with financial information and footnotes. The summary budget will be at the front of your binder with well-organized information and the documentation of expenses will be divided into sections that correspond to the categories on the financial affidavit (housing, utilities, children, and so on). You will follow the same format as the financial affidavit form used in your court system.

I have found that if you understand your own budget numbers it is much easier to make the appropriate financial compromises when you need to. This basic information will give you the control you need to be an active participant in your own settlement negotiations.

I suggest that you have three binders: one for historical spending; one for the temporary budget during separation before the divorce is final; and one for your postdivorce budget.

The historical predivorce binder will consist of the following sections:

Section 1: Financial Affidavit

This is a summary of spending during the year prior to divorce. It should not be longer than five pages. You want to demonstrate that your analysis is thorough and detailed. The actual details will be found in section 2. This summary should give an overview that the appropriate details do exist. If an attorney, court commissioner, or mediator is looking at this information, you want him to know that you are prepared to supply all the details. The summary report is often the only document these professionals read initially. If they question the summary, they may request the detailed data you have in section 2. If there have been unusual sources of income during that time, be sure you note them. Examples might be a gift from parents, an inheritance, exercising stock options, or bonuses. You need to note that these were one-time sources of income and that there may also be some one-time expenses, such as a remodeling project, or a vacation to Europe for the family, for example.

Section 2: Expense and Income Details

You will have files for each of the major categories with your backup documentation. (For example, housing, utilities, insurance, and so on.) These contain statements, invoices, charge slips, and receipts for all expenses and income sources.

Section 3: Calendar and Diary

This is a record of the highlights that occurred during the time period covered in each notebook (historical, temporary, and possibly postdivorce). For example, if you have a child who is active in sports, you might list the games and events you are attending. These dates lend credibility to the detailed records in section 2 that show charge slips for car expenses, as well as your time commitment.

This is also a place where you can mark who has the children and when, as well as the money being spent on each child. Keep a record. You know what the temporary parenting plan specifies about shared time with the children. This is your record of the reality.

Many times I will see a pattern develop where the parenting plan is not followed, and one spouse is taking advantage of the other spouse by not being on time, or returning the children early, for example. I am not suggesting that you forego flexibility, but that you should not become the "doormat." You need your own time and a life to get through the divorce process. This diary can be very effective in your negotiations during the divorce process and also postdivorce when there are requests for revisions of child support.

The second and third binders—for the temporary budget during separation and for the postdivorce budget—will have information organized in the same way as the first binder does for sections 2 and 3. The difference is that the documentation in binders two and three will cover the appropriate time frame involved—during the divorce-separation and postdivorce.

You can put a copy of the historical summary report from the first binder in the other two for reference if you wish.

Remember, the court system is not interested in how you feel, only in the facts. Documentation and good record-keeping skills can work in your favor. You will probably be surprised by what you find out about yourself and your spouse. This is especially true in the discovery of expenses involving a husband's girlfriend. You will be able to trace any "unusual" transactions in the previous year. Be prepared to become your own "Sherlock" about your family finances.

This is also the time to step up and admit whether you have spent discretionary funds freely for clothes or personal expenses in the past. You were married when you did so, and it is assumed that you and your spouse were partners and equally responsible for your lifestyle. Don't hide expenses. Honesty is the best defense. Identify those areas in which you are suggesting changes in your temporary and postdivorce budgets based on your change in circumstances. This is where you want to appear reasonable and realistic about your finances.

The system works both ways. Usually men come into these budget hearings with even less documentation and detail for their living expenses. It can be very effective for you to have your expenses and income placed side by side with his, showing what both of you anticipate spending during the period of separation and in your postdivorce lifestyle. Let's go back to Judith so you can see how this budget process works.

Judith's case demonstrates how important the budget process can be for the temporary alimony order. The preparation of the temporary budget is typically the first step in planning a fair and equitable settlement. This process takes two weeks to one month depending on your involvement and organization.

BUDGETING SESSION ONE

When I first meet with a client, I like to spend time getting to know her. With Judith, I spent nearly half an hour talking about her feelings and about her current situation. More often than not, this dialogue provides me with valuable insights about the spending patterns of the household.

When Judith came to see me, she was about to have a temporary alimony order put in place that would have been inadequate based on her financial needs, especially in the short term. This resulted from her hasty and incomplete analysis of her family's spending habits, representing a gross misinterpretation of her married lifestyle. Had her attorney asked a qualified financial planner to evaluate her historical budget this could have been avoided.

After our meeting, she immediately began to gather as many financial documents as she could—bank and credit card statements, money market accounts, and anything else that showed how she had spent money in maintaining the household.

I look at the historical spending for at least one year prior to separation. All bank checking and savings account statements, money market accounts, and credit card statements are entered into a budgeting computer program. Microsoft Money or Quicken provide the maximum flexibility for the type of reports I need to generate. If you don't have either of these computer programs, you can create your own spreadsheets based on the figure 7.1.

When I look at the bank statements, I am establishing the source of all funds deposited into the checking or savings account. Then I categorize and code all of the checks written out of the account into the expense categories provided on the financial declaration form. Figure 7.2 summarizes these codes as they are listed on the financial declaration.

Home Expenses

Year _____

	Rent/ Mortgage	Homeowners Association Fees	Property Taxes	Telephone	Cell Phone	Pager	Internet	Cable/ Satellite
January								
February								
March								
April								
May								
June								
July								
August								
September								
October								
November								
December								
TOTAL	$	$	$	$	$	$	$	$
Average/ Month	$	$	$	$	$	$	$	$
Projected Monthly	$	$	$	$	$	$	$	$

Copyright © 2005 Miller Advisors, Inc.

FIGURE 7.1   Historical Spending Templates

Home Expenses

	Electricity	Heating Fuel	Water/ Sewer	Trash Removal	Grass Cutting/ Fertilizing	Landscape Maintenance	Snow Removal
January							
February							
March							
April							
May							
June							
July							
August							
September							
October							
November							
December							
TOTAL	$	$	$	$	$	$	$
Average/ Month	$	$	$	$	$	$	$
Projected Monthly							

FIGURE 7.1   *(continued)*

Home Expenses						Food Expenses		
	Exterminator	General Home Repairs/ Maintenance Windows/ Carpets	Home Improvements/ Upgrades	House-cleaning	Misc. Household	Groceries	Snacks	Fast Food
January								
February								
March								
April								
May								
June								
July								
August								
September								
October								
November								
December								
TOTAL	$	$	$	$	$	$	$	$
Average/ Month	$	$	$	$	$	$	$	$
Projected Monthly								

FIGURE 7.1   *(continued)*

	Food	Entertainment Expenses						
	Restaurant Meals	Entertainment (Excludes Dining Out)	Videos/ CDs/ Tapes/ DVDs	Movies and Theater	Hobbies for Self	Classes/ Lessons (Recreational) for Self	Vacations/ Travel	Memberships/ Clubs for Self
January								
February								
March								
April								
May								
June								
July								
August								
September								
October								
November								
December								
TOTAL	$	$	$	$	$	$	$	$
Average/ Month	$	$	$	$	$	$	$	$
Projected Monthly								

FIGURE 7.1   (continued)

	Medical Expenses - After Insurance (Excludes Children)				Insurance			
	Physicians	Dentist/ Orthodontist	Optometry/ Glasses/ Contacts	Prescriptions	Life	Health and Dental (Postdivorce)	Disability	Long-Term Care
January								
February								
March								
April								
May								
June								
July								
August								
September								
October								
November								
December								
TOTAL	$	$	$	$	$	$	$	$
Average/ Month	$	$	$	$	$	$	$	$
Projected Monthly								

FIGURE 7.1   (continued)

| | Insurance | | | Transportation for Self | | | | |

	Home Insurance	Auto Insurance	Other Insurance (Boat, Umbrella)	Auto Payment	Fuel	Repair/ Maintenance/ Car Wash	Parking/ Tolls	Licenses and Other Fees
January								
February								
March								
April								
May								
June								
July								
August								
September								
October								
November								
December								
TOTAL	$	$	$	$	$	$	$	$
Average/ Month	$	$	$	$	$	$	$	$
Projected Monthly								

FIGURE 7.1 (continued)

| | Clothing Expenses | | Miscellaneous Expenses | | | | | |

	Clothing for Self	Laundry/ Dry Cleaning for Self	Postage	Gifts/ Holiday Expenses	Vitamins/ Non-prescription Drugs	Toiletries	Beauty Salon/ Hair/ Nails	Pet Care/ Vet
January								
February								
March								
April								
May								
June								
July								
August								
September								
October								
November								
December								
TOTAL	$	$	$	$	$	$	$	$
Average/ Month	$	$	$	$	$	$	$	$
Projected Monthly								

FIGURE 7.1 (continued)

	Books/ Newspapers/ Magazines	Stationery and Home Office Supplies	Contributions/ Donations	Bed/Bath/ Kitchen Items	Floral Arrangements	Film Developing	Education for Self (Non-reimbursed)	Business Expense (Non-reimbursed)
Miscellaneous Expenses								
January								
February								
March								
April								
May								
June								
July								
August								
September								
October								
November								
December								
TOTAL	$	$	$	$	$	$	$	$
Average/ Month	$	$	$	$	$	$	$	$
Projected Monthly								

FIGURE 7.1   (*continued*)

			Quarterly Taxes and Other Tax Payments	Spousal Support Payments	Child Support Payments	Eldercare Expenses	Professional Fees (Financial Planning, Accounting, Legal)
Miscellaneous Expenses			**Other Payments**				
	Cash	Other Misc.					
January							
February							
March							
April							
May							
June							
July							
August							
September							
October							
November							
December							
TOTAL	$	$	$	$	$	$	$
Average/ Month	$	$	$	$	$	$	$
Projected Monthly							

FIGURE 7.1   (*continued*)

Other Payments							

	Mediation/ Arbitration/ Court Costs	Therapist/ Counseling	Service Fees (Banks, IRAs, Investment Accounts)	Credit Card/ Loan/ Debt Payments			
January							
February							
March							
April							
May							
June							
July							
August							
September							
October							
November							
December							
TOTAL	$	$	$	$			
Average/ Month	$	$	$	$			
Projected Monthly							

FIGURE 7.1 (continued)

Child Related Expenses								

	Education/ Tuition	School Supplies/ Field Trips/ Expenses	Childcare Work Related (After-Tax Credit)	Childcare Non Work Related	Sports/ Camps/ Lessons	Hobbies/ Toys/ Games	School Meals/ Lunches	Clothing
January								
February								
March								
April								
May								
June								
July								
August								
September								
October								
November								
December								
TOTAL	$	$	$	$	$	$	$	$
Average/ Month	$	$	$	$	$	$	$	$
Projected Monthly								

FIGURE 7.1 (continued)

Child Related Expenses							

	Medical (Not Covered by Insurance)	Dentist/ Orthodontist (Not Covered by Insurance)	Prescriptions (Not Covered by Insurance)	Allowances	Transportation	Misc.		
January								
February								
March								
April								
May								
June								
July								
August								
September								
October								
November								
December								
TOTAL	$	$	$	$	$	$		
Average/ Month	$	$	$	$	$	$		
Projected Monthly								

FIGURE 7.1   (continued)

In chapter 6, I reviewed the steps in the preparation of the historical budget so that the information was available to both parties and to their attorneys. Judith could certainly see the benefit of having more detailed information to prepare the budget and to justify proposed expenses. The process begins with Judith providing me with data, usually beginning with checking account statements. An associate inputs each of the checking transactions (deposits, checks, fees, and interest earned) as they appear on the statements. While this occurs, Judith assigns the budget codes (see figure 7.2) to each transaction on her credit card statements. Where possible, she determines to whom each transaction applies. For instance, was a clothing purchase for the children applicable to Judith or Jake?

BUDGETING SESSION TWO

By the time Judith completes her credit card statements, the data for the majority of the checking statements will have been entered. The checking information, however, is still incomplete, since the payees and budget codes for each check are still unknown. Judith had been good about maintaining her check register, but she occasionally neglected to write down the whole payee, substituting acronyms like "M. J. Sit.," which eleven months later

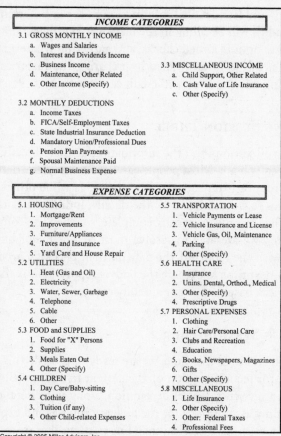

FIGURE 7.2   Financial Declaration Codes

even she couldn't place as "Michelle J., baby-sitting." Session two typically involves meeting to decide the best method of handling the checking accounts and determining which statements, if any, are missing.

In Judith's case, I print out a report that shows the check number, date cleared, and amount for each transaction. She is asked to take the report home to fill in the payees and to determine the appropriate code, which only she can decide. She is also told that there are two pages missing from two separate bank statements that she is to obtain from her bank. Judith indicates that she didn't know what to do with several expenses, so she made up some categories for them, a strategy that works as long as you're consistent. It is quite easy to consolidate the information at any time by reassigning the expenses to the appropriate category on the financial declaration.

Regardless, session two is typically the shortest meeting, with only a few questions and less detailed information to cover. Between session two and three, Judith will be filling in the blanks on our report, locating copies of any missing or unrecorded checks, and gathering whatever other information that needs to be assembled in preparing the historical budget report, including missing bank and credit card statements.

BUDGETING SESSION THREE

The number of sessions and the information discussed really depends on how organized you are. Most people can have a complete, detailed budget prepared in four or five relatively short meetings while others come in six or more times to try to resolve all the details. Judith is a fairly organized person, and her records are mostly complete, so when she comes in for our third meeting, we are able to resolve most of our major questions. She presents us with the report of the data on their checking account, and we plan to meet next time to prepare the budget report. This is the report that will be used as a baseline for our alimony request.

BUDGETING SESSION FOUR

When Judith comes in this time, we are ready to provide this information to the judge for reconsideration of the current temporary alimony award. We prepare a revised financial declaration, along with detailed footnotes that support my assumptions for the budget proposal and explain any significant variances from historical spending patterns. For instance, a change in residence might mean higher mortgage or rent expenses, increased utilities, and possible payments on replacement furniture and appliances.

In addition, the budget will account for projected costs of experts, therapists for both Judith and the children, any immediate educational expenditures, and an estimate of the income tax liability that Judith will incur on her alimony income. Since she already has a court order, the alimony income received after the temporary order is in place is taxable. Waiting to make an estimated payment to the IRS could result in additional penalties and interest.

The budget shown in figure 7.3 is submitted by the attorney with the motion for reconsideration of the original temporary alimony order. The historical budget period included in the report is for the twelve months prior to separation. The proposed temporary budget covers the months of separation prior to the final property settlement and the divorce being finalized. These are the months that Judith and her family experience the financial impact of the divorce on the family's lifestyle and create a new budget for the postdivorce lifestyle.

Proposed Temporary Monthly Budget for Jake and Judith Jessup				
	Historical Yearly Expenses	*Historical Monthly Budget*	Temporary *Monthly Budget* Judith	Temporary *Monthly Budget* Jake
INCOME				
3.1 MONTHLY INCOME				
1. Wages and Salaries	8,500	708	708	
2. Interest and Dividend Income	412	34	17	17
3. Business Income (Jake's Salary)	140,000	11,667		12,500
4. Other Income (Jake's Bonus)	10,000	833		1,250
Total 3.1 MONTHLY INCOME	**158,912**	**13,243**	**725**	**13,767**
3.2 MONTHLY DEDUCTIONS FROM INCOME				
1. Income Taxes	23,117	1,926		1,926
1. FICA/Medicare (Judith)	650	54	54	
3. FICA/Medicare (Jake)	7,755	646		646
4. State Industrial Insurance Deduction	125	10	10	
5. Pension Plan Payments	6,000	500	167	333
Total 3.2 MONTHLY DEDUCTIONS	**37,647**	**3,137**	**231**	**2,906**
Total Income	**121,265**	**10,105**	**494**	**10,861**
EXPENSES				
5.1 HOUSING				
1. Rent, First Mortgage or Line of Credit	34,552	2,879	2,879	1,100
2. Improvements - Repairs	1,277	106		
3. Real Estate Taxes	4,275	356	356	
4. Insurance	593	49	49	237
5. Installment Payments for Furniture	1,725	144	50	75
5. Yard Care and House Repair	1,630	136	125	30
Total 5.1 HOUSING	**44,052**	**3,671**	**3,460**	**1,442**
5.2 UTILITIES				
1. Heat (Gas and Oil)	1,137	95	90	90
2. Electricity	948	79	80	75
3. Water, Sewer, Garbage	621	52	50	50
4. Telephone/Cell Phone	1,826	152	100	125
5. Cable	566	47	25	35
Total 5.2 UTILITIES	**5,098**	**425**	**345**	**375**
5.3 FOOD & SUPPLIES				
1. Food for 4 People	6,746	562	400	300
2. Supplies (Paper, Tobacco)	819	68	40	50
3. Meals Eaten Out	1,847	154	150	250
4. Pet Care	688	57	60	
Total 5.3 FOOD AND SUPPLIES	**10,100**	**842**	**650**	**600**

For settlement purposes only.   Copyright © 2005 Miller Advisors, Inc.

FIGURE 7.3   Proposed Temporary Budget for Jake and Judith Jessup

Proposed Temporary Monthly Budget for Jake and Judith Jessup				
	Historical Yearly Expenses	*Historical Monthly Budget*	*Temporary Monthly Budget* Judith	*Temporary Monthly Budget* Jake
5.4 CHILDREN				
1. Child Care	418	35		
2. Clothing	4,624	385	350	
3. Other Child Related Expenses	12,667	1,056	1,000	
Total 5.4 CHILDREN	**17,709**	**1,476**	**1,350**	**0**
5.5 TRANSPORTATION				
1. Vehicle Payments or Leases				
2. Insurance and License	1,379	115	106	115
3. Gas, Oil, Ordinary Maintenance	2,134	178	125	150
4. Parking	117	10		35
5. Repairs	732	61	25	50
Total 5.5 TRANSPORTATION	**4,362**	**364**	**256**	**350**
5.6 HEALTH CARE				
1. Insurance				
2. Unins. Dental, Orthod, Medical, Eye Care	363	30	35	20
3. Counseling after Copay	1,589	132	240	
4. Prescriptive Drugs	1,160	97	56	30
5.6 HEALTH CARE	**3,112**	**259**	**331**	**50**
5.7 PERSONAL EXPENSES				
1. Clothing/Accessories	5,619	468	250	200
2. Personal Care, Cosmetics, Hair Care	1,535	128	100	50
3. Clubs, Recreation	1,432	119	115	100
4. Education				
5. Books, Newspapers, Magazines	386	32	25	30
6. Gifts	1,760	147	75	50
7. Entertainment, Vacations	867	72	70	100
Total 5.7 PERSONAL EXPENSES	**11,599**	**967**	**635**	**530**
5.8 MISCELLANEOUS				
1. Bank and Credit Card Fees	298	25	10	60
2. Donations	638	53	25	
3. Professional Fees	5,213	434	125	150
Total 5.8 MISCELLANEOUS	**6,149**	**512**	**160**	**210**
TOTAL HOUSEHOLD EXPENSES	**102,181**	**8,515**	**7,187**	**3,557**
ADJUSTMENTS: Jake's separate expenses	6,000	500		
TOTAL EXPENSES	**108,181**	**9,015**	**7,187**	**3,557**
INCOME LESS EXPENSES	**13,084**	**1,090**	**(6,693)**	**7,304**

For settlement purposes only.   Copyright © 2005 Miller Advisors, Inc.

FIGURE 7.3   *(continued)*

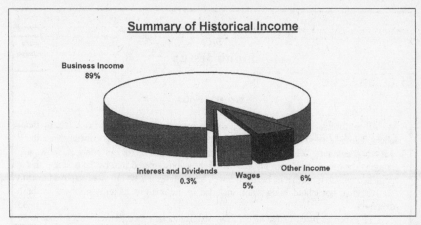

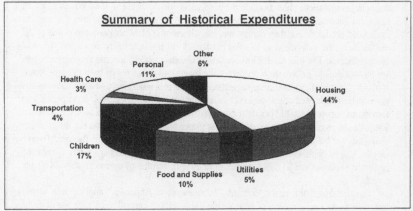

Copyright © 2005 Miller Advisors, Inc.

FIGURE 7.4   Historical Income and Expenditures

The temporary budget, as shown with accompanying footnotes, is the foundation for the postdivorce budget. While the final budget amounts for the temporary and postdivorce reports may differ (often due to asset transfers, tax liabilities, and income variances), the objective is to be accurate the first time through so that costly adjustments will be unnecessary in the future.

BUDGET MAINTENANCE

I will continue to keep Judith's record spending current—and in the same format as the historical spending binder—until she goes to trial or is in the position of making or receiving a property settlement from her husband

Footnotes to Proposed Temporary Budget
for
Judith Jessup

General Notes

All information contained herein has been provided to Miller Advisors, Inc. by the client, Judith Jessup. The data has been entered into our accounting software from the account statements. We have used a full year as the baseline for our analysis, showing household expenditures from all sources. Transactions entered into by Jake Jessup that pertained only to him (that is, business travel, his clothing, and so on) were removed from the historical household budget and included in the analysis as an adjustment to the expenses.

The expenses listed under Jake's Proposed Temporary Budget were taken from his financial declaration. The budget proposal does not include a detailed analysis of historical income. There are complete records of monthly deposits into the various household accounts, but they do not indicate the income of either party since it is at the discretion of the individual as to what portion of income is actually deposited. We will use our Income Tax and Cash Flow models in determining our income projections when we have adequate information regarding the assets and liabilities of both parties. Please note that budgeted expense requirements cannot be met assuming that Jake receives the agreed-upon (first mediation session) business income of $150,000, with an expected and also agreed-upon $15,000 "bonus" (extra payments to Jake should the business generate adequate revenues). Judith's expected gross wages are $8,500. Based on the information available, we believe that the net income available to both parties in the next twelve months will be approximately $140,000 or approximately $11,666 per month. Combined budgeted expenses are $11,244, resulting in a slight surplus of approximately $420 per month.

The section of the report entitled "Adjustments to Expenses" applies only to the historical budget as a means of reconciling the historical expenditures with the account information compiled by Miller Advisors, Inc. The line for "Jake's Expenses" attempts to segregate expenses belonging to Jake, which do not pertain to the household in any way. As such, no allocation is made in the budget proposal. These expenses are assumed to be included in Jake's budgeted expenses.

FIGURE 7.5   Budget Footnotes

Cash Expenditures:

Unless otherwise noted, checks written for cash were allocated among the following estimated percentages:

Allocation of Cash Expenditures

CATEGORY	SUBCATEGORY	JUDITH'S ESTIMATE	% OF TOTAL
5.5 Transportation	5.5.3 Gas	$100	17.7%
5.3 Food & Supplies	5.3.3 Meals Out	150	26.5
	5.3.1 Groceries	70	12.4
5.7 Personal Entertainment	5.7.7 Personal Entertainment	35	6.2
5.4 Children	5.4.4 Other Child-Related Expenses (Personal, Sam)	15	2.7
	5.4.4 Other Child-Related Expenses (Personal, Frances)	15	2.7
	5.4.4 Other Child-Related Expenses (Personal, Jacob)	15	2.7
	5.4.2 Clothing—Sam	25	4.4
	5.4.2 Clothing—Frances	25	4.4
	5.4.2 Clothing—Jacob	25	4.4
	5.4.4 Other Child-Related Expenses (Piano, Sam)	10	1.8
	5.4.4 Other Child-Related Expenses (Personal, Sam)	30	5.3
	5.4.4 Other Child-Related Expenses (Personal, Frances)	25	4.4
	5.4.4 Other Child-Related Expenses (Personal, Jacob)	25	4.4
TOTAL ESTIMATED CASH EXPENDITURES:		$565	100%

NOTE: Judith has indicated that she believes that the above amounts accurately reflect her monthly expenditures from cash machine withdrawals. Total withdrawals were $8,930 from the previous twelve months, which is $744.16 per month. Her estimates resulted in a total of $730, which is 2 percent below the actual monthly average. We applied the percentages listed under "% of Total" to every cash machine withdrawal transacted by Judith (as indicated in their joint check register). Cash machine transactions recorded as belonging to Jake totaled $6,200 and were included in the budget under Jake's Separate Expenses.

FIGURE 7.5   (continued)

Notes to Subcategories

5.1 HOUSING

4. Taxes and Insurance

Judith will pay the property taxes on the residence from her combined wages and maintenance. Property taxes are approximately $4,275 on the family residence, for a monthly average expense of $356. Judith will be paying homeowner's insurance premiums of $50 per month until the residence sells. Total expenses for this category are budgeted at $406 per month.

5.2 FOOD and SUPPLIES

General

The historical budget for food and supplies did not differentiate between groceries and supplies on some of the larger checks written to a local discount shopping organization. They were allocated 50 percent to each subcategory, resulting in food expenses that were too low and supplies that were too high. We have adjusted the budget figures accordingly.

5.4 CHILDREN

4. Other Child-Related Expenses

Judith pays in cash each month child-related expenditures totaling $210, as noted above in the "Allocation of Cash Expenditures." In addition, she spends approximately $1,560 additional dollars on various check and charge card purchases, including school supplies, sports fees sports equipment, movie theater and video rental expenses, travel/vacation expenses, personal expenses, and so on.

5.5 TRANSPORTATION

2. Vehicle Insurance and License

Judith will continue to drive the van since it is paid for. We estimate her monthly cost for insurance and licenses to be $410.64 twice per year for auto insurance plus $450 in license fees. The total annual expense is expected to be $1,271.28 for a monthly average expense of $106.

3. Vehicle Gas, Oil, Maintenance

The monthly average expense for gas, oil and maintenance is $177.80. However, this total includes several small charges made by Jake on the family gas card. Most (approximately 90 percent) of Jake's gas and maintenance costs are paid by the company. We estimate that Judith's portion of gas, oil and maintenance to be $125 per month.

FIGURE 7.5   *(continued)*

5.6   HEALTH CARE
1. Insurance
Judith will continue to be covered under Jake's plan until the divorce is final.

2. Uninsured Dental, Orthodontic, Medical
Judith will be paying her costs only for health insurance in the temporary period. We assume that Jake will pay for the children since they will be covered under his plan. This reduces potential problems with filing claims and handling of insurance reimbursements. If it is determined that this is the best method of handling medical expenses, an adjustment will need to be made to Jake's budget. The historical total does not incorporate Frances's recent need for orthodontia and the current payments of $115 per month. We assume that Jake will pay this cost. We recommend that Jake's budget for uninsured medical expenses be approximately $50 per month (Note: projected and agreed-upon income levels will support this figure).

3. Other: Counseling
Judith has been seeing a counselor and would like to continue to do so. The weekly cost for each visit is $60, or $240 per month.

5.7   PERSONAL EXPENSES
6. Gifts
During the budget period, all gifts that were assumed to be from both Judith and Jake were allocated to Judith in attempting to isolate Jake's separate gift purchases. For the proposed budget, we allocate approximately half of the historical average expense.

5.8   MISCELLANEOUS
3. Federal Taxes
We estimate Judith's income tax liability to be $537 per month on maintenance income of $54,000, wages of $8,500, bank interest of $200 and a $4,000 deductible IRA contribution. There is a Federal Income Tax saving of more than $3,000 if both parties file separately. She will be filing as head of household with two exemptions, one for her and one for Frances, as agreed upon in their second mediation session. Jake will file as Single with three exemptions.

FIGURE 7.5   *(continued)*

and his attorney. Judith will periodically drop off the coded budget information for data input. This is an ongoing process during the third and fourth phases of the integrated process outlined in chapter 6.

A fairly solid understanding of the cash flow requirements of the household prior to the dissolution should have been established by now. If it hasn't in your case, start asking questions. The responsibility of maintaining the financial balance is in your hands, and the less you understand about your financial future, the harder it will be to keep it from toppling. Always keep in mind your goals, your financial future, and your career. During the preparation of the postdivorce budget, we work toward establishing the best course of action in achieving the financial goals you identified at the beginning of the budget process.

You may recall that the temporary budget usually differs from the historical spending patterns of the household. The same is true of the temporary budget and the proposed postdivorce budget. Your perception of how things have changed since the temporary budget was prepared, along with incorporating the long-term financial goals, may result in yet another "compromised" financial plan. Once you've established a temporary budget, it becomes more relevant to consider the effects of such factors as inflation, increased income taxes, salary changes, and other economic conditions that affect the long-term needs of the household. The use of financial planning models can provide a simplified means of showing what the most likely outcomes are for both parties for the various settlement proposals that are presented.

I will meet with Judith about the other financial and tax issues in her case and for the purpose of helping the attorney with the data-gathering, financial and tax analysis, and property settlement proposal. Judith, her attorney, and I, will be doing "what-if" projections, creating various scenarios for Judith to look at to prepare her for her settlement negotiations or trial.

During this time, Judith will evaluate her future financial needs and try to answer some of the following questions. Judith is doing her own guided research to determine what her postdivorce lifestyle will be—she wants to be able to speak about the details of her new life rather than taking what is left over. This is not Jake's plan for Judith, but Judith's plan for Judith and her family.

POSTDIVORCE BUDGET QUESTIONS

Housing

- Will Judith keep or sell the family residence?
- Will Judith refinance the family residence?

- What kind of a loan is best for her, a fixed or variable mortgage?
- What are the current mortgage rates available and what are the points on these loans?
- What income is required for Judith to qualify for a mortgage? She needs to meet with a mortgage broker, take notes, and bring those notes back to our meeting. She will want to get prequalified for a mortgage, preferably a fixed-rate mortgage. She will quickly find out what kind of income is required for her to qualify for a new mortgage on a house. This information will be helpful when negotiating the property settlement.
- Will the current lender refinance the mortgage and on what terms, with what fee?
- Since Judith and Jake are selling their house, she must look for new housing. She should bring in the listings on three houses that could work for her and the children.
- Judith needs to have three real estate firms provide her and Jake with a market analysis on their current home.
- What will the monthly costs for gas, electricity, water, sewer, and garbage expenses be at this new home? Judith can call the power company. When given the address, they will provide her with information regarding the average expenses.
- What will the real estate taxes be in this new home?
- Will Judith need to replace furniture or appliances or make improvements to this new home?
- What is the cost of the homeowner's coverage for this new house?

(Note: If Judith decides to rent for the long term, the above questions will need to be adjusted for that scenario.)

Children

- How will day care, education, and other child-related expenses change postdivorce?
- Does Judith need day care for the children while pursuing her career?
- What are the after-school and summer day-care costs?
- What sports activities and hobbies do the children participate in currently? Which will they continue with in the future? (She needs to be very detailed about these anticipated costs.)
- Will the children see a therapist in the future? How often, at what cost, and for how long?

Transportation

- What is the cost of insurance coverage on Judith's car?
- Will Judith have parking fees while attending school and during any internship?

Health Care

- What is the estimated cost for comparable health insurance for Judith—either under COBRA or under a new individual plan? Judith needs to get at least two comprehensive bids for her sole health insurance coverage. Oftentimes, COBRA coverage is more expensive than buying an individual insurance plan. Know the costs when negotiating your property settlement.
- How will Judith be reimbursed for uninsured medical costs she pays for herself and the children even though the children are under Jake's health insurance policy?
- What are Judith's costs for visits to her therapist? How long does she plan to continue these sessions; how often will they meet?

Personal Expenses

Put yourself in Judith's shoes and ask yourself the questions below that she had to answer.

- Specifically, how will your clothing expenses change from the time you are in school to the time of full-time employment?
- What are your educational costs listed in the career plan prepared by your vocational expert?
- What vacation budget do you have for one trip for yourself and a major trip with the children annually? (Be detailed: travel costs, lodging, food, entertainment, and automobile rental.)
- How have you adjusted your purchases of gifts for family and friends? Itemize your costs by the holiday and each person receiving the gift.
- Are you taking up any new sports with your children? Have you joined a health club as a family or are you planning to maintain your current club membership?

Miscellaneous

You will be maintaining a life insurance policy on your husband's life securing death benefit coverage for you and the children for the time period during which he has an obligation for child support and alimony. What is your estimated monthly premium cost?

- Is your husband insurable, with limited health problems?
- Will you continue with the current insurance coverage or have you looked into new coverage?
- What are the costs of these policies? Are they term or whole life insurance?
- What do you estimate your annual tax preparation fee to be in the future?
- Will you need ongoing financial planning services? What are the fees for these services?
- What is the cost to have your new will prepared by an attorney?
- What is the cost to have a durable power of attorney and directive to physicians documents prepared?
- Are you paying your legal bills as you go through this dissolution process? What does your attorney estimate these costs to be before your first settlement conference, to prepare for trial, going to trial, writing the divorce documents and/or reviewing these documents, coordinating the transfers for your retirement and nonretirement assets, and for the court filing of your decree?
- What are your current credit card balances by card? What is your minimum payment and interest rate charged on each card? Close all joint credit cards and if possible, pay off all credit card balances at the time of the divorce. Start your postdivorce lifestyle credit card debt-free.
- What have you paid in attorney fees to date and what do you currently owe to the attorney and any experts who are working on your case?

Information in this chapter is designed to help you get started with the financial details of your divorce. If you do not have an attorney and are not in the process of gathering the data I've identified, you should begin assembling the information listed at the end of chapter 6 so that your budget can be prepared in conjunction with the other tax, cash flow, and asset allocation models.

Once the divorce becomes final, it would seem that the budget process ought to be complete, but the budget does need to be evaluated. You need to see how what you thought you would spend compares to what you did spend.

Cash Management System—Today and in the Future

For some the budget process is instinctive, which speeds up the process of gathering and processing the data. Others fear it and avoid the process. Complications generally arise when there are too many accounts used in maintaining the household. In a surprisingly large number of cases, three or four checking accounts and six to twelve credit cards are being used simultaneously to pay bills and make household purchases. It is no wonder these clients have no idea what their household expenses are. Getting on a budget and determining whether or not the budget is working is much easier when a simplified approach to handling deposits and paying household expenses is implemented.

The following twelve-step approach to cash management is an excellent way to deal with future budgeting issues. While the process is laborious, it is important for you to utilize the budget that has been prepared and to update it periodically. If you are uncertain about how to complete a step, seek help from your financial planner or accountant. The cycle for this system is twelve months long, although it is intended to create spending habits that last a lifetime.

Here are the steps to follow to create a cash management system:

1. Categorize your expenditures over the previous year.
2. Think about your financial future and what you would like your financial picture to look like in five years. What are your goals? Write them down.
3. Forecast your living expenses over the next year and create a twelve-month cash flow calendar that will allow you to reach your financial objectives.
4. Identify all sources of income. Determine net income from each source.
5. Add up all fixed expenses and subtract them directly from net income.
6. If you don't already have a money market checking account into which all your income flows, establish one. (These federally insured accounts allow the bank to invest your money in relatively secure short-term securities that pay a higher interest rate than regular checking accounts. They may have some restrictions on how and when you can withdraw your funds.) Hold on to only one checking account. You should also have two separate investment accounts: one for your periodic payments (see figure 7.6), and one for retirement and savings.

7. Deposit all income into the main account. Pay all mandatory living expenses directly from this account and set aside an amount each month in your first investment account that will allow you to make your periodic payments.
8. Keep track of your expenses for at least twelve months. Make sure you are staying within the budgeted amounts.
9. You may want to allocate specific income to specific expenses.
10. Monitor withdrawals from the investment accounts.
11. Review the budget each year to determine whether or not the goals and objectives set forth are being met. Look at inflows and outflows in your money market account and identify any excesses or deficiencies. Excess funds are transferred to your retirement or savings account. If there are deficiencies, go back to step 3.
12. Once the budget has been successfully maintained for twelve months, go out and treat yourself to something fun.

You don't need to categorize your expenses again, nor do you need to redefine your financial goals. This system is intended as a follow-up to all the preparation and hard work you've already done. In addition, the system is designed to accommodate changes in living expenses as well as any changes in your financial objectives through periodic reviews and updates.

As suggested in step 6, the system proposed in this chapter includes the use of three accounts. Figure 7.6 summarizes the structure of the accounts and the flow of funds through them.

You should find yourself a money market account that allows you to write checks and deposit all income you receive into the account. Only two types of checks should be written from the money market account. One check per month is written to you for deposit into your checking account. The amount of the check should equal the total expenses determined at your last budget review, minus your periodic payments. These payments occur either once per year or at regular intervals and cover such expenses as auto, life, and homeowner's insurance, and property and quarterly income taxes. These periodic payments are the other type of check you should be writing. Pay these expenses directly from the money market account, since it will be much easier to make sure that the payments are made and much more obvious when your budget is working effectively.

The balance in the main money market account should always be at least one-half of the total living expenses (from step 3, p. 148) required to maintain the home for three to six months. The other half of your emergency funds may be kept in a third account, which we haven't yet discussed. This last account is your reserve parachute. It might hold the

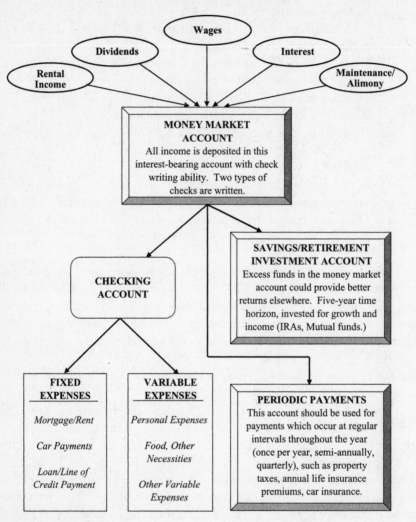

CASH MANAGEMENT SYSTEM

Wages

Dividends

Interest

Rental Income

Maintenance/ Alimony

MONEY MARKET ACCOUNT
All income is deposited in this interest-bearing account with check writing ability. Two types of checks are written.

CHECKING ACCOUNT

SAVINGS/RETIREMENT INVESTMENT ACCOUNT
Excess funds in the money market account could provide better returns elsewhere. Five-year time horizon, invested for growth and income (IRAs, Mutual funds.)

FIXED EXPENSES

Mortgage/Rent

Car Payments

Loan/Line of Credit Payment

VARIABLE EXPENSES

Personal Expenses

Food, Other Necessities

Other Variable Expenses

PERIODIC PAYMENTS
This account should be used for payments which occur at regular intervals throughout the year (once per year, semi-annually, quarterly), such as property taxes, annual life insurance premiums, car insurance.

Copyright © 2005 Miller Advisors, Inc.

FIGURE 7.6   Cash Management System

money you intend to spend in reaching your longer-term financial objectives or your retirement funds. You might even set up two accounts, since retirement funds withdrawn early often have a penalty and an income tax consequence.

In either case, you should review the balance in your money market account periodically to see: 1) if the money you spend from your checking account is really enough; and 2) if you have excess money sitting in your money market account. Your excess funds could be providing you with better investment return if you put the money into a mutual fund or other slightly higher risk investment. This higher risk is often acceptable in light of the increased earnings potential. We will discuss this and other types of accounts in chapter 12.

You should be setting aside something each month for the achievement of your long-term financial objectives. The question is, how much should be used for goal funding? A good rule of thumb is to deposit the greater of 10 percent of net income or one-half of the money you have left after you pay all of the bills and pay for your budgeted variable expenses such as food, entertainment, and clothing. You should set up your budget so that there is some money left, no matter how small, to put in your investment account.

I like to use the example of two investors, call them Mr. A. and Ms. B.

Mr. A. believes that at age thirty-five he has plenty of time to start saving for his retirement. He spent every dime he made until he was forty-five when, realizing he couldn't work forever, he began to put $6,000 per year into his retirement plan (perhaps an *annuity*) for the next twenty-five years for a total investment of $150,000.

Ms. B., also thirty-five, decides that now is the time to think about retirement and makes a ten-year commitment at the same $6,000 per year level starting immediately. In ten years, she will have made a $60,000 investment. Let's assume they both invest in assets that earn 8 percent after taxes or 8 percent tax-deferred. (Most retirement accounts, pensions, IRAs, and annuities are tax-deferred, which means you pay taxes on the earnings when funds are withdrawn after retirement.)

The after-tax value of Mr. A.'s account after his last $6,000 deposit, if he were to take all the money at once is $552,555, while Ms. B. has $694,317 in after-tax dollars, with $90,000 less having been deposited in the account! The cost of waiting is evident in this example.

Use the information I provided to create your own cash management system. Your plan must be monitored so that the results may be measured against the objectives defined in creating the plan, in addition to helping you stay on your budget. Any time there is a variance it should be investigated, understood, and then either corrected or incorporated into future plans. Reviews should be made periodically so that changes may be made, and a major update of the plan should be done at least annually.

Make sure you continue to monitor your spending. Not only does this confirm you are following your budget, but it also ascertains whether any child support being received is sufficient for the needs of the child. Child support figures are adjusted every two years or by agreement, and the ages of the children and the requirements of your household are part of the facts being considered. Your organization of the facts in a concise format will save everyone time and money.

The cash flow analysis discussed in this chapter really has a dual purpose. A legal document is prepared that clearly indicates the cash flow requirements of the household in both the pre- and postdivorce settings. At the same time, the identification of the financial goals as well as a potential means of achieving them have been defined. These tools are invaluable in this time of transition, and a clear understanding of your future financial picture can help reduce the level of emotional distress brought about by a divorce.

Judith was not unique in her budgeting process. The family spent most of the money earned each year. Judith did not keep a detailed family budget during her last few years of marriage. The family business paid for such discretionary expenses as vacations and meals. When Jake filed for divorce, Judith was immediately put on an "allowance," with no training to prepare her for the challenges of budgeting and downsizing from the family's married lifestyle. The budgeting system I implemented with Judith got her back on track financially and helped her regain the control she needed to complete the process.

PROTECTING YOURSELF FINANCIALLY DURING AND AFTER DIVORCE

This chapter would not be complete without addressing two topics that are increasingly significant concerns in contemporary divorce—credit protection and identity theft. I provided some pointers earlier about dealing with credit, but I want to expand on the subject in the next section.

Identity theft is an area few people think about during divorce. They should. This is a time of increased vulnerability, and the effects of becoming a victim may not be noticed until serious financial harm has been done.

How to Protect Your Credit in Divorce[1]

If you are contemplating divorce, or in the midst of one, you need to start thinking like a single person. You need to understand your and your spouse's credit rating and how these credit scores will be affected by the divorce. If you don't have children, the separation could be relatively easy. If you have children, real estate and mortgages, and/or lines of credit and credit cards, you need to be working with your attorney from the very beginning. You will be:

- Separating shared bank accounts, shared credit card accounts, and shared insurance coverage
- Establishing utilities in your own name
- Changing the guarantors of motor vehicle loans and the titles to those vehicles
- Transferring real estate mortgages and ownership in real estate
- Splitting up investment and retirement accounts and stock option awards

. . . and much more.

Beware if your decree says one spouse is "100 percent liable for debts and bills" listed in your property settlement because, unless your creditors agree to it (and they are not legally required to agree), they won't exclude you from being liable for the debt. Further, if you do allow your former spouse to assume these bills 100 percent, even if ordered by the court, and he does not make the payments in a timely manner, it is your credit rating and score that may be harmed, not only his. Separate the jointly held checking accounts and credit cards as soon as possible and start establishing your own credit right away. Try to refinance your real estate loans and automobile loans, if possible, and get your name off the old loan. I have seen houses go into foreclosure and both people who signed the loan are held accountable, even though the spouse who gave up the house may not have known it was in default until it was too late for her credit rating to be saved.

The Institute of Consumer Financial Education (ICFE) suggests you take the following steps to protect yourself if you are contemplating separation or divorce:

- Learn what lenders see in your credit report by ordering a copy today, either online or by phone, from the three major credit reporting agencies:
  - Experian (1-888-397-3742)
  - Equifax (1-800-685-1111)
  - TransUnion (1-800-888-4213)
- Begin to separate and/or close out shared and joint accounts, including checking, savings, IRAs, charge cards, doctors, dentists, health care, life insurance, and also motor vehicle loans, real estate mortgages, and student loans. Some separation of car loans or home mortgages may require refinancing or an outright sale to pay off your loan obligations.
- Make all of your payments before the due date. Missing or being late on a payment, even to the phone company or a book or music

club, can be very costly if it makes it on to your credit report. It may be much more than a $30 or $40 late payment fee, because of a clause that may be in your credit card or other loan agreements known as universal default. In essence, universal default stipulates that if you are late on one account, you are late on any account that includes the universal default clause. It may also trigger much higher fees and interest charges and lower credit scores. Prevention is easy. Pay your own monthly obligations at least a week or more ahead of the payment due date.

I like to see all current credit card debt paid no later than the date of the divorce. In your postdivorce planning, you can work with your financial planner to come up with a payoff strategy.

IDENTITY THEFT AND DIVORCE

The Federal Trade Commission estimates that 27 million Americans were victims of identity theft between 1998 and 2003. Though the rate of occurrence has stabilized, the number of cases is still staggering.

Everyone has some risk of being victimized—you don't have to lose a purse to fall prey to a thief rifling through your loan documents on a car dealer's desk. Unfortunately, the process of dissolution can substantially increase your exposure. Divorce is a legal process that usually involves filing documents that are considered "public records." Most courts automatically treat certain information as confidential, including data about minor children. State laws vary widely in what is labeled confidential, and judges and other court officials often have considerable latitude in interpreting what should be shielded from public access. Even potentially protected data can be revealed under various exceptions to the standard rules. Once a judgment is finalized, it is almost impossible to have the court impose additional restrictions on the records. In many jurisdictions, prevailing law requires the court to invoke "special considerations" to shelter divorce documents. Because of the high demand for public access in our society, only limited protection is available to divorcing couples.

Before you submit documents to the court, particularly the financial affidavit and asset descriptions, talk to your attorney about what protections are available. Ask about requesting that certain data be "sealed" by the court. **Never assume that financial records, which may include account numbers, PINs, passwords, and even Social Security numbers, have been secured from public access.** The effect of sealing depends on state law and local court rules. Some seals may last only a few months; others may remain effective for years. A number of courts allow personal data entered into the record to be abbreviated, commonly by showing the *last four digits only* of your Social Security number or financial account numbers. In some situations just the amount of the final judgment is sealed, while the other information is not. Be sure you understand what information will be available to whom and under what circumstances. If you cannot shield the information, at least you can anticipate how it may be used. Remember you cannot protect your data under the restrictions imposed by the Federal Right to Information Act, which only applies to data held by the U.S. government, not state or local resources. Keep a record of all information submitted to the court. You can use this to create a tracking system to monitor account activity during and after the divorce.

Protect Your Credit Report

Credit reports often contain sufficient information to allow a thief to pose as you, so it is important to guard access to them. If you believe you are the victim of identity theft, there are three levels of fraud alerts you can place on your credit report.

The *initial alert* is activated by contacting any one of the three major credit-reporting agencies (Equifax, Experian, or TransUnion). They will place a ninety-day alert on your record and notify the other two agencies. This makes you immediately eligible for a free credit report (you may have to request it), and you will have to provide some personal information such as a telephone number and your Social Security number so creditors can confirm your identity. During this time you may not be able to obtain additional credit.

An *extended alert* is more serious. It lasts for seven years, and to invoke it you will have to file proof of loss, such as a police report or the FTC's ID Theft Affidavit. This alert can be removed in less than the full seven years if you provide a written request that includes sufficient data to prove your identity.

A *credit freeze* blocks all access to your credit report and prevents thieves from opening any new accounts in your name. New creditors are required to contact you before obtaining your report. Members of the armed forces serving on active duty may request a military fraud alert. This specialized alert does not require proof of loss.

If you are concerned about your credit rating, but have no real proof someone is tampering with your accounts, you can use a credit monitoring service. All three major reporting agencies provide this for a fee. It is designed to notify you if there is any change in your credit status, such as new accounts being opened or a credit inquiry. Federal law now allows residents of all states to request a free credit report annually from each of the credit reporting agencies. By spacing these requests over twelve months, you can get updated information every four months for free.

THE BEST DEFENSE IS VIGILANCE

Most experts agree the single most effective protection against ID theft is personal monitoring. Check your credit report regularly—three or four times per year is not too often. Other steps you can take to minimize your exposure include:

- Never carry your Social Security card with you, and don't provide the number to anyone without verifying why it is needed and how it will be used. Request a different ID number in place of it if insurance cards, driver's license, or other commonly referenced documents use it.
- Minimize the number of credit cards you carry and keep a record of all cards and identifying documents you have in your purse or wallet.
- Guard your financial transactions from observers in public places such as ATMs and pay phones.
- Never leave receipts for purchases lying around, particularly at the point of sale.
- Use a shredder to destroy statements and other documents containing personal data.
- Use a secure mailbox to deposit outgoing mail. Pick up incoming mail promptly, especially if it is delivered to an unlocked mailbox.
- Don't conduct financial transactions on public computers, and keep your personal computer safe by updating its antivirus and spyware-blocking software. Use a firewall program when connecting to the Internet and keep abreast of e-mail and other Web-based scams.
- Be conscious of billing cycles and immediately contact any creditor whose statement is late or reflects unknown charges.
- Never give out personal information (especially SSN and account numbers or passwords) over the phone or online if you have not initiated the call or are not sure to whom you are speaking. Always verify what the data will be used for.
- Shred unsolicited credit card offers and limit those you receive by calling 1-888-567-8688 to opt out of these offers.
- Don't put your telephone number, driver's license number, or SSN on your printed checks. Pick up blank checks and deposit slips at the bank if they are not delivered to a secure mailbox.

- Check out what personal information on you is available over the Internet. You can perform searches for your telephone number, address, date of birth, and other data. If you find references you don't want listed, contact the Web site administrator and demand it be removed.
- If you suspect you are the victim of identity theft, use the resources below to initiate appropriate action. Don't ignore the signs!

There are a number of good sources available for more information on this subject. One of the best is the Federal Trade Commission's Web site at *www.consumer.gov/idtheft*. Another excellent nonprofit site is *www .privacyrights.org*.

8

Closing In on Disparity: A New Era Deserves a New Divorce Model

*The best career advice to give the young is
"Find out what you like doing best
and get someone to pay you for doing it."*

—KATHERINE WHITEHORN (BRITISH JOURNALIST AND WRITER)

In earlier chapters I have commented on the plight of divorcing women who have been financially dependent upon their husbands. Their difficulties are not always due to a man being the sole "breadwinner" in the family. The sad reality is that many working women earn less than their male counterparts. In this chapter, I am going to address this disparity of earnings between men and women. Particularly after divorce, women—often removed from the workforce through marriage, by the mutual choice of both spouses for the benefit of the children and the family—reenter the workforce in a position far below their former spouse in earnings and in their capability to catch up.

Most of the material presented here is adapted from a 2006 article I wrote with Janice E. Reha, CMHC, MA, who provides career services to companies, colleges, and career changers. For more information, visit *www.careerdiscoveryinc.com.*

Twenty-five years ago, America was at the tail end of the Manufacturing Age. At that time, most people worked in one company for the duration of their work lives. During the height of the Manufacturing Age, one person (usually male) could support three or four other people in a household. Women traditionally raised children and kept up the home. If they did work outside the home, it was generally in lower-paying jobs than their husbands.

Twenty-five years ago, life planning was simple and defined much more in linear terms. Society and our economy have become more complex than ever before.

Today, the United States participates in the Global Age. Technology has produced new occupations, many of which have no defined titles. People change jobs seven to nine times in a lifetime due to technology, economic concerns, and restructuring within companies. The United States has moved from a more predictable, consistent workplace to one that is constantly forming, dismantling, and reforming to compete internationally. Yet we still are using the same mind-set of twenty-five years ago when addressing divorce and the implications of dividing property. This societal shift requires a more dynamic, multifaceted, individualized model for divorce settlements to reflect current social and economic trends.

A NEW ERA NEEDS A NEW MODEL

One of the major changes needed in the new divorce model is when and how much alimony will be paid. There simply is no set amount to how much alimony you can expect to be awarded. You need to understand your state's statutes and its case decisions. I have found there are two primary themes in court cases concerning alimony laws that determine the amount of alimony awarded: the economic lifestyle of the parties during marriage and the length of marriage.

Alimony awards vary widely and are affected by judges looking carefully at income disparity. The longer a couple is married, the greater the predisposition for a longer period of alimony.

ALIMONY THEORIES: OLD AND NEW

Transitional or Rehabilitative

It is not unusual, even in a marriage of modest length, for a trial court to award alimony of short duration, so as to provide interim financial assistance to one spouse. Terms given to such support awards are *transitional* or *rehabilitative.*

At the other end of the spectrum are awards of lengthy, even permanent alimony in a situation where a spouse, most typically the wife, is concluding a long-term marriage (as in, thirty-five years or longer) primarily as a homemaker with no marketable skills or professional training for the workplace. The longer the marriage and the longer a spouse is out of the workforce, the greater and more permanent is the loss of that spouse's earning capacity.

Restitution or Compensation

When a spouse interrupts their professional advancement by doing part-time clerical work, or acting strictly as a homemaker to enable the other spouse to complete advanced degrees and establish a career, the expectation is that both parties will eventually enjoy economic benefits derived from this arrangement. The concept may work if the parties stay married. In the event of a divorce, however, in the absence of spousal support, the spouse who has interrupted a career is at an economic disadvantage, regardless of the length of the marriage. That spouse often is awarded alimony on the "compensatory" or "restitutive" theory, to provide payment for the lost economic opportunities experienced during the time when the other spouse was advancing a career.

The Partnership Model

Long-term marriages can be characterized as partnerships in which each spouse has an important role to play. If the wife operated primarily as the homemaker, for example, or worked in a low-paying position while the husband earned an advanced degree and significant income, those contributions should be considered of similar or equal value.

The partnership theory assumes that both spouses make substantially (although not necessarily identical) contributions to a marriage. If so, they should receive substantially equal benefits from the marriage and should not be left in a widely disparate position after the marriage ends.

Under this theory, spousal alimony should be utilized to level the playing field by providing ongoing support to the spouse whose economic position is significantly inferior. This support, in combination with an equitable distribution of the property, should place her in a financial position comparable to that of her husband.

The courts tend to base settlements on the assumption—often false—that both spouses can be equally self-sufficient. In reality, marriage often creates economic inequality. Consider the following research.

- Following divorce, mothers typically experience a sharp decline in economic status and often descend into poverty with their children. Nearly 40 percent of divorced mothers are poor. And even if the children of divorce do not end up in literal poverty, they are less

likely to reach their parents' social and economic level or obtain a college education.[1]
- Women who interrupted their careers, were full-time homemakers, didn't create their own retirement accounts, and who are divorced at an older age with a longer life expectancy, often have inadequate financial resources during the most vulnerable time in their lives.

The new divorce settlement model needs to focus more on the division of income for a longer period of time, taking into account the career assets, rather than simply the length of marriage. To divide marital property equitably, the major breadwinner's career and the associated earnings that go with it must be acknowledged as property by the courts. Assets including salary, stock options, health and disability insurance, vacation and sick pay, education, and potential earning power are all assets that were earned during the marriage and should be accounted for during a divorce settlement.

Of course, assessing economic value of the career assets and forecasting their value to both parties in the future is a much more difficult task than simply applying a length of marriage test. Under this divorce settlement model, every divorce negotiation requires a unique and innovative approach given the career and economic circumstances of the parties involved.

It also requires a more sophisticated understanding of the employment, retirement, and investment trends in the twenty-first-century workplace and economy. The goal here is to outline some of the driving social and work trends of our time and illustrate through case studies how understanding the trends can lead to more equitable settlements for both parties.

CULTURAL TRENDS AND THEIR EFFECT ON DIVORCE

Social Trends

Despite a growing female workforce and increased education, women are still at an economic disadvantage when compared to men, particularly following a divorce. The divorce rate has not declined and multiple marriages mean more divorces. There also is research indicating that people in second and third marriages are even more prone to divorce. As a result, many women enter their senior years divorced. For women who were born between 1951 and 1955, a projected 20 percent will be divorced by age sixty-seven, according to a study published by the University of Michigan.[2]

Meanwhile women continue to interrupt careers to raise children. Roughly 30 percent of U.S. children under the age of fifteen have a mom at home full time, while less than 1 percent of men are stay-at-home parents. Among male managers and professionals who are working, more than 30 percent work fifty or more hours a week in order to advance their careers. Ninety-five percent of mothers work fewer than fifty hours per week during the key career-building years because those are also the key child-rearing years. Ultimately, many are finding the work-life balance too difficult to achieve, so they quit their jobs.[3]

Women also are at a disadvantage when it comes to saving enough for retirement. Social Security is still a mainstay of their financial security. Women earn less than men, save less than men, and are less likely to have a pension than men. Yet they will likely outlive men. Earnings are what make retirement savings possible and these earnings are the yardstick used to calculate Social Security benefits. With a history of unemployment or underemployment, women are stuck in a cycle that will provide them with less Social Security and retirement income despite their greater need.

Workplace Trends

Outsourcing jobs from the United States is accelerating. According to *Outsourcing Times,* 406,000 jobs left the country in 2004. This acceleration is expected to continue for years to come. Job losses also have occurred due to mergers and acquisitions.

Meanwhile, the weakness in the labor market means a growing number of temporary jobs. Temporary staffing practices that were considered short-term fixes in the early 1990s are now commonplace in many businesses. By using temporary help, employers find it easier to hire and fire, which saves them the cost of paying health care and other benefits of full-time employees.

Health insurance benefits also have decreased in coverage. Employers are transferring more of the costs of health care to the individual worker, including the premium cost and payment of out-of-pocket expenses and prescriptions.

Another trend, which becomes more apparent when job loss occurs, is the increase of small businesses or self-employment. According to the Small Business Administration (SBA), small firms employ half of all private sector employees and generate 60 to 80 percent of new jobs annually.

A declining proportion of workers can count on defined benefit payments to see them through lengthy retirements. Pensions are being replaced with self-funding plans such as 401(k) accounts that may have a profit-sharing or matching component. The risk of the investments has been transferred to the employee from the employer. The problem is that many people mismanage these assets.

The soaring stock market of the late 1990s lulled many workers into complacency with regard to saving in their 401(k) plans for retirement. The bull market of the 1990s fueled a crazy kind of optimism regarding retirement. Those who invested heavily in technology and the overall stock market in their 401(k) plans have seen the erosion of 50 to 70 percent of their retirement savings.

The decline in stock prices then, along with the outlook for only modest returns going forward, have caused baby boomers and other workers to reassess whether they really have enough saved for retirement. Most have not.

With job security and benefits less concrete than in the past, divorcing parties need to realize that the income they relied on during their married life is more at risk than ever before.

Longevity Trends

The American worker is aging and life expectancy continues to increase the danger of outliving one's asset base. For many years, the economy, pension plans, and the government supported the concept of a mid-sixties retirement. Over time, demographics, economic forces, and divorce will make this standard harder to achieve, increasingly leaving it up to the individual to build a nest egg large enough to avoid the late retirement trend.

The average life span for a male at age sixty-five in 1940 was just under seventy-eight years; today it is greater than eighty years. The average life span for a woman in 1940 was sixty-five years; in 2004, it was nearly eighty-four, according to the Social Security Administration.

As a result, the government is enacting pension reforms. They are delaying the age one can receive full Social Security benefits and Medicare; they are sharing Medicare premiums payments between the government and the retiree, increasing the restrictions with Medicaid, and encouraging the older worker to be responsible for his own retirement and stay in the job market longer.

Demographic changes also will drive up the cost of home health care. The number of people needing help from family caregivers is expected to skyrocket in the next few decades, and leading the change will be the baby boomers who are looking for help with their parents, and later on, for themselves.

Retirement Trends

As the fear of being insolvent in the later years increases for today's mid-career workers, the genesis of a solution is emerging. Either many baby boomers will retire later than they expected to or they simply won't retire at all.

For many decades, rising affluence allowed the average age at retirement to fall. Since the mid-1980s, this trend has reversed with labor force participation among older American workers rising dramatically.

In 1984, just 27 percent of the income of people aged sixty-five to seventy-four came from wages and salaries. By 2002, this had jumped to 37 percent. This surge in the older workforce has continued unabated in the last few years, even as other age groups have pulled back from the labor market in reaction to a sluggish economy.

More important, companies will need to utilize baby boomers due to the growing number of aging baby boomers in the population and the much smaller number of younger people who follow behind them. The exodus of baby boomers will start in 2009 when the oldest of the group turns sixty-three.

Divorce attorneys and their clients need to become better at estimating how much they will need in retirement based on how long they expect to live. Workers facing much weaker job security than ever before need more education and flexibility in career choices. They will also need to take a closer look at their medical expenses and long-term care as well as any obligations they may have to care for aging parents. That means settlements must be more flexible to accommodate the postdivorce financial needs of both spouses.

Most divorcing spouses will not have any choice—the majority of them will need to work longer to pay for the costs of dividing the household assets and income as well as supporting their children.

Housing Trends: Keep or Sell the Family Home?

This area of postdivorce financial planning warrants particular attention because it is a flashpoint for tension and controversy. For most married couples, the family home is the highest valued asset they will divide in their divorce. A home is difficult to value; it is not readily converted to cash; it costs a substantial amount of money to maintain; and it has implications of federal and state tax liability. Add to that all of the emotional attachments and the ensuing decision process can become costly and divisive.

Home prices nationwide have climbed an average of 40 to 75 percent in some areas during the past five years. Homeowners have tapped into their low-interest home equity to take vacations, remodel, and purchase second homes. Many banks have allowed home buyers to get loans when their mortgage payments total as much as 50 percent of their monthly income, up from the more customary limit of about one-third in past cycles. This debt eventually needs to be paid off. If the home equity has aggressively been tapped, there is less to divide between the spouses at the time of divorce.

Often, the spouse who gets the house can't afford to maintain it. This is known as being "house poor." Child support and alimony can help for a time, but if all of the money is going into the house and little to savings and to a career plan, the end result is not good. This situation often leads to a poorly maintained home and a loss in the value of the equity. It can also result in an overall reduction in the standard of living of the owner if the money is diverted from personal uses to the home's upkeep.

Too many times, clinging to the family home means delaying education for career advancement and no funding for retirement. Downsizing at the time of the divorce and investing in a career plan may be emotionally painful, but is often the best long-term decision for financial security.

SECURING AN EQUITABLE AND STABLE POSTDIVORCE LIFE

The following two case studies are representative of the complex social, financial, and career situations that we are seeing in modern divorce cases. Under the old model, length of marriage and age were given the most weight. A modern settlement should bring greater balance yet address the unique circumstances of each couple. Each scenario considers:

- Salary and wage information
- Education levels
- Occupational choices and trends
- Age
- Health
- Dependent children
- Length of marriages
- Remarriage patterns
- Longevity

As our society continues to change and evolve, we must broaden the way we look at divorce and the financial implications for all parties involved. My hope is that attorneys and their clients will realize that equitable divorce settlements can be achieved for both parties when they are willing to address the significant social and economic changes of our time.

CASE STUDIES

The following two cases illustrate the "nuts and bolts" of how a professional team of divorce specialists applied the information supplied earlier in this chapter.

CASE 1: MID-TERM MARRIAGE

DIVORCE SETTLEMENT ANALYSIS
Marriage: 18 Years

SCENARIO

Andrew, fifty-two, is a midlevel manager at a manufacturing company that has just merged with a larger company. His educational background includes an MBA with a specialty in finance completed twelve years ago. His salary is $125,000 plus a $10,000 bonus per year. His employer matches 3 percent of his income in a 401(k) profit-sharing plan.

His wife, Jeanne, fifty-one, has been a stay-at-home wife and mother for the length of the marriage. She has an associate of arts degree in business and was an administrative assistant at the company at which they met nineteen years earlier.

They have two children, ages fifteen and thirteen. Jeanne has been raising the children and helping to coordinate her elderly parents' care as they are moved to assisted living facilities. Her mother and father are seventy-seven and eighty-four, respectively, and they live in a small town thirty miles away. Jeanne's father's health has been declining, and he is in the early stages of Alzheimer's disease. Since he will require more care than his wife, he lives in the extended care wing of the same facility where the mother has a small apartment. Jeanne's parents sold their home and used the $175,000 equity to prepay the cost of housing for the rest of their lives.

Andrew's widowed mother is seventy-eight and lives out of state. She is in an interim care facility after having hip surgery, and she will not be able to return to living in her former home. As a result, Andrew is planning to have her move to an assisted living apartment. His sister, who works full time, lives near their mother and has provided help with her physical care.

Their agreement has been that Andrew will pay for domestic help and his sister will give more time to their mother. The mother has sufficient assets to maintain herself for approximately four years in the retirement home, but if her health deteriorates more rapidly, assets from the sale of her home will have to be used to provide care. The family expects to net approximately $200,000 from the sale of her home.

Jeanne had been married at age twenty-two for three years with no children—a "starter marriage." She had no separate assets at the start of the second marriage. This is the first marriage for Andrew and he has separate assets from a previous 401(k) rollover retirement account. He used $8,000 in funds from the sale of the house he had owned prior to marrying Jeanne to purchase the current residence in their joint names.

DISCUSSION ISSUES

- Both parties must reduce living expenses.

- Since she gave up a career to be the primary caregiver to their children, Jeanne will need to increase her education to support herself over the long term. She is competing for education funding with her soon-to-be college-age children.

- Each party will have to work longer and retire much later.

- Neither party participates in a pension plan—only a profit-sharing plan for him and a **Roth IRA** for her.

- The Social Security life expectancy table updated June 2004 gives a life expectancy of 81.7 years for Jeanne and 77.9 years for Andrew.

- Based on their mutual experiences with aging parents and the trend of employers passing more responsibility for heath care costs to workers, the increasing cost of medical care is a concern for both spouses.

SOLUTIONS

Career Plan
Due to Jeanne's age and previous work experience, she intends to go back to community college and take courses in accounting and

business. She wants to start a small business providing concierge services for the elderly. She has enjoyed her exposure to the field of elder care the past four years with her parents and her mother-in-law. She is aware of the need to provide financial planning services for the elderly and would like to become a consultant in elder care issues. Her plan is to offer bookkeeping management with insurance and Medicare, help families find the appropriate health care facility, and help baby boomers like herself manage the health care solutions for their elderly parents.

Upon completing her career assessment with the help of a career counselor, Jeanne discovered that she has a clear interest in being an entrepreneur, with skills in social work and data management. She intends to complete an associate of arts degree in accounting at her local community college and become licensed to sell long-term nursing care insurance.

She will attend college full time for two years and develop a business plan. During the next three to five years, she will be networking with various associations and groups to promote her business. She will look for employment through temporary help services as well as seek employment in the elder care field.

Jeanne will need two years of alimony while attending college full time. An additional three years of alimony will be required for her to promote her business and work part time. The last year will be at a reduced rate. The career and financial plan will afford her the flexibility to attend to her teenage children's needs.

Finances and Alimony
The couple enlisted the services of a financial planner to help them divide their assets. They will sell the family home, and each party will downsize to a $200,000 home or condo with a $100,000 mortgage. Jeanne will rent a home at first, because she will earn more over the long term by investing in education rather than investing in a home and foregoing her education.

They have agreed to live in the same neighborhood near the children's schools and share caring for the children. Andrew will pay child support of $600 per month per child until they are eighteen or graduated from high school, whichever is longer.

Jeanne will file her taxes as head of household and Andrew will file as single. Each party will claim one child as a deduction.

College funding will be split between the parties based on their pro rata share of earned income when the children are enrolled in a community and/or state college. They would like the children to go to the community college for two years, work during the summer, and use school loans for the difference.

He will provide health care coverage for the children. She will fund her health coverage with an individual policy based on her health. Otherwise, she will take COBRA coverage under his plan, typically more expensive coverage, and she will apply for health care coverage with the AARP. They are each planning to purchase a minimum long-term nursing care policy and will jointly apply before the divorce is final to qualify for preferred health and couples discount. They anticipate an annual premium of $1,500 per year for each policy.

Their investment assets in the retirement plans and individual holdings were depleted by more than 50 percent during the 2000–02 market decline. After meeting with their financial advisor, they have each created a disciplined asset allocation plan with their remaining assets. Their diversified equity portfolio is limited to a maximum of 75 percent of the investment assets.

They will divide their retirement assets fifty-fifty and the overall division of property is 55 percent to Jeanne, 45 percent to Andrew. Meanwhile, he will have significantly more funds in his Social Security plan at full retirement—age sixty-seven under the current rules. She will fund a Roth IRA while receiving alimony to offset this difference. He will contribute 3 percent into his 401(k) plan for the next five years rather than the maximum allowed contribution. As a result, each party will have to work into their early seventies to fund their retirement.

Using the data from this case I created projections of the cash flow and net worth for Jeanne and Andrew. Figure 8.1 shows these projections for ten years following their divorce. Note the difference between the two parties in both figures at year five compared to year ten. This illustrates the importance of extending such projections beyond the typical five-year span.

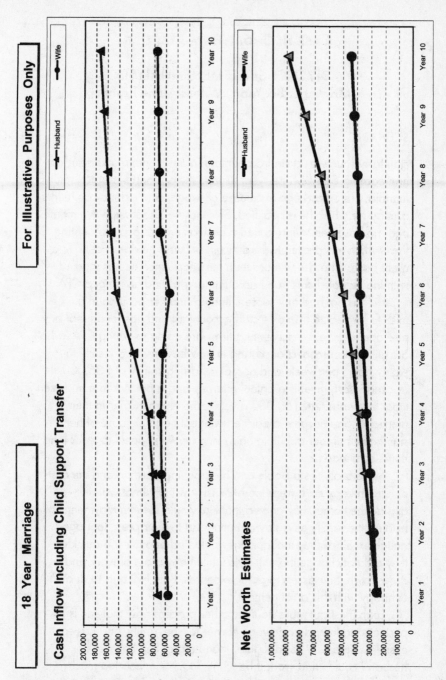

FIGURE 8.1 Comparison of Cash Inflow and Net Worth

CASE II: SHORT-TERM MARRIAGE

DIVORCE SETTLEMENT ANALYSIS
Marriage: Six Years; Wife Is Alpha Earner

SCENARIO

Hal, forty-four, was a staff accountant in a national manufacturing firm earning $55,000 per year. Due to the outsourcing of tax returns to India, there has been a squeeze on wages and actual jobs in this country for which he is qualified. Since losing his job eighteen months ago, he has been trying to find a position with a local accounting firm, which has proven to be difficult, because he does not have a client base. It has been more than ten years since he has worked with individual clients in an accounting firm, and he is not a CPA.

He has not had any success finding another position in a mid- to large-size firm as a staff accountant and has found that any new openings in the accounting firms are going to young CPAs who are willing to prospect and bring in new business, work sixty to eighty hours per week, and accept a starting salary of $36,000.

Leah, forty-five, is a patent attorney and a partner in a midsized legal firm earning $150,000 a year—the alpha earner in their marriage. She became a partner two years ago because of her significant number of billing hours and her willingness to work long hours as needed.

Since Leah has a stable and high-paying position and the costs of full-time day care were too expensive with Hal not working outside the home, they agreed that Hal would seek employment while helping the family as a stay-at-home dad to their preschool-aged daughter. Since they thought Hal would find another job quickly, they did not change their lifestyle while he was out of work and drew down their assets to cover expenses. Both Hal and Leah are unhappy with this arrangement.

Leah must put more hours into her practice now that she is a partner and the primary wage earner for the family, and has spent even less time with her daughter than before. She believes her husband could "find work if he wanted to." She feels too much pressure and resents having less time with their daughter. Leah has always wanted a career and was happy with the marriage when they were a dual-career couple. She now knows she wants a financial partner in marriage.

Their daughter will start full-time school in the next year, and her day-care needs will be reduced to after-school care five days a week. Each parent plans to share the evening and weekend care of the daughter after the divorce is final. They have seen a mediator and have negotiated a flexible temporary parenting plan.

The family home is valued at $450,000 with a $350,000 mortgage and a fixed interest rate of 5 percent over the twenty-eight years remaining on the loan. They each have separate property, and each will keep this money separate from their overall property division.

DISCUSSION ISSUES

- Nontraditional marriage—the wife is the higher wage earner while the husband needs career counseling and further education.

- Offshoring of jobs and self-employment model changes educational and career plan.

- The husband chooses to invest in education and a new business versus buying a new home.

- Their six-year marriage would qualify as short term under the currently accepted legal definition of marriage. However, they will focus on the need for a career change and support of the child rather than the length of marriage when coming up with the division of assets and the amount and duration of alimony.

- Both parties will need to reduce living expenses and will work past their traditional retirement age to age seventy or beyond.

SOLUTIONS

Career Plan

Hal has always had an interest in investments and personal financial planning and would like to earn his license as a certified financial planner (CFP) and open his own financial planning practice to provide him with the opportunity to own and control his own business and have the potential for more earning capacity. He chooses self-employment over a corporate position, because even if he could find corporate work, he does not want to face downsizing. He also has been envious of his wife's career advancement and her ownership in the law firm.

Upon completing his career assessment with a career counselor, Hal confirmed his career direction. One recurring career theme was his strong sales orientation, so he is entertaining the possibility of starting his own financial business. He will enroll in an intensive certified financial planner correspondence program and the H&R Block® tax course, which will take eighteen months to complete. He will create an intense flexible study schedule for the next two years that will allow him to drive their daughter to and from school and provide three days of afterschool care.

Once Hal completes his course to become a CFP, it will take him two to three years to build up his practice. It is assumed that he will make net earnings after expenses of $20,000 his first full year and $45,000 the second. He believes that he will be earning $100,000 net within five years of completing his education.

Finances and Alimony

After discussing their assets with a financial planner, Leah agrees to pay Hal alimony of $4,000 per month for two years. Hal will pay Leah $300 per month for child support, an arrangement that will be reviewed every three years, with mediation if necessary. Leah will also pay a reduced alimony of $2,000 per month for an additional year to get Hal to the point in his new business where he makes close to the salary he earned during the marriage. Hal will use investment assets to fund his education over and above the alimony or supplement with part-time work, as his schedule permits.

Leah will keep 29 percent of their joint retirement assets and Hal will take the remaining 71 percent. They will retain separately the retirement assets they had prior to the marriage.

Leah will keep the family home and have primary custody of their daughter. She chose to keep the home in lieu of more current retirement assets. Hal will rent instead of buy a home and invest in his career. A vacation home they own jointly will be sold and they will split the proceeds fifty-fifty.

They will renegotiate child support in three years after Hal has completed his education and has started to develop his business. By agreement, they will adjust the child support annually based on the Consumer Price Index for the next three years and beyond.

Leah will file as head of household and keep her daughter as a deduction. Hal will file as single with one deduction.

Hal will be responsible for his medical coverage benefits package by purchasing an individual health insurance policy. The daughter will be covered on Leah's medical plan at work. They will share the medical costs for their daughter fifty-fifty after insurance payments.

Hal does not anticipate funding any money toward his retirement for at least three years. Leah plans to contribute to a Roth IRA versus her 401(k) plan for the next three years. This will give her a tax-free source of income at retirement without any penalties for early withdrawal and will not force her to start taking distributions at age seventy and a half. Neither has a pension plan and they have always funded their retirement through contributions to retirement plans at work.

Both expect to work to age seventy or beyond, although under the current Social Security rules based on their ages, the full retirement age is sixty-seven for each of them.

RECOMMENDATIONS FOR SETTLEMENT PROPOSALS

It is critical to the financial well-being of divorcing couples to strive for settlement proposals that incorporate the features described in the previous case studies. The following features should be included whenever they are appropriate.

A career plan that:

- Analyzes an individual's strength and weaknesses.
- Evaluates an individual's suitability for various types of work.
- Identifies appropriate career opportunities.
- Prescribes necessary training and/or education.
- Estimates associated costs and projects expected wages over time.

A Comparative Financial Analysis for both spouses that includes:

- Historical spending analysis, temporary spending review, and post-divorce budget planning
- Comprehensive list of assets and liabilities
- Listing of community and separate assets
- Asset allocations to each spouse considering after-tax consequences
- Income tax and cash flow analysis (ten-year projection)
- Valuation of all assets including career assets
- Analysis of division of retirement assets including pensions

AN ULTIMATE SOLUTION TO THE DISPARITY OF EARNINGS?

I am not naïve enough to believe that changing our divorce laws and incorporating the features described in this chapter is a cure-all for the disparity of earnings. The solution requires changes in employment practices, government programs, and even fundamental social values. Perhaps the most effective initiative starts with redefining financial relationships at the beginning of marriage. If you and your spouse are sensitive to the issues I've discussed, you can work to create a more equitable financial environment before divorce looms.

Financial and Tax Checkpoints Along the Way to the Property Settlement

Any one may so arrange his affairs that his taxes shall be as low as possible; he is not bound to choose that pattern which will best pay the Treasury; there is not even a patriotic duty to increase one's taxes.

—Judge Billings Learned Hand (American jurist, 1872–1961)

What Will Postdivorce Life Be Like?

This is a question every person who goes through a divorce should ask before signing the property settlement agreement. Each week I meet with clients who bring in their divorce decrees and ask for financial planning help. Too many times, I find they have not met with a competent financial planner prior to signing the final decree. They have relied on their attorney and/or family accountant to provide tax and investment planning advice. These professionals may not have the training and information to provide comprehensive financial planning advice. Frequently, a professional was consulted for one part of the divorce, but was not involved in the analysis of the overall property settlement. This results in such items as the early distribution from IRAs to pay legal fees, deductibility of some of the costs of the divorce, and the tax basis on all of the investment assets not being discussed prior to settlement. When this happens one or both parties are saddled with unnecessary postdivorce expenses.

With a comprehensive financial and long-term cash-flow analysis, longer and/or larger amounts of alimony can be awarded, systematic withdrawals from pension plans can be initiated, or the house can be sold, with the expense of the sale being shared by both of the parties, and current taxes can be either substantially reduced or completely eliminated.

This chapter will cover several important tax, cash flow, and investment and retirement planning questions you will want to understand before agreeing to a final property settlement.

Sale of the Family Residence—Are You Money Poor and House Rich?

The family residence is the first asset we consider. The best time to deal with your housing is before the divorce. The foundation of your post-divorce lifestyle is your home and the costs that go with home ownership.

Young couples in short-term marriages of fewer than ten years generally have big mortgages and little equity. It is usually a struggle for either party to keep the house. If the wife is home raising young children, generally only minimal liquid funds are available to be divided. Often, the wife will need to be retrained to enter the job market or go back to school.

Mid-term marriages of ten to twenty-five years often are characterized by large homes and large mortgages. The wife most often retains custody of the children, who are typically in the later years of high school, and she wants to keep the kids in the same school their friends attend. After the kids leave home, she is left with a large house that is too expensive to maintain.

In long-term marriages of twenty-five years or more, the children have generally left home. In some situations, the wife wants to keep the large residence so the children will have a place "to come home to." Even when there is large equity in the home, houses are expensive to maintain. After being in the house for a few years, the resident spouse may find the expense is more than his or her budget can handle and decide to sell it. If this occurs after the individual has been in the house for some time, the cost of sale and income tax consequences of the sale are not so important. If it is within one to five years after the divorce, the timing of the sale can be critical to the long-term financial well-being of the individual.

What are some of the financial considerations of selling a home? The following are a few of the key issues you should consider:

- Will the sale result in a taxable gain, and if so, how much of a gain?
- What will it cost to sell the home?
- What information do you need to assemble for the IRS?
- How long will it take to sell the property?

- If you find a replacement home and buy it, how will you cover the expenses of two homes if your original home takes some time to sell?
- What if the real estate market goes down?

Unless an asset is to be disposed of as part of the divorce, the sale costs are not included in the property settlement. The party receiving the asset takes it at the full market value. With the family residence, taxes and costs of sale could represent 10 to 25 percent of the gross value of the home. If the home has a mortgage or if the mortgage has been refinanced, I have seen situations in which the costs of sale and income taxes were greater than the equity in the home. Costs of sale and income taxes can materially alter the actual property settlement you thought you were making.

Most homeowners have only a general idea of how much their home is worth. With changing market conditions, values of homes go up and down. If you haven't done so, get two or three real estate agents to do a market analysis. This will give you a better idea of how much your home is really worth. I also recommend you determine the tax basis of the property. The tax basis is what the IRS uses to determine whether you will realize a gain or suffer a loss when you sell the property. Even if you do not sell your home, it is important to establish the tax basis for future transactions. The most common mistake I see people make is assuming that the difference between the mortgage and the sales price is what is taxed. The mortgage is there either because funds were needed for the original purchase or home equity was taken out with refinancing and used for other purposes. The mortgage has nothing to do with the taxable gain.

Determining the tax consequences of selling the family home as part of a divorce is not a simple process. Consult a qualified tax expert or financial planner who is experienced in divorce. The terminology alone can be overwhelming. My intent in providing the information in this chapter is not to make you an expert in the field. Rather, I want to point out those issues you should be prepared to work through with the appropriate member of your professional team.

In 1997, the Tax Relief Act of 1997 (TRA '97) was passed and the complex rules governing the sale of a residence were dramatically changed. For many of today's sellers, the capital gains tax upon the sale of their residence has been reduced or eliminated. For example, current law under the Internal Revenue Code now provides that:

- Single taxpayers can exclude up to $250,000 from gains.
- Taxpayers who are married and filing joint returns can exclude up to $500,000 from gains.

Generally, taxpayers can exclude from gain only one sale every two years. Exceptions include:

- A change in the taxpayer's place of employment. The home seller's new place of work must be at least fifty miles farther from the sold home than the former workplace was from that home.
- Health reasons—to qualify for health reasons the early sellers need to show that the sale was related to a disease, an illness, or injury of an owner or coowner of the property. If a physician recommends a change in residence for health reasons, that will qualify.

Exclusions due to unforeseen circumstances include the following:

- Death of a taxpayer, spouse, co-owner, or family member.
- Divorce or legal separation of an owner or co-owner.
- Job loss that makes an owner or co-owner eligible for unemployment compensation.
- A change in employment that leaves an owner or co-owner unable to pay mortgage or basic living expenses.
- Multiple births resulting from the same pregnancy.
- Damage to the residence caused by a natural or manmade disaster, or an act of terrorism or war.
- Condemnation of the property by a public entity.
- Taxpayers must have owned and used their principal residence for two of the last five years prior to sale. The two years do not need to be consecutive (IRC 121).

There are several options to consider when deciding how to dispose of the family residence. These could include:

Sell the House and Split the Proceeds

In this situation you share the cost of the sale and the tax liability with your ex-spouse. When the house is sold, your involvement with your ex-spouse is over, which can be a major advantage. Under IRC Section 121, between you and your ex-spouse there is an exclusion of up to $500,000 of gain.

Keep the House and Buy Out Your Ex-Spouse's Share

You continue to live in the family home. When the house is sold the taxes and sales cost will be incurred. You want the house to appreciate during this time to offset the sales costs in the future that will be paid by you alone. All maintenance costs and repairs are your responsibility. When you sell the house, if the gain exceeds $250,000, you will pay the taxes due upon the sale.

Sell the House to Your Ex-Spouse

Under Section 1041 of the IRC, any transfer of property between spouses during marriage or any transfer of property between spouses or former spouses if incident to a divorce is tax-free. No gain or loss is recognized at the time of sale. Your ex-spouse would assume your basis and holding period. When you go to buy a new house, a new tax basis will be established. Make sure you receive enough cash in the property settlement to buy another house. See a mortgage banker prior to the final settlement to know what kind of loan you will qualify for with the new home. Make sure you meet the qualification requirements for a new loan before you make this agreement. Clarify any assumptions the lender is making regarding your down payment, interest rate on the loan, term of the loan, and sources of income. Alimony and child support will count as part of your income sources as well as employment income. I suggest you get a prequalification letter in writing from the mortgage broker. Make sure that the specific assumptions are listed on this prequalification letter.

Interest rates can start to move upwards and the lender's requirements change. The loan you thought you would qualify for might not be available any longer. This letter needs to be kept current and shared with your realtor.

If your ex-spouse has a new girlfriend, you will need to assess your level of emotional distress with someone else living in "your house" with your children.

Own the House Jointly Until the House Is Sold to Your Spouse or a Third Party in the Future

This can be done, but it requires a comprehensive written agreement between you and your spouse in which you define who will pay the mortgage, how specific repairs and maintenance expenses will be shared, the sources of funds for payment, timely payment of these expenses. Some points to consider:

- In the past, you may have done all of the yardwork together in addition to the housekeeping. Who will do this work when you are working full-time or pursuing your education?

- What will trigger the sale of the house? What is the term of this arrangement?
- Make sure your agreement meets tax law requirements.
- What is the formula for sharing the sales proceeds at the time of sale, after you've paid taxes and all sales costs?
- If your ex-spouse is paying the mortgage, will this qualify as alimony?
- Each mortgage payment has part applied to principal and part applied to interest. Does the person paying the mortgage get a credit for these principal payments at the time of closing? Who gets the tax deduction?
- How is this agreement enforced if there is a dispute? Who pays the legal costs?
- Can you go to binding arbitration?
- If you are going to jointly list the house for sale, make sure your agreement covers how you will handle disputes over price, listing agent, improvements prior to sale, closing costs, and excise taxes. You do not want to incur future legal costs to get your agreement interpreted.

Unless you and your ex-spouse can be civil, I would not recommend joint ownership, particularly for the sake of the children. If either spouse is under daily pressure from the costs of operating a home or the sale of a home, children will feel that tension. In my experience, children can adapt to a lower standard of living up front much more easily than witnessing one parent become angry, bitter, and overstressed, because he or she cannot handle the home financially, physically, or emotionally.

Be very careful of any agreement that guarantees one spouse will pay the other a fixed appreciation rate for each year the house is jointly owned. I have seen very unfair agreements in which the equity in the house is inadequate to make this future payment. This could occur when the value in the house has not appreciated at the projected rate, or if the person living in the house has not had sufficient funds to maintain the house in prime condition.

As you can see, the questions can go on and on as well as the opportunities for misunderstandings and disagreements in the future. Factor in a new partner and the emotional issues can significantly complicate the financial ones already addressed.

At this point you need to be asking yourself some serious questions about your future housing:

- What are the actual costs to your keeping the house—both today and in the future?

- Have you and your children looked at alternative housing arrangements that will keep you in the same school district that are affordable?
- Have you separated the emotional and financial aspects of this decision?
- Do you have sufficient investment assets to provide for an emergency reserve fund to cover the repairs, maintenance, gardening, and other costs going forward and an allowance for a major repair in the next five years, like repainting the house or replacing the roof?
- If you have an adjustable rate mortgage, can you afford the interim increases in your payments over the next five years?
- Have you looked at what assets make the most sense for you to take in the divorce settlement? Ideally, you will have money in your home, retirement assets, and more liquid assets in investments and cash reserves. What kind of a return can you expect with other alternative investments vs. home ownership net of the costs at time of sale?
- Do you need to invest in your career and education plan now instead of the home to ensure long-term financial security for yourself and your children?
- Have you looked at the costs of alternative housing in your area or are you considering moving out of the area?
- What kind of future interactions—emotional, financial, and shared parenting—do you want to have with your ex-spouse? How easily can the two of you communicate and come to a decision? Do you even want to communicate with your ex-spouse?

Until 1998, the Internal Revenue Service required Form 2119 (Sale of Your Home) to be completed and attached to an income tax return each time an individual sold a primary residence. This form was mandatory whether or not there was a gain recognized on the sale. Due to the new changes in the tax code, this form is no longer required. Your CPA may want to see these forms to help determine your cost basis for the current residence, so be prepared to show these forms from prior income tax returns. You will also want to make a list of improvements that you have made to the current residence to see if these expenses will adjust the cost basis. For many clients, these issues are less important than they were before August 1997. If your home may have appreciated more than $250,000 and your house is selling for more than that amount, this is a tax planning issue to discuss with your CPA. This information should be gathered early in the divorce process so you have adequate time to evaluate the various financial and tax scenarios around your home. Be prepared to separate the tax implications from the other economic considerations. By that I mean you should keep tax issues in perspective. They are not the only consideration.

You may defer tax on the sale and purchase of a mobile home, trailer, houseboat, cooperative apartment, and condominium apartment you use either as a principal residence or a rental property.

You can exclude $500,000 gain on two homes if you meet the following qualifications:

- One spouse retains ownership of one house and sells it.
- The other spouse moves into another house for two years, and then sells it.
- Any depreciation claimed after May 6, 1997, must be recaptured as income upon the sale, subject to the 25 percent federal tax rate on depreciation recapture.

Once again, there may be tax advantages to this type of move but not practical emotional benefits. The chart below summarizes a sample analysis for a couple trying to decide whether to sell their house as part of the divorce, or keep it and sell later.

If you compare the "Net Net Proceeds," which is the after-tax result of selling now or four years from now, you might assume it would be better to sell the house later. However, this does not take into account any increase in maintenance costs, like replacing the roof or a new furnace. Any additional future costs will subtract from the available profit. Also, there is no guarantee the real estate market will appreciate at the assumed rate of 5.5 percent. The tax laws could also change in the future, which might reduce the available proceeds.

Given these uncertainties, waiting to sell is not necessarily the best choice. How do you decide? You must determine what assumptions you are comfortable with and whether more cash in the future is worth the risks in waiting. In some cases it is wiser to sell now and invest the proceeds in your career plan.

What If There Has to Be a Note to Divide the Assets Equitably?

In this scenario, the house is awarded to one spouse who then, over time, buys out the former spouse's interest in the property. The former spouse effectively becomes the banker to the party that receives the residence. In this situation, the purchase of the former spouse's interest is considered a

Sell Now or Later

Assumptions

▷	Current Value of the house	$ 675,000
▷	Cost basis 20 years ago	(230,000)
▷	Growth Rate of house over 20 years	5.53%
▷	Mortgage - Currently Refinanced	(400,000)
▷	Mortgage in 4 years	(376,637)
▷	Cost of Sale %	8.50%
▷	Assumed Growth Rate	5.50%
▷	Extra capital gain tax on lost exclusion	(37,500)
▷	Actual annual growth rate after	1.56%
	Capital Gain Tax on the Lost Exclusion if sold at the end 4 years	

If house is sold with an 8.50% cost of sale and a 15% capital gain rate, net proceeds would be:

Now	Sales price	$	675,000	Sales Price	$	675,000
	Cost of sale 8.50%		(57,375)	Cost Basis		**(230,000)**
	Net before tax		617,625	Gain		445,000
	Tax @ 15%		-	**Exclusion**		**(500,000)**
	Net Proceeds		**617,625**	Taxable Gain		(55,000)
	Mortgage		**(400,000)**			
	Net Net Proceeds		**217,625**			

If house is sold with an 8.5% cost of sale and a 15% capital gain rate, net proceeds would be:

Four	Sales price	$	755,493	Sales Price	$	755,493
Years	Cost of sale 8.5%		(64,217)	Cost Basis		(230,000)
	Net before tax		691,276	Gain		525,493
	Tax @ 15%		(41,324)	**Exclusion**		**(250,000)**
	Net Proceeds		**649,952**	Taxable Gain		275,493
	Mortgage		**(376,637)**			
	Net Net Proceeds		**273,315**			

FIGURE 9.1   Sell Now or Later

transfer of property incident to a divorce. Under this section, principal payments to the former spouse are not taxable and payments do not increase the basis of the home. The spouse who keeps the home retains the same tax cost basis in the home that the couple had.

TAX CONSIDERATIONS OF OTHER ASSETS IN DIVORCE

Though the family home is often the largest asset, there may be a number of additional taxable assets with substantial value. The tax implications of some of these, like a family business, professional partnership, rental property, or time-share are beyond the scope of this book. Only a qualified tax professional can properly identify all the tax issues associated with such assets. I will cover limited partnerships, stock options, stocks and mutual funds, and retirement and pension funds.

Jointly Owned Limited Partnerships

Limited partners are part owners of a business, but do not have a right to manage or control it. They are liable only to the extent of the capital they have invested in the partnership. Think of yourself on a cruise ship. You go wherever the cruise ship takes you. You may or may not make it back to port. You could run into major weather and mechanical problems along the way. You are together in this to the end. Since there is often no active financial market for limited partnerships, it is very difficult to determine their value. Many attorneys recommend their clients with less financial and economic independence assign them to their spouse. Doing so could be giving away either a future headache or a future bonanza. Partnerships need to be evaluated very carefully. On large public partnerships, it may be best to simply divide the investment equally between the parties.

If you are going to have an interest in a limited partnership such as equipment leasing, real estate, or oil and gas, you need to have the historical tax information on the investment. Contact the general partner and request current information on your partnership interest. Your annual tax information is reported on an IRS Schedule K-1 (Partner's Share of Income, Credits, Deductions). Since tax information from the partnership will be needed to complete your income tax return, and it often takes several months to get the ownership reregistered, you should begin the reregistration process before the ink has dried on your divorce papers.

If your prior year tax returns have been prepared by a professional, there should be a record of what the IRS calls "passive activity losses" with the return. Such losses arise from investments such as limited partnerships in which you are not an active manager or participant. If your spouse has been preparing your return, be sure to obtain the worksheets from his files. This can be a very complicated area of tax, so I do not recommend that you try to get all the answers by yourself. Hire a professional tax accountant.

Stock Options

Getting your fair share from stock options can be tricky. The National Center for Employee Ownership states there are more than 10 million workers who have option plans. Experts still disagree on the best way to divide them, especially when the precise value cannot be determined. They are either awarded to the employed spouse or allocated to the other spouse in the divorce decree. Stock options cannot be assigned through a Qualified

Domestic Relations Order (QDRO). Be sure and talk with your tax advisor to clarify the taxation of these stock options and to determine how best to transfer or take ownership of them in your property settlement agreement.

One common method, especially involving situations with nontransferable options, calls for the spouse who owns the shares to give his exspouse a percentage of the proceeds when they are sold. It is usually best to wait for the options to be sold. This way both parties share in the investment risk, tax consequences, and net cash after exercising the options. If you can, get the company to issue a separate W-2 to each spouse for the stock proceeds so you both share the tax burden.

The real problem comes with unvested stock options. The rights to buy stock in an employer's company at a future date and at a price less than market value are often activated (that is, "vested") over time. Options that have not yet become vested are called "unvested." Find out how these options are handled by the laws in your state when there is a divorce. Your attorney will be able to advise you on how your state views unvested stock options as marital property.

Sale of Stock and Mutual Funds

After the divorce, assets have to be retitled to the name of the spouse who received the asset. No taxes are due with this transfer as it is incident to divorce. The problems surface when you decide to sell the security. Make sure you know what the cost basis of your security was prior to the divorce becoming final. Get a copy of the original confirmation from your files, ex-spouse, or the brokerage firm. You will then be able to track this paper trail from the original purchase date through the transfer between spouses, and any sale of a portion or all of the assets. Do not sign your final divorce decree until all cost basis information has been shared in writing.

Stocks, bonds, and mutual funds are often sold during separation or after divorce to cover cash needs, expenses, or accommodate changes in the owner's risk tolerance. A sharp attorney details in the decree how these transactions are to be reported by the divorcing parties. Too often it is easier for the attorney to ignore the tax consequences of such transactions and leave it to the clients to argue it out when it comes time to file income tax returns. Make sure the decree states how the capital transactions in the year of the divorce are to be reported. Figure 9.2 is an example of a worksheet you can use to collect the information you will need for recording the asset values described in this chapter.

Stocks, Bonds and Other Assets

	Name of Security	Purchase Date	Number of Shares (A)	Cost Per Share (B)	Total Cost (A*B)	Total Value	Gain (Loss)
1							
2							
3							
4							
5							
6							
7							
8							
9							
10							
11							
12							
13							
14							
15							
16							
17							
	TOTALS:						

Mutual Funds

	Name of Fund	Purchase Date	Original Cost (A)	Reinvested Dividends (B)	Total Cost (A+B)	Total Value	Gain (Loss)
1							
2							
3							
4							
5							
6							
7							
8							
9							
10							
	TOTALS:						

Real Estate

	Name/Location of Property	Purchase Date	Cost Plus Improvements	Less Depreciation	Adjusted Cost	Total Value	Gain (Loss)
1							
2							
3							
4							
5							
6							
	TOTALS:						

Copyright © 2005 Miller Advisors, Inc.

FIGURE 9.2 Asset Worksheet

Taxation of Withdrawals Made from Qualified Retirement Plans, Annuities, and Modified Endowment Contracts Prior to Age Fifty-nine and a Half

Abby and Craig, both forty-eight, had been married for twenty-two years. An engineer, Craig had been with his present firm for twenty years. As a senior manager, he received a substantial salary and annual bonuses. Abby and Craig had been separated four and a half years. During that time Abby had returned to school to complete a master's degree in education.

She was teaching part-time and looking for a full-time teaching position. The couple had four children, all of whom attended private schools. Both husband and wife were committed to continuing the children's private-school education.

The family residence had a small mortgage that would be paid off in six years. The husband had shared custody of the children and wanted to purchase a home for himself and the children. Although he had been living in a condominium they had purchased four years previously, there was no equity in that property. The couple's assets were primarily in the equity in the house, his 401(k) retirement plan, and his earning capacity.

Abby initially requested 60 percent of the assets, alimony for ten years, and the family home paid for in six years. Craig felt he had paid alimony for four years at a level representing half his income and bonuses, the costly private school education for their children, and his wife's master's program.

With creative planning and the allocation of Craig's 401(k) plan, we were finally able to settle the case. Abby and Craig continued to share his income and bonuses for the next four years with alimony decreasing annually. If Abby found full-time employment, alimony would decrease sooner. Until she obtained full-time employment, Craig would continue to pay the children's private school education costs. After she obtained employment, they would share education costs in proportion to their total income. In addition, she would receive 65 percent of his 401(k) plan and make a cash settlement to him. Under the QDRO, Abby took a lump sum distribution of 15 percent of the plan. After paying income taxes on the distribution, she made a cash settlement to Craig. This strategy saved the 10 percent IRS penalty on early distributions.

As Abby fell in a lower tax bracket, the total income tax was reduced, and the cash payment provided the funds Craig needed to purchase a home. It was a win-win financial and tax strategy for each of them.

In general, if you take funds from a qualified retirement plan or annuity prior to age fifty-nine and a half under IRC Section 411(a)(11) or 417(e), the part of the distribution that must be claimed as gross income is generally subject to an additional 10 percent tax. This penalty does not apply to certain withdrawals specifically excepted by the code. One of the exemptions is for payments made directly to a former spouse under a Qualified Domestic Relations Order. Retirement accounts covered under a QDRO must be "employer sponsored qualified retirement plans." IRA accounts do not qualify.

For example, the husband passes part of his company 401(k) plan to his wife as a transfer of property incident to divorce. The wife is able to take a withdrawal from this plan and not pay a 10 percent penalty on it.

The husband cannot qualify for this exemption on distributions from his plan. When the wife receives these funds she will have to pay taxes on these funds as ordinary income. Sometimes this strategy is used to provide liquid cash to one or the other of the spouses to allow for both of them to own a home. If this strategy is used, the income tax obligation is taken into account in the overall property settlement prior to the divorce. Be sure that your distribution paperwork is prepared correctly. The plan administrator would issue two checks in this example—one to the spouse for the early withdrawal without penalty, and the other amount is deposited with the organization that will be acting as the new IRA custodian for the retirement assets. Remember, even though there is no penalty, there are income taxes.

INCOME TAX RETURNS

No matter how complex your tax return was in the past, it will be even more so during divorce. What status is best to use, what liability you may have on prior returns filed by your spouse, who can claim the children, or the effects of alimony and child support are a few of the numerous issues to consider.

Choosing a Filing Status

The four possible tax statuses on an income tax return are:

1. Married Filing Jointly (or Qualifying Widow/Widower)
2. Married Filing Separately
3. Head of Household
4. Single Taxpayer

You tell the IRS how you are going to file in the block labeled "Filing Status." Your marital status as of December 31 determines your filing options. Neither marriage nor divorce comes under the jurisdiction of federal laws. Marriage, remarriage, divorce, prenuptial agreements, and community property rules as they relate to marriage are all strictly domestic affairs. Tax implications are determined based on family laws in the state where you live.

In navigating your divorce, filing status is another area in which you need to hire a professional or do some research and outside reading. In November, you may have agreed to and signed property settlement, alimony, and child support documents, but for tax purposes decide to wait and file your final divorce decree until January 1 of the following year. This would be done if both parties realize such action would save tax dollars, and they agree how the tax savings would be shared. To obtain more complete information on your filing status options, call the IRS and request a copy of their Publication 504.

Liability on Prior Joint Income Tax Returns

If you suspect your spouse of fraud or other inappropriate claims or deductions, you may choose not to file a joint return. For tax returns that have been previously filed, there is the possibility of being considered an "innocent spouse." A spouse can be relieved of liability in certain cases. If you suspect your spouse of foul play, you should discuss this with your attorney and/or accountant.

Pull out a copy of any of your returns and turn to page two of the return. Look for the signature block near the bottom of the page that says: "Please sign here." You have probably never read the small print above the white space for your signature before signing your name. It reads: "Under penalties of perjury, I declare that I have examined this return and accompanying schedules and statements, and to the best of my knowledge and belief, they are true, correct, and complete."

Unless you can prove that you are an innocent spouse, the IRS holds you liable for any errors, penalties, or interest due on the return. The IRS is looking for the quickest way to collect its money and can assign tax liabilities to assets of either party of a jointly filed income tax return. You will then have to go to civil court to dispute payments your spouse should have made.

If your spouse was the one who handled all the business, financial, and tax affairs of the household, I urge you to have language put into your decree that holds this spouse financially responsible for any future tax problems. You may have to share in inadvertent mistakes on the returns, but you should have some protection from intentional misrepresentations of which you had no knowledge. Though this language may not save you from the IRS taking some of your funds, it will give you recourse against your former spouse.

Who Can Claim the Children as Dependents on the Tax Return?

This issue is normally addressed in parenting plans and child support agreements. If the dependency deduction is not discussed in your child support documents, by default the deduction goes to the custodial parent. Since the noncustodial parent is generally the one with the highest income, this parent would like to claim the children as exemptions on his or her income tax return. With the current income tax law, if income goes over a certain level, the dependency exemption is limited. When this is the case, the parties may agree to share income tax information annually by March 15. If the noncustodial spouse does not receive a tax benefit from the exemption, it is passed over to the other spouse. Spouses will sometimes alternate the deduction between their returns from year to year. The custodial parent can transfer the right to claim the exemption to the noncustodial parent by signing a written release (IRS Form 8332—Release of Claim to Exemption for Child of Divorced) and the noncustodial parent must attach this form to his tax return for each year the exemption is claimed. It is best for the attorney to have the waiving spouse sign Form 8332 at the same time the judgment is ordered. The child must be in the custody of one or both parents for more than one-half of the year to qualify to take this exemption.

The settlement wording used to describe what conditions must be met for the noncustodial spouse to claim this deduction is important. The language should specify a minimum dollar value of deduction or tax savings must be met. Otherwise the noncustodial parent could obtain the deduction by claiming as little as $1 of tax savings, leaving the custodial parent with an unfair tax burden because she couldn't use the deduction.

It is best to agree on this issue before the divorce is final. Financial circumstances can change between divorced parents. If you have been given the dependency exemption in your child support agreement and want to release this exemption, use IRS Form 8332 to change your prior agreement. Instructions on the form permit release for the current year only, for a specified number of years, or for all future years. I prefer an annual signing since attitudes and conditions can change.

Alimony Versus Child Support

Alimony, or maintenance, provides an income tax deduction for your husband's payments and is taxable income when you receive it. Child support and payments made pursuant to a property settlement are neither deductible to him nor taxable to you and are not even reported on your income tax return. Given the income tax considerations of alimony and child support, you will want to have the major portion of your payments considered child support, and your husband will want the major share to be alimony. Since he will be making the payments, and an income tax savings will make more funds available for both of you to share, your negotiations should encompass the tax and cash flow for both of you. Another point to remember, child support continues until the child is either eighteen or twenty-one. Check with the laws in your state.

There are five requirements for a payment to qualify as alimony:

1. The payment must be in cash, check, or money order.
2. The payments must be made under a written divorce decree, separation agreement, or a temporary alimony award. There must be a legal obligation to pay via a court document.
3. The payments must cease in the event of the receiving spouse's death.
4. The ex-spouse or soon-to-be ex-spouse may not be a member of the same household or file a joint return.
5. The payments must not be deemed to be child support.

Your final property settlement will address the amount and duration of alimony and its taxability. If you have been receiving payments during your separation, and the payments were ordered under an alimony order from the courts, these payments will be taxable to you.

Sometimes, the courts will award a specified amount of money to be transferred during separation, and they will state that the money you receive is not differentiated between child support and alimony. This is done, as one settlement stated, "so that the decree can have some room for negotiation and flexibility." Unfortunately, too often the decree does not address the taxability of the temporary order. Since you will not want the income to be taxable, and he will want the income tax to be tax-deductible, disagreement will follow. If your separately filed income tax returns do not list the same amount of alimony payments, the IRS will be contacting both of you, and you will have to explain the difference.

I do a great deal of postdivorce planning in which a client will come in to see me just before or shortly after signing the final property settlement. It is not unusual for the client to have received alimony income for several months. Too many times the client was taken by surprise to find that not only does she have a large income tax liability owed on the alimony income, but since no quarterly payments have been made, there will be IRS penalties assessed when the income tax return is filed. No professional ever told her about the tax consequences of receiving alimony. Don't let this happen to you. If you are receiving alimony income, taxes will be owed. You should ask your attorney, accountant, or financial planner to estimate what the tax obligation will be and when the tax is due without penalty. If taxes being withheld from wages are not sufficient to cover the tax on alimony income, you will need either to increase the amount of tax withholdings or to make quarterly tax payments. When working with a client to complete a financial affidavit, I always make sure there is an allowance for income taxes and provide payment vouchers so that the taxes are paid in a timely manner.

As income taxes on alimony reduce the amount of cash flow available to the receiving spouse, it can increase the cash flow of the paying husband. If the same amount of taxes are being withheld from your husband's paycheck after beginning alimony payments as was withheld before alimony payments, there could be a big tax refund when he files his tax return. By adjusting the amount of taxes withheld from the wage now, next year's refund is available to the parties for current needs.

Front-loading is a term describing arrangements in which very large alimony payments are made in the first few years, then drop off dramatically. The IRS sees this as a disguised property settlement and will apply additional taxes.

What Happens if Alimony Declines Substantially in the First Three Years?

If alimony payments are stopped or reduced by more than a certain amount—currently $15,000 per year—during the first three years, the IRS will apply "recapture rules." These rules change the tax deductions available to both you and your former husband. The rules do not apply if:

- Payments are made under a temporary support order before the divorce or separation.
- Payments made over at least three years represent a percentage of the business or property income.
- Payments end due to the death of either spouse, or the receiving ex-spouse remarries within the first three calendar years of payments.

If you experience a significant change in alimony payments during the first three years after your divorce, you should review the circumstances with a tax professional.

When to File Form W-4 After the Divorce

Technically, an employee must give an employer a new Form W-4 within ten days after a divorce if certain changes occur in the number of allowed withholdings. You should check with a tax professional to see if enough tax will be withheld for the year by comparing the total withholding from your pay with what you expect your tax to be. You probably will have too little withheld if you have more than one job at a time, if you are receiving alimony, or if you have income from foreign investments or certain moving expense reimbursements that are not subject to withholding. If too much tax will be withheld and you don't want to wait for a refund, decreased withholding by claiming more exemptions is possible.

If you are having too little withheld, you may need to start making quarterly estimated tax payments. These are due April 15, June 15, September 15, and January 15. It is never too late in the year to start making these quarterly payments. If you have missed one or two payments, start as soon as you have the funds available and don't wait for the end of the quarter. To make an adjustment to the W-4, employees must give a new form W-4 to their employers. The deductions and adjustment worksheet that is part of the form can be helpful in determining the number of allowances, but an in-depth tax analysis done with your advisors will be more accurate.

Deductibility of Legal and Expert Fees on Postdivorce Returns

No deduction is allowed for personal, living, or family expenses, according to Section 212 of the IRS code. The cost of getting a divorce is considered a personal expense. You can deduct all of the ordinary and necessary expenses paid or incurred during the taxable year:

- For the production or collection of income.
- For the management, conservation or maintenance of property held for the production of income
- In connection with the determination, collection, or refund of any tax.

If you itemize your deductions, some of your attorney fees will qualify as a deduction on your income tax return. The fees are deductible in the year paid. Request a letter from your attorney and other experts that will assist you and your accountant in determining the deductibility of fees paid to the legal firm in connection with your dissolution proceeding.

In some instances, fees that are not deductible under Section 212 may be treated as a capital expense and added to the cost basis of property awarded to you in the dissolution proceeding.[1] Ask your accountant if your expenses may qualify.

Many accountants and attorneys are not aware of these expense deductions. You need to reference Section 212 and have your advisors tell you how this rule applies to your own situation. If they are unfamiliar with the code, or unwilling to explore its applicability to your case, I would suggest finding a new advisor. Generally, your expert fees are deductible in the course of the divorce, as they will meet one of the conditions.

Establishing Guidelines with Your Financial Planner and Accountant

Tax laws are changing all of the time, annually at the very least, and when this is combined with the trauma of getting a divorce, you need to realize that a tax plan developed today probably won't work tomorrow. Because of these changes, develop a working relationship with the financial planner and accountant prior to the divorce and continue with this relationship for at least two years postdivorce. This team of experts will have the background of your case as well as the divorce decree and will be able to work out future problems.

Dealing with the tax consequences of divorce is time-consuming and complex. Don't accept shortcuts, excuses, or substitutes for the results you need to win a fair settlement. Pretending you can make up later for losses incurred in a poorly devised agreement will penalize you and your children for years after the divorce is final. Remember that old adage, "Anything worth doing is worth doing right," and add to it, "the first time."

Divorced Women, Pensions, and Avoiding Poverty in the Golden Years

From birth to eighteen, a girl needs good parents.
From eighteen to thirty-five, she needs good looks.
From thirty-five to fifty-five, a good personality.
From fifty-five on, she needs hard cash.

—SOPHIE TUCKER

RETIREMENT BENEFITS ARE NOT WHAT THEY USED TO BE

The following chart summarizes the typical sources of income available to women after retirement. Additionally, if retirement benefits, IRAs, *Keogh*s for self-employed spouses, and defined benefit and profit-sharing plans were earned during a marriage, you can expect them to be divided equitably at the time of divorce.

All women may be at the mercy of their life patterns, but women who divorce in midlife or later are pushed with sudden force into a vulnerable subset of the female experience. It is those women who have done what was expected of them and led traditional middle-class lives who may be the least prepared to face the reduced circumstance in which they will very likely find themselves in old age. There are ample statistics to suggest that marriage—the financial bulwark for such women—is no longer necessarily "forever," leading many women to view their prospects of financial independence in later life with apprehension.

There are strong indicators that women will continue to rely heavily on Social Security as a cornerstone of their long-term financial security.

Sources of Post Retirement Income by Age				
AGE 55 —— 60 —— 65 —— 70 —— 75 —— 80 →				
Sell Family Residence Qualify for $250,000 per Person Exclusion of Capital Gain	Retirement Distributions Penalty Free at Age 59.5 Widow's Social Security Benefits Social Security Income Allowed at Age 62	Social Security Income Allowed Between Ages 65 & 8 Months and Age 67 Depending Upon Date of Birth	Maximum Social Security Benefits	Life Expectancy Based Upon Social Security Tables Updated 6/27/2006 Female at Age 65 Expected Life: Age 84.09 Male at Age 65 Expected Life: Age 81.15

Copyright © 2005 Miller Advisors, Inc.

FIGURE 10.1   Sources of Post-Retirement Income by Age

Thomas Bethell, a writer and editor in Washington, D.C., gathered the following statistics using resources provided by the Social Security Administration and the National Women's Law Center:

- Workforce participation rates remain lower for women in the age range of twenty-five to fifty-four (75 percent versus 91 percent for men).
- Women earn less than men (about 76 cents on the dollar).
- The typical woman's 401(k) balance is 40 percent lower than the typical man's.
- Social Security's actuaries estimate that, forty years from now, 40 percent of women will rely at least in part on spousal benefits for their income.
- The Gerontological Society of America forecasts that poverty rates among those women who become eligible for Social Security benefits in 2020 will be unchanged from 1991.
- Social Security provides 90 percent or more of total income for more than four in ten women over sixty-five.

These studies send women a strong message about their long-term value as mothers and caretakers of the family and about their retirement years and financial independence during those years.

Many experts on pensions and divorce say changes in matrimonial law since the advent of no-fault divorce generally have not worked to the benefit of women. Although the courts once used alimony or maintenance and tangible assets to punish and reward, they now focus on distributing property fairly. They have expanded the definition of property to include such intangibles as potential earning power and pensions. In the process, women have come to receive alimony or maintenance less often and for shorter periods.

The last thing a woman may be thinking about as she contemplates her immediate lower postdivorce income is a pension. Women with children may have other priorities. They choose to solve a three-year problem at the expense of a ten-year problem by ignoring a spouse's future retirement benefits in favor of receiving a higher short-term maintenance payment.

I see women ignore the pension issues in their property settlements without realizing the economic impact on their postdivorce lives. The pension and retirement issues are very important in the divorce process. You need to be thinking about the pension benefits that were earned from a defined benefit plan and accrued during your marriage years. These pension benefits—although earned by your husband—are marital assets that can be provided as a lump settlement to you or that can be shared in the income paid during retirement alongside your husband. You need to be aware of the risks of potential changes, like remarriage or the death of your ex-husband, which could occur before his retirement and nullify your agreement, leaving you with nothing.

What are the messages we are giving out today in our society with the rising divorce rates and increasing poverty for women? The major ones are "Marry rich and stay married as long as possible" or "Go to work, but don't leave the workforce to raise your child or care for an elderly parent, because if you do, your contribution to Social Security and a future pension will be meaningless."

Understanding Social Security Benefits

Social Security came about in the 1930s during the Great Depression and was presented as a social insurance program to help the nation's elderly population remain financially solvent after leaving the workforce. It was sold to voters as a supplement to retirement for those who needed help. The key word is "insurance." Social Security was not called an investment account.

At that time, the American family consisted of a wage-earning husband and a wife who stayed at home to raise the children. By 1988, just one in five families fit this traditional description. Today, more than 50 percent of families have two wage earners. In the event of death, the survivor of a dual-income couple, usually the widow, almost always gets a lower Social Security benefit than a single income couple with the same total earnings. Women under the age of sixty are more likely to be collecting spousal benefits early, because of outdated job skills and age discrimination. This decreases their lifetime benefits by as much as 30 percent.

Today, Social Security benefits are the foundation of many women's

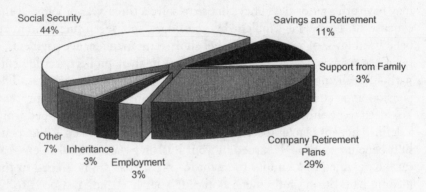

Actual Sources of Income for Retirees

Social Security
44%

Savings and Retirement
11%

Support from Family
3%

Other
7%   Inheritance
3%   Employment
3%

Company Retirement
Plans
29%

Source: Employee Benefit Research Institute and Mathew Greenwald & Associates, Inc.
2005 Retirement Confidence Survey

FIGURE 10.2   Actual Sources of Income for Retirees

retirement and long-term financial security. A divorcée is entitled to benefits as long as her former husband is receiving them and only if the marriage lasted at least a decade. No benefits are awarded if the marriage
dissolved before ten years.

In figure 10.2, Social Security is identified as the single largest source
of retirement income for men and women. By comparison, the retirees in
this 2005 national survey said only 11 percent of their income after retirement comes from savings and personal retirement accounts.

There are also problems with corporate pension plans for women. The
odds are stacked against a woman's long-term financial security because
female workers are more likely to hold low-wage, service, part-time or
nonunion jobs for which retirement coverage is less likely.

Many people are arguing for an overhaul of the Social Security system. There will be significant changes to this system for women in the
coming years. Already, we have seen Congress advance the date of retirement incrementally toward age sixty-seven by the year 2027, and Social
Security benefits are being taxed in cases where recipients have income
above certain levels ($25,000 for a single person and $32,000 for a married
couple filing jointly). Those with high total incomes must include up to 85
percent of their benefits for federal income tax purposes. There are special
separate thresholds that determine the amount on which you will be taxed.
See your accountant for the specifics in your personal tax situation.

Social Security as a Percentage of Income

Unmarried Women, Widows	52%
Unmarried Men, Widowers	38%
Elderly Couples	35%

FIGURE 10.3   Social Security as a Percentage of Income
Source: Social Security Administration, September 2004.

Women are living longer. As recent census data clearly shows, longevity is a reality and women are the leaders in the trend. In 2001, the overall life expectancy in the United States was 77.2 years, and the life expectancy for women was 79.8 years compared to 74.4 years for men. As baby boomers reach retirement age, the number of women eighty-five and older is expected to mushroom from 2.2 million today to more than ten million by midcentury.

If you want to calculate your own life expectancy, go to Social Security Online Actuarial Publications at *www.ssa.gov,* or for a different perspective look at *www.livingto100.com.* This latter site has interesting information that will show how changing your lifestyle may influence your life span. The site has a calculator that is based on the findings by the Boston University Medical School.

The question is whether living longer is really an advantage for women. "Women's longevity is not all good news," says Nancy McConnell, who is studying the issue for the National Institute on Aging. "It is frequently ten years of poverty and declining health."

Cynthia Tauber, a demographer with the U.S. Census Bureau, has written, "Most women should be planning and financing to live into their mid-eighties or longer, often alone. The life that one leads as a younger person greatly affects the life one leads as an older person." Getting your fair share on the pension is going to be a major part of your financial security if you are currently fifty or older and getting a divorce.

A Deeper Look at Social Security Benefits

With the change in federal law that went into effect in 1983, it became much easier for a divorced person, married for ten years or more, to receive benefits on a former spouse's work record regardless of whether the worker has retired and taken benefits for himself or has chosen to continue working.

To receive one-half of your ex-husband's Social Security benefits at retirement, you must be at least sixty-two, have been married for at least ten years, and not have remarried when you claim your benefits. These rules do differ if you are disabled or if your ex-spouse has died. I often see women who don't get the benefits they earned in their first marriage, because they have remarried or because the spouse in the second marriage did not earn as much as the first.

If you qualify, you can start getting reduced benefits as early as age sixty-two. For people born after 1937, normal retirement age will increase. For example, if you were born in 1940, full retirement age is sixty-five and six months; born in 1950, it is sixty-six. Anybody born in 1960 or later will be eligible at age sixty-seven.

If you claim benefits early, you are penalized. At age sixty-two, your benefits used to be reduced about 20 percent, but now it gradually goes up to 30 percent. If you are within five years of age sixty-two, I would definitely recommend that you call your local Social Security office and ask some questions. Remember, Social Security benefits do not automatically start coming in the mail the first day of your normal retirement age and definitely not if you are taking early retirement. You must apply for benefits.

A woman was in my office a few weeks ago, concerned that her ex-husband was struggling financially over their property settlement. He is an engineer, and she is a therapist. Let's call them John and Sheila. John earns an average of $210,000 per year, and Sheila will make up to $35,000 in a good year. Sheila earns money only if she is working, billing on an hourly basis for her time or her supervision of others.

John owns a building and is a partner in a small local engineering practice. Sheila received 52 percent of the property and three years of maintenance. Part of her maintenance was designed to be paid as a settlement note from the valuation on his business. It was advantageous to pay her this money as maintenance so it would be tax-deductible for him. She is in the 25 percent marginal income tax bracket, so she is giving up a substantial part of her maintenance payments in taxes.

Together John and Sheila have two grown children. One is employed, and the other is in her last year of college. They are sharing the tuition costs in proportion to their gross wages. Money is tight for John while he pays Sheila the maintenance, makes payments on the property settlement note, and foots the bill for the daughter's remaining college costs. Sheila has agreed to defer the property settlement payment until their daughter is out of school, since she is afraid John will stop paying his share of the tuition if she does not agree.

Sheila is still responding to John's emotional manipulation. She is worrying about him and submitting to his anger and rage over the divorce. He hates her and her attorney for uprooting his life and causing him short-term financial setbacks. He feels his whole financial difficulty is entirely Sheila's fault. He is the victim.

At this point, I pulled out the postdivorce cash flow and income tax spreadsheets I had prepared for Sheila a few months earlier. This was the kick start that Sheila needed to get a grip on her finances and her responsibility for John's future. John was making choices and getting on with his financial and personal life. She couldn't change anything about his life and choices, but she could look at her own. Sheila was very nervous about her finances and the need to make money in order to meet her financial obligations. She knew she had to be at work to earn money and was frightened about becoming ill and taking care of herself. Sheila knew that she would eventually receive a substantial inheritance from her mother's estate, but she was concerned about the interim years. Her son had married, and her share of the wedding costs was a lot more than anticipated. She had acquired considerable credit card debt and worried about how she would pay off those bills.

Sheila and I reviewed the facts and discussed cash-flow management for the next year: what debts to pay off and with what funds. The money was scheduled to come in from various investments over the next three years. She would be okay. Sheila also wanted to discuss giving up part of her Social Security benefits. She did not understand how these benefits worked for her and John. Let me explain.

We did some postdivorce planning, and I showed her each of their postdivorce lifestyles projected over the next three years. The disparity of income between them had not gone away. I informed her that at age sixty-two, she would be able to qualify for 100 percent of her eligible benefit or 50 percent of his benefit (both discounted for early retirement), whichever is greater. She understood that if she chose to take the 50 percent benefit, this would reduce John's benefit to 50 percent, and she felt bad that she would be a burden on him for the rest of her life. This is not the case. John would still get his 100 percent, meaning 150 percent would be paid out. Remember, since the 1983 law change, you and your ex-husband each qualify separately for your Social Security benefit. There is a limit to the amount of benefits that can be paid on each Social Security record, a "Maximum Family Benefit." It is generally around 150 to 180 percent of the worker's benefit. If this limit is exceeded, the family benefits are reduced. This could be an issue if your husband has been married for ten years or more to several women who, for whatever reasons, are all trying to qualify under his worker's benefit.

If you feel you are taking financial advantage of your ex-spouse and have the urge to step back into your role as the caretaker, look at the disparity between your earnings and try and put a value on your time at home raising your children. One sobering method to use in this process is to write to the Social Security office nearest your home and request a Personal Earnings and Benefit Estimate Statement on form #7004. Order one for yourself and your husband—since each of you needs to sign your own form. It takes the Social Security office about six weeks to process this report, although it does send out the report on an annual basis, and has been doing this for a number of years. You should have a copy already available if you and your spouse have kept the information and are willing to share.

If you do not find and correct errors in your Social Security record within three years, they become part of your permanent record. Therefore, you might want to check on them every three years or so. I gave a corporate retirement seminar a few years ago at a major manufacturing firm and during that workshop the employee group discovered their wages had been incorrectly reported to the Social Security Administration for one year. It took time and effort, but eventually the appropriate corrections were made to the employees' permanent records.

You can work during retirement, but if you earn too much it will reduce the size of the benefits you are receiving from age sixty-two up to your full retirement age. The limits on such earnings in 2005 are $12,000, and increased to $12,480 in 2006. This amount is adjusted annually.

You can even receive Social Security under your spouse's earnings if your spouse is not retired. The divorce must have occurred at least two years prior to your receiving the benefits. The policies on these entitlement benefits as a divorced spouse do change, so it is important to make sure you are dealing with current information. The last change relating to divorcing spouses was in October 2002. Your financial planner, your attorney, and other advisers should have the most current information.

A few months ago I was in a mediation setting in which the mediator wanted to structure the property settlement as follows:

Both spouses were turning sixty-five within a few weeks. The husband was a doctor and did not intend to retire at sixty-five. The mediator assumed that the wife could start receiving half of his Social Security benefits when she turned sixty-five, but this did not meet the criteria at the Social Security Administration. She was told she had to wait two years from the date the divorce was final before she could collect, unless her soon-to-be ex-husband started taking his Social Security at age sixty-five. We were able to illustrate to the husband the economic benefits for him to start taking his Social Security at sixty-five, which would allow his wife to start receiving her benefits. He would have to pay taxes on up to 85 percent of the benefits he received, but he would not see his benefit amount decreased and would be able to have unlimited earnings after turning sixty-five. This meant he would not be required to pay increased maintenance for these two extra years. We postponed the final property settlement until each of them started receiving their Social Security benefits as a married couple.

If there is a long marriage, I advocate that the two Social Security benefit checks be combined and then divided equally between the two divorcing spouses for as long as they are each alive. The person who receives the larger check sends a portion to their ex-spouse in the form of maintenance, minus an allowance for income taxes.

To illustrate this point, Darin receives $1,800 per month from Social Security. His ex-wife Regina receives $900 per month. The average benefit is therefore half the sum of these, or $1,350. That is $450 more than Regina is getting. Darin is in the 25 percent income tax bracket and will have to pay taxes on the $1,800 he receives. To adjust for the difference in benefit amounts and offset the taxes Darin must pay on the benefit portion he sends Regina, Darin sends Regina a check for the $450 minus 25 percent of that amount. In other words he sends Regina a check for $337.50 each month. She will claim this as maintenance (and will pay taxes on it), while Darin claims it as a tax deduction.

Social Security has an annual Cost-of-Living adjustment (COLA) or inflation increase on the benefit amounts. In 2004, the increase was 2.7 percent, and in 2005 it jumped to 4.1 percent. Most company pensions don't have a COLA clause, and we all know what happened to many retirement account values between 2000 and 2003 as a result of the downturn in the stock market. This COLA increase means real money and an increase annually on the Social Security benefit you will receive. Remember, originally it was designed as insurance and not an investment.

If the spouse takes Social Security at sixty-two, she will receive 32.5 to 35 percent of the spouse's full retirement benefit, not 50 percent. If your ex-spouse predeceases you, and you have been married for more than ten years, you can qualify for widow's benefits when you turn sixty. Don't lose his Social Security number—ever.

In many middle-income families, pensions are the most valuable marital assets to be divided, sometimes exceeding the equity that the married couple has accumulated in a family home.

There are three main kinds of retirement assets:

- **Savings Plans.** IRAs are examples of savings plans.
- **Defined Contribution Plans.** A defined contribution plan involves specified contributions to the plan. The employee and employer

may contribute to this plan. Since these plans do not commit to payment of a fixed amount, both employer and employee contributions may lose value with market fluctuations. A 401(k) plan is an example of a defined contribution plan.

- **Defined Benefit Plans.** A defined benefit plan promises the employee a specific amount of money at retirement, usually based on the salary and years of employment of the employee. Some benefit plans allow employees to contribute, but most are funded completely by the employer, who is solely responsible for selecting the investments used in the plan. In either event, there is no investment risk to the employee, because the employer is guaranteeing the amount of the final benefit. Most of these plans now provide benefits after five years of work. If your husband has been employed in government or military service, you will need to find out about the different rules that apply to those pensions.

You may have a hybrid qualified plan that combines features of both the defined contribution and defined benefit plan.

Here are a few more important terms related to retirement benefits.

Vested Interest Versus Nonvested Interest

Benefits are vested if they cannot be forfeited when the employee quits or is terminated. Once the benefits are vested, the only condition to receiving them is that the employee survives until retirement age. The employee's interest is nonvested when it is contingent upon continuation of employment with the employer sponsoring the plan. Many 401(k) plans are set up so the employee "vests" a certain percentage of the total benefit over a period of years.

Unmatured Benefit

Benefits may be unmatured, even though vested. They are matured when the employee has an unrestricted right to receive the benefits at the time they retire. A certificate of deposit (CD) that has not yet matured when the employee retired could be vested but unmatured.

Contributory Plan Versus Noncontributory Plan

A contributory plan is funded by contributions from employer and employee. A noncontributory plan is funded entirely by employer contributions.

Pension Checklist

What follows is a checklist of pension questions to ask in planning for your financial future. Get the answers to these questions in writing and document the answers whenever possible. This is one area of investigation where you must trust, but verify. Start early with your investigation. There are many bureaucratic hoops for you to pass through on the way to your answers.

There are three sets of questions you will need to answer.

Ask yourself:

1. How much Social Security will I receive?
   To get an estimate of future Social Security Benefits, call (800) 772-1213 and request a Personal Earnings and Benefits Estimate statement. You can also order one on your spouse's earning history. On the Internet, you can request this information at *www.ssa.gov.*
2. What are our annual earnings from investments?
   This includes dividend and interest income. Check Schedule A on your income tax return, look at your W-2s, and look at all brokerage, savings accounts, and credit union statements for information. You may or may not have this annual income distributed to you.
3. Is my pension or my husband's a defined-benefit plan, which pays a set amount based on salary, or a defined-contribution plan, like a 401(k)?
4. When am I eligible to retire?
5. How will these benefits be paid? Lump sum or paid over time?
6. Is there a survivor benefit for the divorced spouse and when does it take effect? How does my spouse's age, remarriage, or departure from the company affect the survivor benefit?
7. What is the earliest date I can qualify under this plan (as a spouse and as an ex-spouse)?
8. What is the lifetime cost if I retire early?
9. How many employer plans have I or my husband participated in, and where is the pension information from all the jobs we held?
10. Does either of us have a military pension?
11. What documents have I signed previously relating to these pension benefits?

Ask your employer and your husband's employer:

1. For an individual benefit statement and a summary plan description from each plan in which either of you have been a participant.

2. For copies of your annual summary benefits statement. Get them for as many years back as possible on your own and your husband's plans.
3. Do I or does my spouse participate in the employer-sponsored plan? Are we each vested in our plans? If not, what are the requirements?
4. Is the pension guaranteed by the federal government Pension Benefit Guaranty Corporation?
5. By what amounts are the benefits reduced for early retirement?
6. Is the pension integrated with Social Security?
   If it is integrated with Social Security you will not receive the full amount of the pension, as Social Security benefits will be subtracted.
7. Is the pension benefit amount calculated based on the length of service and/or average earnings?
8. Is there an automatic cost of living adjustment in the retirement benefits?
9. What is the effect of being away from the job—can either of us have a break in service for months or years and not lose pension credits?
10. How will the retirement benefits be paid out?
    a) in monthly payments?
    b) in a lump sum?
    c) in monthly payments until death (for example, an annuity)?
    d) a choice from a, b, or c above to be determined later or at retirement?
    e) a survivor benefit for the divorced spouse?
11. How are the 401(k) dollars invested?
12. Are the 401(k) funds invested consistent with my goals?
13. How often can the investment allocation be changed on these funds?

Ask your spouse:

1. What is the death benefit on all of our life insurance policies, both those at work and our privately owned policies? Go to *www.finance.cch.com* and print their Insurance Policy Inventory Toolkit to organize your information and have it available for your attorney and financial planner.
2. What will I receive at your death as long as we are married?
3. What percentage of our pension will I receive at your death?
4. What kind of disability insurance do you have from work?

5. Will I get a benefit if you die before you retire? How much?
6. What are the terms of your military retirement?
7. Is there any life insurance death benefit from the military since your retirement?

How to Value a Pension Benefit

The two primary methods of allocating pension income benefits in a divorce are by:

1. Preparing a present value calculation, and
2. allocating the future pension benefit as either a fixed dollar amount or as a percentage of the ultimate benefit.

The primary purpose of a present value calculation is to account for the effects of inflation on funds to be received in the future. The present value calculation works best when you know exactly how much the monthly benefit will be. For those with several years left in the workforce, present value calculations aren't as meaningful, since any major event, such as a prolonged illness or disability, will affect the ultimate pension benefit. Even slight changes in the monthly benefit or in any of the assumptions used can have significant effects on the present value of the benefits. If there is a pension in your divorce, I recommend you hire an actuary or a qualified accountant specializing in these valuations to provide you and your attorney with an opinion letter of the fair market present value of your husband's retirement benefit. Experts can use various assumptions that can give substantially different results.

The following case illustrates how the present value calculation is applied.

Thomas and Gina have been married for thirty-five years, and Thomas has been employed with his company since the year they were married. He has a significant accrued pension benefit. In their case, a present value analysis would be presented as follows.

In making this calculation, the following assumptions were used:

- Retirement Date: January 1, 2012, Thomas's age at sixty-five
- Valuation Date: January 1, 2003—their date of separation
- Accrued monthly benefit: $6,500
- Thomas has an actuarial age of 15.84 years at age sixty-five based on the Social Security life expectancy tables, updated on June 16, 2004. That means the benefit is estimated to be paid for 15.84 years.

- The discount rate is 6 percent per year compounded monthly. This rate can be obtained at *www.PBGC.gov.*

Based on these data and assumptions, the value of Thomas's pension at retirement age is $800,025. This will need to be adjusted for inflation again to reflect the value of the pension on January 1, 2003. The present value of Thomas's pension on January 1, 2003, is $466,840. This benefit could be allocated to one spouse or the other in the property division, providing that the value is agreed upon.

In an allocation of future pension benefits, there can be an allocation of either a fixed-dollar amount or an allocation of a percentage of the ultimate pension benefit. Traditionally, a fixed-dollar amount was allocated to the nonemployee spouse. More recently there has been a trend toward the participatory allocation method.

- If the fixed-dollar amount method is used in allocating the pension, the nonemployee spouse is not fully compensated for the years that the parties were married. Instead, the final pension benefit is calculated by multiplying the average annual compensation by the average annual final salary, which is then multiplied by an adjustment factor.
- When applying the participatory allocation method, the ultimate pension benefit is allocated to the divorcing parties based on the percentage of the benefit earned during the marriage versus before or after marriage.

In appendix B, you will find an actual divorce settlement that includes calculations for allocating future pension benefits. This case study will help you understand not only how this method is applied in real world circumstances, but it will also illustrate its long-term effects.

To ensure that you receive your fair share of these future earnings, your financial planner, attorney, and you will need to review the implications of each approach—present value and allocation of future pension benefits—to see which best suits your situation. Regardless of the method used, the division of a future pension is an important consideration in a divorce settlement.

Once the divorce decree is filed and your share of the pension benefit is determined, a Qualified Domestic Relations Order (QDRO), pronounced "kwa-dro," is filed with your ex-spouse's company. A QDRO is a legally binding written agreement between a divorcing couple that spells out who gets what when it comes to retirement money held in a company pension plan such as a 401(k) plan, a 403(b), and most ***private pension*** *plans* in companies. Your benefit formula will segregate your future pension benefit from this point forward. You will need to call the corporate pension office annually to get an updated estimate of the pension benefit or request this information in writing. Some corporate benefit offices are more responsible than others. It is important that you notify your husband's employer's office of any change of address so they can contact you regarding the distribution of this pension benefit in the future.

RETIREMENT ASSETS DIVIDED WITH A QDRO

QDROs were created and are governed by the federal Employment Retirement Income Security Act of 1974 (ERISA) and control pensions and company-sponsored retirement accounts. In contrast, your divorce proceedings are a function of state courts, and a judge cannot require anything that a federally regulated retirement plan's own rules do not permit. When your QDRO is completed, it must be sent to the administrators of the company plan. The QDRO is then approved by the plan administrator and later by the divorce judge and it becomes the final word on who gets how much of the retirement plan assets.

Some Facts About QDROs and Common Mistakes Women Make

Some pension and retirement plans are not required to accept any court order transferring benefits to a former spouse. These include many benefit plans for highly paid company executives, as well as certain deferred compensation plans for state and local government employees. Likewise, federal government retirement systems have unexpected requirements for paying pensions to former spouses. For example, the government won't pay you a military retirement benefit awarded as marital property unless you are married for at least ten years of your husband's military service. Also, a federal civil service survivor pension is usually not available if the pension order is signed by the court after the divorce is final and the employee has retired.

The information summarized in the following points is taken from Anne E. Moss, J.D., author of *Your Pension Rights at Divorce*.

- QDROs are complicated and require an expert to draft the documents regarding the plans. Be aware that no two plans are alike. For example, John Deere's pension plan for salaried employees is drastically different from Dr. Smith's profit-sharing plan, or Dow Chemical's plan for hourly employees, or General Motors' stock savings plan. Make sure you and your attorney start the research on the company retirement plans early in the divorce process. Ask for a summary plan document of the pension plan and for the plan's procedures for "domestic relations orders." The rules for most government retirement plans (federal, state, and local) are usually found in publicly available statutes and regulations rather than a plan document. Your attorney should be familiar with these laws.

- Do not retain the same person to draft each spouse's QDRO. This document is not a neutral document, but one that advocates comprehensive benefits for you. Be careful using the sample QDRO document provided by the company. Have your expert read the document to check that all the provisions needed to protect your interests are included.
    - Make sure the agreement addresses preretirement and postretirement survivor benefits if your spouse predeceases you.
    - Clarify any employer provided early retirement assumptions.
    - Ensure that cost-of-living adjustments are on both parties' pensions.
    - Determine on what date the pension or profit-sharing plan is to be divided.
    - Establish what happens if the market goes down before the official division date if no date is stated in the QDRO.
- Try to have your QDRO simultaneously filed with your divorce decree. If not, make sure you have protective language in your decree that allows this issue to be kept open if there are problems with the QDRO being accepted by the administrator as anticipated at the time of the divorce. I have seen attorneys taking months to get an accepted QDRO signed by all parties. This is a problem if you need money from the qualified plan soon after the divorce or your spouse predeceases you.
- Follow up with your attorney to be sure a QDRO order is filed with the courts and that the pension plan officials receive and approve the final pension order promptly after the divorce is final. Ask for a notification in writing from the plan administrator that the order has been accepted.
- A few months after you divorce, you should call the plan administrator and verify that the paperwork has been received, everything is in order, and all of your personal information has been entered correctly in the system. This is an important loose end that you must follow up.
- Verify that the order clearly specifies what amount is to be paid to you. The amount can be stated as a fraction or percentage of the

pension. It can be based on the total benefit earned as of the separation date, the date of divorce, the date your ex-spouse is eligible for retirement, or the date he retires. There may be a separate property interest in the plan that is excluded from the final calculation.

- Make sure you are specifically named in the QDRO order to receive survivor benefits.
- Ask whether your former husband's death will have any effect on your benefit. What if he dies before he starts collecting his own benefit? In many situations, a former spouse will share in her husband's pension only as long as he is living, unless the court has also specifically awarded her a survivor pension. However, some state and local government plans won't pay survivor pensions to divorced spouses under any circumstances.
- You need to know how your retirement income will be affected. If you learn that pension benefits won't continue after your husband's death, you may want to try to get him to buy a life insurance policy with you as beneficiary to protect your retirement income, or you own the policy and pay the premiums. Do this before the divorce is final.
- Your husband might also never apply for his pension, or he may be injured on the job or become disabled, or he could waive his rights to the pension. Find out from your attorney how these or other acts would affect your benefits and what legal recourse you would have. May sure your property settlement agreement allows you some options if the worst happens. As an example, you may want to ask the court to require your former husband to pay you alimony or other property if he interferes with your right to the pension benefits.

Find out what effect your remarriage may have on your benefits. Some federal, state, and local government employee benefits will stop if the former wife remarries. For example, federal civil service and military survivor pensions terminate if the former spouse remarries prior to age fifty-five. Any pension benefits that have been awarded to you as alimony or spousal support, rather than marital property, will likely terminate upon your remarriage.

RETIREMENT ASSETS DIVIDED WITHOUT A QDRO

No QDRO is needed to divide an IRA, Roth IRA, or SEP-IRA. The transfer of a taxpayer's interest in these IRA accounts to a spouse or former spouse in a divorce is not considered a taxable transfer. You can roll over any distributions from an IRA to a spouse or former spouse's IRA and avoid the 10 percent early withdrawal penalty if you are under fifty-nine and a half.

There are many arguments for both a deferred division and a present division for the nonemployee spouse to consider. Talk with your attorney, the plan administrator, and your financial planner to list the pros and cons of each decision.

OTHER TYPES OF RETIREMENT PLANS

The previous sections have dealt with the most common types of pensions, and the issues involved in gaining a fair share of them during a divorce. Now we will concentrate on less frequently encountered retirement plans.

Military Pensions

If there is a military pension as part of your property settlement, find an attorney who is familiar with this type of retirement plan. Military pensions are subject to the Internal Revenue Code (IRC). The treatment of military pay differs from state to state. In most community property states the nonmilitary spouse will be entitled to one-half of the portion considered the property of both spouses. The portion will generally be based on the number of years the retirement pay was earned during the marriage, divided by the total years of service. Most noncommunity property states also will award a portion of the retired pay to the nonmilitary spouse.

You will qualify for direct enforcement of this benefit if you were married for at least ten years while your spouse was on active duty. You will receive payment directly from the military finance office.

As an example, the Survivor Benefit Plan (SBP) is an annuity that allows retired members of the military (either active duty or reserve) to designate a beneficiary to continue receiving up to 55 percent of the member's income after the member's death. The benefits are funded by nontaxable premium payments drawn from the retiree's paycheck. Payments to a member's spouse will cease upon the member's death without this SBP coverage.

A married active service member must make the SBP election at or before retirement. Reservists can make the election upon the completion of twenty years of service or upon reaching age sixty. The decision to participate is irrevocable. State courts can order a member to elect SBP coverage. A current spouse will be notified of the election to provide coverage for a member's former spouse, but she cannot veto that election.

If a military pension is part of your settlement, write for a copy of *A*

Guide for Military Separation or Divorce for you, your attorney, and your financial planner if they don't already have the publication. Write to, *A Guide for Military Separation or Divorce*, EX-POSE, P.O. Box 11191, Alexandria, Virginia, 22312.

The publication includes excellent information on benefits to which an ex-spouse may be entitled under the Uniformed Services Former Spouses Protection Act. Particulars about the Survivor Benefit Plan are explained, along with how to prepare for divorce court, the complete survivor benefit plan, miscellaneous benefits available to you, and other pertinent information.

You also will want to contact the military finance centers for the appropriate branch of service. Check resources at the end of this book for addresses to find the center nearest you.

Public Employees Retirement System (PERS)

These plans are used by many employees working for state and local governments and sometimes for employees of public educational institutions. These plans are covered under IRC sections as with military pensions. You will find that some agencies will permit the assignment of pension benefits or allow for the creation of a separate account in each party's name for their employees; some will not. Work with your family law attorney to determine how you can best share in these benefits.

Federal Employee Retirement System (FERS)

FERS is administered under its own set of rules with the Office of Personnel Management. As a general rule, the spouse will receive her share of a benefit as the participant receives it. This means you, the spouse, cannot elect early retirement and cannot receive an annuity based on your spouse's or your own life expectancy. FERS has published a booklet that discusses how you can divide retirement benefits, survivor benefits, and contribution refunds under their system. The booklet, as well as a handbook for attorneys and several other related publications, is available at *www.opm.gov/retire/html/library/other.asp*.

Civil Service Retirement System (CSRS)

These plans follow the same guidelines and rules in effect under FERS. Remember that both FERS and CSRS plans cannot be divided by a QDRO. You will need a court order containing very specific legal language before the Office of Personnel Management (OPM) will act on your request to divide either type of retirement plan. A third program, called the Thrift Savings Plan (TSP) is administered by a different agency than the OPM, and also requires a uniquely worded court order to divide in a divorce.

457 Plans

These are unfunded, nonqualified, deferred compensation plans for some state and local government workers. They cannot pay out benefits before an employee leaves the job, reaches seventy and a half, or has an unforeseeable emergency that does not include divorce. These plans cannot be rolled tax-free into an IRA account as is allowed in a 401(k) plan.

Nonqualified Deferred Compensation in the Private Sector

Don't forget to look at deferred compensation packages. The employer may have given your husband the opportunity to defer current income. This money is backed by the full faith and credit of the company for which he works when deferred compensation is elected as a "nonqualified" retirement benefit. Nonqualified simply means the plan is not subject to federal ERISA or IRC regulations, particularly for tax purposes.

The major objective of a deferred compensation plan is to postpone the tax on compensation to a year in which the recipient will be in a lower tax bracket. The IRS will generally treat amounts paid under a nonqualified deferred plan as taxable to the person who earned the compensation, rather than the person who receives it.

In the nonqualified plan, the employer is rewarding the employee compensation beyond that which is provided to the rank-and-file employees. These benefits are usually part of the retirement package and are corporate perks. These benefits can include: health insurance, paid time off, tuition reimbursement plans, deferred bonuses, stock options, *stock appreciation rights*, golden parachutes, *secular* and *rabbi trusts*, and *phantom stocks*. Many of these plans also have benefits centered on life insurance. Some common types of insurance arrangements are key employee insurance, group life insurance, *split dollar* plans, and reverse split dollar plans. These plans may be funded or nonfunded.

ACCESSING RETIREMENT FUNDS POSTDIVORCE

I often work with clients who find themselves in a situation where it makes sense for the nonworking spouse to start taking a distribution from the husband's qualified plan prior to the minimum age of fifty-nine and a half. She can do so without penalty under Section 72(t) of the Tax Code. There are three methods allowed by the IRS in calculating this distribution amount—life expectancy, *amortization*, and annuitization. This is a complicated retirement planning area with many rules, exceptions, and recalculation conditions. If you are considering this strategy, you will want to hire a knowledgeable accountant and/or financial planner to help you do these calculations to determine whether this is the right strategy to generate cash flow in your divorce.

However, the recently divorced woman may need to tap retirement funds for a different reason, perhaps to cover bills incurred during the divorce. As discussed earlier, incident to divorce and pursuant to a Qualified Domestic Relations Order (QDRO), you are allowed to take a one-time, penalty-free distribution from your qualified plan, such as a 401(k) plan. Make sure you budget the amount you need and include the taxes that will need to be paid with this distribution. This income will be added to other income for the year in which the retirement funds are withdrawn and is taxable. Again, you need the professional guidance of a financial planner and tax advisor to help you minimize your overall income tax liability. And don't forget to pay your quarterly estimated taxes after taking this withdrawal!

11

Preparing for Life After Divorce: Restricted Securities, Insurance, Housing, Debt, and Estate Planning

What lies behind us and what lies before us are tiny matters, compared to what lies within us.

—RALPH WALDO EMERSON

Looking back with regret because you failed to act aggressively on your own behalf to secure your future is one of the saddest acts of nostalgia. While retirement benefits from your marriage can be a substantial postdivorce asset, there are a number of other assets to consider. This chapter will explore several other common assets. We will also examine provisions for managing risk, housing, debts, and your estate.

STOCK OPTIONS AND RESTRICTED STOCK

Stock options can be one of the most contentious areas of negotiating a settlement, and it is an increasingly common asset. Employers often use them as incentives to attract and retain key employees. A few of the most common plans include qualified incentive stock options, employee stock purchase plans, nonqualified stock options, nonqualified employee stock purchase plans, and restricted stock. These assets cannot be assigned to the other spouse with a QDRO, but they are transferred on the records of the employee or they are held by the spouse. You will want to have all of these benefits analyzed to determine their value as a marital asset and how they will be taxed. If any of these are part of your marital assets, be sure to see a tax expert and securities analyst to determine the value of the stock.

Each asset has restrictions on the holding period, taxation, and ownership. For example, a corporation may provide its executives with Incentive Stock Options (ISOs) to acquire its stock or the stock of its parent or subsidiaries. These ISOs are not taxed when granted or exercised. Instead, the gain is taxed when the employee decides to sell stock options that have already been exercised. The ISO agreement will usually indicate the holding period required for an appreciation in stock value to qualify as a capital gain, and whether it is usually taxed at a lower rate, or treated as ordinary income. The corporation issuing the ISOs will also have restrictions regarding the transfer and exercising of these options.

Start gathering information early on these marital assets. It is a difficult area from which to get a fair settlement. There is a great deal of disagreement on valuing these assets and then dividing them equitably, since they stay with the employee and are typically nontransferable. These forms of compensation are one of the key incentives of the twenty-first century. If you have any of these assets in your marriage, be sure to ask your attorney about his experience in dealing with them. You will want an experienced attorney arguing on your behalf or one that works with an expert in this area of planning.

REVIEWING YOUR INSURANCE NEEDS

Many people think of having life insurance, yet not everyone needs it. For example, an older, divorced woman with a modest estate and no children at home or other beneficiaries might not need life insurance, but she may need long-term care insurance to help replace lost income and pay estate taxes.

The first step in determining what types of insurance you need is to identify and analyze possible risks in your life. Then assess how much insurance you might need to cover those risks and how much of the risk you are willing to carry yourself. What property and assets do you own? Do you face potential estate taxes? Are you a partner in a business in which you may need to buy out the heirs of a deceased partner?

Some types of coverage will be obvious. If you own a car, you'll need auto insurance. The same for a home. But how current is the coverage for your rental property, jewelry, and artwork?

People often overlook personal liability coverage over and above that offered by auto and homeowner's policies. Personal liability policies are relatively inexpensive. They cover accidents involving your property, as well as claims usually not covered by other policies such as libel, slander, or invasion of privacy.

Many people buy life insurance but not disability insurance. Though they know they'll die someday, they don't think they'll become disabled. **You are at least four times more likely to be disabled for at least ninety days before age sixty-five than you are to die.** Social Security benefits typically won't be enough, if they are available at all. Disability insurance will provide monthly income during the disability period.

Long-Term Nursing Care Insurance

LTC or Long-Term Care also includes custodial or institutional care in skilled care and assisted living facilities, home-based care by health professionals, respite care, adult day care, and care management services to evaluate, coordinate, and monitor care delivery. The coverage may include nonmedical support services such as personal assistance and homemaker services, as well as rehabilitative therapy. It does not include disability income protection, which replaces income and does not pay for medical expenses, nor is it the same as health care provided under group or individual medical policies.

Though Medicare and Medicaid have some provisions for LTC, they are restrictive compared to the scope of protection usually included in quality, private LTC plans. LTC protection is usually designed to activate at the onset of certain "triggering events" as certified by a medical professional including a cognitive impairment such as a loss of capacity in memory, orientation, or reasoning due to Alzheimer's or other forms of dementia, or the inability to perform two or more of the standard Activities of Daily Living (ADLs), bathing, dressing, toileting, eating, continence, and transferring. LTC protection is not reserved for particular age groups or employment conditions and covers circumstances initiated by accident, illness, or other non-self-inflicted disability. Unlike typical medical coverage, most LTC plans do not assume the individual will recover.

This specialized form of disability insurance is important in divorce. If owned by either spouse, it is an asset that must be considered in the property settlement. It is a form of protection against catastrophic financial loss and may be important to either spouse after the divorce. Compared to other types of insurance, long-term nursing care insurance can be relatively expensive and must be carefully evaluated from a risk-benefit perspective well before it may be needed. Many companies today are providing managers and executives with LTC policies as a corporate perk. If one spouse has such a policy, he may want to avoid having it claimed as a career asset subject to the property agreement.

To determine if LTC insurance should be part of your postdivorce financial plan, you need to consider its costs, how it would be paid for, and what your potential for needing it is. This last factor involves assessing your own health and the historical patterns of your parents and older siblings. From a statistical point of view, here are some numbers to consider:

- There has been a 400 percent increase in severe disabilities for those age seventeen to forty-four in the last twenty-five years.[1]
- 43 percent of those age sixty-five in 1990 will spend time in a nursing home (25 percent will spend more than one year; 9 percent more than five years). Three times more women than men spend five or more years in nursing homes.[2]
- 80 percent of single people entering a nursing home are impoverished within one year.[3]

Long-term care insurance should be considered in the context of a total financial plan, not as a stand-alone issue. You should discuss it with your financial advisor and make certain that your attorney and advisor know of any existing policies. It is especially important to find out if an existing policy has a "pooled benefit," whereby two spouses share the same total benefit amount, instead of each having individual coverage. It is not likely one spouse will want to continue paying for such coverage after divorce, nor is it necessarily in the best interest of the nonpaying spouse.

Health Insurance and COBRA

Health insurance is also a major consideration for you. Under the **Consolidated Omnibus Budget Reconciliation Act of 1985 (COBRA)**, you are allowed to continue on your husband's policy for three years, but you must pay the conversion premium cost. Health insurance is currently under major reform. You will need to do your research to determine the best health insurance alternative for you. Find out the cost of the COBRA coverage versus an individual policy in your name. Often, the COBRA coverage is much more expensive. Don't give up the COBRA coverage until you have a suitable individual policy in your name. If you have health problems during the COBRA three-year coverage period, you may find that you are uninsurable or have high premiums because of changes in your health.

Check with more than one provider and get quotes on your coverage so that you know your facts when it comes time to negotiate the property settlement. No one is going to know the basics of your situation better than you.

One area in which I encourage very careful documentation is uninsured medical costs. Document these expenses for each individual in your household. What have they been historically, who is to pay them in the future, and what is the method of payment?

Study your health care coverage from work carefully. These plans are changing their coverage on an almost annual basis. Companies have dependent care, educational assistance plans, cafeteria plans, and other features. Ideally, you and your spouse would try to find the most cost-effective coverage for your children. The employee generally pays for more of their family health care costs.

Know your family issues. Many families have specialized health care needs and you need to quantify the risks and costs after the dissolution to try to come up with an equitable division of these rights in your property settlement.

When assessing your insurance needs, don't determine them piecemeal. Work with your financial planner to see where each type of insurance fits into your overall plan, postdivorce.

Life Insurance

Meredith was fifty-seven years old and had worked only part time during her thirty-year marriage. Meredith's husband, Robert, was a doctor who had been in and out of the military three times during their marriage. They had lived in twenty-four houses in several states during the course of the marriage. They had a daughter; Robert also had a grown son from his first marriage.

At age sixty, Robert retired from both the military and their marriage. Meredith was emotionally devastated. Prior to her husband's departure from the military with full retirement, Meredith had signed a waiver of any pension benefit coming to her in the event of his death. This is not uncommon with senior military personnel involved in second or third marriages. It is viewed as an abbreviated form of a prenuptial agreement. This was an irrevocable election. However, the property settlement provided that Robert split his pension income on a fifty-fifty basis with Meredith for the remainder of his life. Upon his death, the pension benefit would stop.

Meredith understood a major portion of her pension income would disappear when Robert died. She had very little Social Security benefits of her own coming, as Robert had never wanted her to work. Even though she was able to maintain a part-time position with an airline over the years, her wages had been low.

As part of the final property settlement, Meredith asked for the right to purchase a term insurance policy on Robert's life. Robert opposed this.

He insisted he wouldn't live to be seventy, saying, "I don't want Meredith to become a rich widow at my expense." Since Robert had no medical evidence to support this claim, Meredith's attorney argued that Robert was just trying to minimize his support obligations.

Meredith won the right to buy an insurance policy on Robert's life. Though she has been paying the annual premiums on this term insurance policy, it has given her peace of mind regarding her long-term financial security. Owning this policy has allowed her to enjoy more of her assets during her lifetime, rather than living in fear that Robert will predecease her and she will lose a substantial portion of her retirement income.

I believe, as Meredith does, that Robert had a definite plan in mind when he asked Meredith to sign off on the military pension. He saw no breach of trust on his part when he encouraged Meredith to waive her rights to a future pension. Less than a month after the divorce was final, he took a new job and within a year had remarried his first wife from whom he had been divorced thirty-six years previously. He intentionally tried to thwart Meredith's plan to guarantee her portion of his pension beyond his death by insurance. Her ability to buy that insurance policy became a key component in her long-term financial planning.

Women often ask me whether they should buy term insurance or permanent coverage. Meredith sought to protect her pension income from Robert through insurance. In essence, she was betting that he wouldn't outlive the term of the policy. Only you can determine the value of this peace of mind.

In a current case, the spouse was awarded lifetime maintenance and an assignment of her husband's state pension at his retirement. Since there is no survivor benefit if he dies prior to retirement, she is totally unprotected in the event of his death. We are now negotiating for her to purchase an insurance policy on his life and to have him pay the premiums as maintenance until he retires. She will have the option to terminate the coverage after his retirement as the additional maintenance will cease, and she will receive one-half of the pension benefit—whatever the amount. My client came to me after the divorce was final. She and her attorney discovered our state pension structure does not have a provision to pay the divorced spouse a survivor benefit if the employee dies prior to retirement, even under a QDRO.

I cannot emphasize too strongly that you need to get all the facts before your divorce is final.

Disability Insurance

Failing to anticipate a postdivorce need for disability insurance can be disastrous. While many employers provide some form of short-term disability

	Annual Rate of Price Inflation in the United States		

Year	Consumer Price Index	Year	Consumer Price Index
1986	1.1%	1996	3.3%
1987	4.4%	1997	1.7%
1988	4.4%	1998	1.6%
1989	4.6%	1999	2.7%
1990	6.1%	2000	3.4%
1991	3.1%	2001	1.6%
1992	2.9%	2002	2.4%
1993	2.7%	2003	1.9%
1994	2.7%	2004	3.3%
1995	2.5%	2005	3.4%

FIGURE 11.1   Historical Rates of Inflation
Source: U.S. Department of Labor, Bureau of Labor Statistics

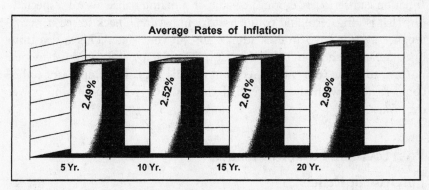

FIGURE 11.2   Average Rates of Inflation
Source: U.S. Department of Labor, Bureau of Labor Statistics

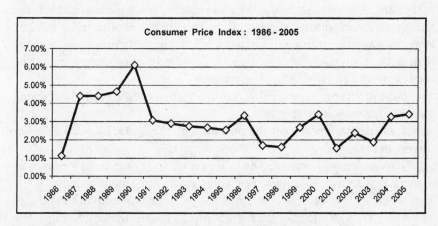

FIGURE 11.3   Consumer Price Index 1986–2005
Source: U.S. Department of Labor, Bureau of Labor Statistics

insurance, there are usually restrictions on spousal or family coverage, and rarely is an ex-spouse covered. Effective long-term disability insurance, usually considered for disabilities lasting more than six months, is even more rare.

If this is an issue, find out how disability insurance is treated in your state. The special circumstances of a disability can make a difference. Did it occur during the marriage, when the two parties were legally separated, or after the divorce? Were the premiums paid while the couple was married? See whether the disability benefits are deemed to be marital property.

Adjusting Maintenance for Inflation

Inflation can seriously erode the value of a maintenance award, especially one that is long-term and compensatory in nature. Check to see if maintenance awards have an escalation clause in your state. This varies from one state to the next, but that doesn't mean that you and your husband are not free to make your own agreement on this issue. It is important to become familiar with the concept of maintaining your purchasing power over time.

Postdivorce Housing Issues

Purchase or Rent?

The decision whether to buy or rent is different for every divorce case. When there are children, there is almost always a home purchase for the wife, often a home that is smaller and requires less maintenance than the family residence during the marriage. Usually the mother and children want to stay in the same school district. This can sometimes pose a problem if the family has lived in an upscale suburb, since there may not be houses within an affordable price range.

Here are some guidelines to consider in determining whether buying or renting is in your best interest.

1. Is the *total return* on the purchase of the house as good as other investments?

This means you evaluate the purchase of the home from a purely financial perspective. When you rent there are no large down payments, real estate taxes, improvement costs, and mortgage or homeowner's insurance payments, though you may elect to obtain renter's insurance coverage. The real question is what kind of a return do you get on the money you have saved monthly by not making the down payment. Many say a renter has nothing to show for her investment at the end of her lease, but I disagree. She has the return on the money that has not gone into the home maintenance and house payments, and may have invested a portion of the difference in career training that will increase her future income.

2. What about the tax savings that I am giving up?

These tax savings may not be as big as you think. It is true that your mortgage interest and local real estate taxes can be used as a deduction on your income taxes and that renters do not have these deductions. These deductions are of benefit only to the extent that they exceed the standard deduction.

16.7%

Let's suppose you buy a house for $300,000 and pay $50,000 as a down payment. If home prices go up and the house is worth $400,000, you have just made $100,000 on a $50,000 investment. Your equity can be wiped out quickly. If you make a $50,000 down payment on a $300,000 house and prices drop 20 percent, your equity is gone. This is a real possibility.

A house is a relatively fixed asset. It isn't so easy to get all your money back out quickly, due to expenses such as real estate commissions, closing costs, maintenance, and repairs. The house can be a forced savings tool, collateral if you need to take out a loan, and a safe haven for you and your family from the outside world. I don't believe a home should be bought as an investment, even though it can turn out to be quite a good one. Remember, we are talking about renting and investing the difference. Buying a house can be as much of an emotional decision as a financial decision.

Other questions to ask yourself about buying versus renting:

- What kind of a neighborhood are you living in?
- Are there a lot of houses up for sale?
- What will this neighborhood be like in five years if there is a recession or downturn in the economy?
- What kind of improvements will this house require in the next five years?
- Will these improvements enhance the resale of your house or will they be considered normal maintenance to the new buyer?
- Do you put money in a new deck or in a treasury bill? Ask yourself which one will give you your principal back plus interest in five years.
- How long do you want to live in this large house? Until the children are out of school, until you finish school?
- Where are you likely to find a job after your education and training?

- Owning a home can be a way for you to build equity over time. You can systematically pay down your mortgage by using your excess cash and not spending this money. How will you spend any excess funds?
- If you have a fixed mortgage, your payments remain the same, whereas an adjustable rate mortgage or rent will probably be going up over time. Which situation is right for your circumstances?
- Is it right for you to rent for a year or two after selling the family home, complete your education, and find employment before purchasing a home?

These questions are intended merely as guidelines to help you make an objective financial decision regarding your living situation. You must make the ultimate determination as to what works best for you. Ask your financial planner to model the specific numbers on a purchase versus rent scenario in your circumstances. She will be able to show you the bottom line or cash flow impact of owning versus renting in your specific situation.

Should You Pay Off Your Mortgage?

You should decide whether to invest your investment assets from the dissolution or use your settlement to pay off the mortgage. John Waggoner wrote a column on this subject in *USA Today*. The return on paying off the mortgage is assumed to be the same as the current mortgage rate of 5.91 percent, the amount you would be saving in interest payments on your principal over the term of the loan. Without having the mortgage, you have no cost, and you are saving the entire amount you would otherwise pay out for this interest.

This last assumption comes with several caveats to consider:

Taxes. If you pay off your mortgage, you will lose the mortgage deduction. Typically this deduction is greater than the standard deduction on your federal income taxes and you would be able to itemize deductions and pay less in taxes.

Leverage. If you pay off your mortgage, you will lose the advantage of using someone else's money to invest. If your mortgage is paid off and your home gains 5 percent in price this year, to $210,000 from $200,000, you have gained $10,000. If you had $20,000 in equity in your home and a $180,000 mortgage and you sell your home for $210,000, you'd repay the $180,000 loan, keep the $20,000 in equity and pocket the $10,000 without tying up $200,000 of your own money.

Liquidity. If you suddenly need money, you could use an equity line of credit to access cash, but then you would be right back in the same place with a loan with an adjustable interest rate, probably moving upward. You must ask yourself if there will be a bubble in the real estate market and consider how it would affect your timing.

Rising Rates. Every quarter-point increase in mortgage rates eliminates potential buyers from the market. The thirty-year fixed rate mortgage was actually 5.63 percent in June of 2005, and 6.71 percent in June of 2006. This 1.08 percent difference means that a $200,000 mortgage financed over thirty years would cost $50,378 more at the higher rate. That represents a 12.15 percent higher monthly payment. At the 6.71 percent interest rate, you would be paying $1,292 per month for 360 months.

Cooling Prices. Home prices, like stock prices, don't normally double in a year or two. Typically, home prices rise 1 or 2 percentage points above inflation. The twenty-year average on inflation is slightly more than 3 percent, according to the investment management firm Ibbotson and Associates. This includes the high years of 12 percent or higher in the mid-1980s to the low inflation rate of under 2 percent in the last few years.

Soaring Expectations. In 1999 people were talking about how much they made from their tech stocks. This has been replaced today with how much money they have made on their houses. They would only have made that money if they sold the house and reinvested the money. Should home prices actually start to drop, the magic of leveraging will work in reverse. If you buy a $200,000 house with $20,000 down, you'll be in trouble if your home price falls 10 percent to $180,000.

To decide whether or not you should pay off your mortgage, meet with your financial advisor and do an integrated net worth, tax, and cash-flow analysis to determine the best answer for you. Look at the decision-making models with both optimistic and pessimistic assumptions, and evaluate your risk tolerance.

DIVIDING DEBT

Most couples will accrue some debt during their marriage—on the home mortgage, home equity lines of credit, credit cards, student loans, and car loans. Debts incurred before the marriage or after the divorce are the responsibility of the individual who incurred them. Debts you take on during the marriage are generally the responsibility of both spouses. It is in your best interest to pay off as many debts as possible before or at the time of the final decree. To accomplish this, you can use liquid assets from bank accounts, stocks, or bonds. In addition, it might make sense to sell some of your "luxury" possessions such as an extra car or a vacation home to raise cash. If you cannot pay all of your debt off at the time of the divorce, your divorce decree should state who is liable for which debt and when each debt will be paid. However, this does not relieve you of your personal liability to the third-party creditors, regardless of what the court order states.

There are two main types of debt to consider: secured debt and unsecured debt.

Secured Debt

This kind of debt includes the mortgage on your house or vacation property and loans on cars, trucks, and other vehicles. The lender has been promised that if they are not paid in accordance with the contract terms, they have the right to take some other asset, such as cash, property, or a vehicle, from you in lieu of the payments they were promised. If your spouse gets the debt, and you get the asset in the divorce, be aware that the creditor could come after you if the debt is not paid as promised.

Unsecured Debt

These debts include credit cards, personal bank loans, and lines of credit as well as loans from parents, friends, or relatives. The borrower in these cases has not pledged to surrender other assets if he fails to make the required payments, but there are still specified penalties if the borrower does default. Either of you could be assigned this debt in the final decree. Usually the court will look at which party can most afford to pay it in light of the total financial settlement dividing the assets, liabilities, and income.

Your final separation agreement needs to include a "hold harmless" clause. This is designed to indemnify the nonpaying spouse and allows that person to go after the ex-spouse if he is in default for missed payments. In some circumstances, you can sue for damages, interest, and attorney fees if the payments were not made. This happens often with credit cards. If a joint card is not terminated at the time of the divorce or the debt is not paid in full and new charges are added, you will be liable for this debt with the credit card company if your spouse defaults. This will also damage your credit rating.

Just cutting up your card and tossing it in the trash will not close the account. Ask the card issuer to close your account and to report your account to credit bureaus as "closed by the customer." You can close your account even if the balance is not paid in full. Be aware that some creditors are raising the percentage rates to the highest rates possible on closed accounts with unpaid balances.

You should receive a letter in approximately ten days confirming that your account is "closed by the consumer." If you don't receive the confirmation letter, follow up by calling the card issuer to make sure it closed your card and is reporting it properly to the credit bureaus.

A creditor cannot close an account just because your marital status has changed. They may require a new application to be reviewed to verify your ability to pay. If you have joint credit card charge accounts with your spouse, you will have the same credit history.

Your divorce property settlement may include an unsecured note between you and your spouse to come up with the overall property division. If your spouse defaults and the promissory note is not secured against another asset—for example, a piece of real estate—you may not be able to collect if your spouse files bankruptcy. In some special circumstances this secured debt can even be included in the bankruptcy action. When possible, pay off as much of the joint debt as you can at the time of the divorce.

Another type of debt to be aware of comes from a possible future tax liability. For three years after the divorce is final, the IRS can audit a joint return, and after that, if there is good cause, they can go back seven years or indefinitely if they suspect fraud. It is typical that the divorce agreement will state what would happen if there was money owing to the IRS, and how any additional interest, penalties, taxes, and professional costs would be shared between the divorced spouses. If the tax return was filed jointly, you are both responsible and individually liable. I have seen the IRS take assets from a spouse's bank account or put a *lien* on real property to cover this tax liability. There is no warning. If you are not in contact with your ex-spouse, you may know nothing about the problem. Though you have protective language in your decree as to which spouse is liable, it will be up to you to go to civil court to try to collect from your ex-spouse. It will cost you time and money to collect.

Make sure your final property settlement outlines who will be paying the debts incurred with the divorce and how they will be paid. These expenses will be for your attorney, court filing fees, appraisals, experts, and mediation fees to name a few. I have found that most divorcing spouses are liable for most of their own legal fees, but there may be an allowance provided for one party to pay a portion of the other's expenses. This can be negotiated in a mediation setting or ordered by the court.

The legal briefs filed by attorneys for each spouse in a divorce action almost always ask for the opposing party to pay court costs and attorney's fee. I seldom see the court assign one spouse's attorney's fees to the other spouse in the settlement.

Divorce can get very expensive in the last few weeks, and then there is the cost of preparing the final decree, property settlement, QDROs, and property transfers. See your financial planner to devise a comprehensive repayment plan. This may seem like one more expense, but a qualified advisor can make sure that you understand the cash flow and income tax implications for your individual situation.

DIVORCE AND BANKRUPTCY

According to research conducted by Harvard law professor Elizabeth Warren, single women account for nearly 40 percent of all bankruptcy filings. Warren reports the number of filings by single women with children is more than triple that of unmarried men—21.3 cases per thousand compared to 6.3. By comparison, the rate for married couples with children is 15.3 cases per thousand. Why are women more susceptible to this financial hardship? It is not because they are financially irresponsible. Ninety percent of women filing for Chapter Seven or Chapter Thirteen protection were forced into bankruptcy by divorce, medical emergency, or loss of employment.

Like most women facing divorce, you have probably never considered the possibility of having to file for bankruptcy. I am not raising the topic here because I believe there is a significant chance you will have to face such a situation. You should be aware that women do experience this trauma as a result of divorce. There are some precautions you can take to avoid bankruptcy.

- Accept the reality of your postdivorce financial condition and adjust your lifestyle quickly to the required changes in cash-flow management and expense controls. Don't wait until the decree is final to reduce discretionary spending.
- Learn all you can about the debts you and your spouse have accumulated and ensure that your attorney and financial advisor have full knowledge of them as well.
- Take control of your credit. Cancel all joint credit accounts. Keep only one or two essential charge cards in your own name. Close department store accounts if they are not absolutely necessary to maintaining your new lifestyle.
- Make sure your name is on the title of all appropriate assets that may be subject to the property settlement in your divorce, including the family home, investment accounts, and vehicles.
- Start working on a career plan immediately.

Filing for bankruptcy is a very serious decision. It can affect your credit for years. If either you or your spouse is contemplating this step, particularly during a divorce, meet with an experienced bankruptcy attorney first. Bankruptcy is governed by federal law, which takes priority over a state's divorce laws. If either spouse files for bankruptcy during the divorce, the divorce may be effectively put on hold until the bankruptcy is finalized. A family law court can establish alimony payments, child support payments, even grant the final decree, but the final disposition of assets and debts cannot be completed prior to the bankruptcy court finishing its work.

There are divorce cases on record in which an angry spouse filed for bankruptcy in an attempt to avoid transferring assets to the other spouse or canceling disputed legal fees. When this happens, all of the nonexempt assets and debts of the filing spouse plus all of the couple's community property are subject to bankruptcy law. You can imagine how complicated the divorce becomes. If you suspect your spouse is considering such a move, discuss it with your attorney immediately.

When divorcing spouses face overwhelming debts, bankruptcy may be appropriate to establish financial stability after the divorce is final. In such cases an attorney specializing in bankruptcy in your state of residence should be consulted. The law is complex and a misguided decision or erroneous assumption can have disastrous consequences. Deciding whether to file under Chapter Seven or Chapter Thirteen of the Bankruptcy Code requires careful analysis by an experienced professional. Keep in mind the code was amended in 2005 and a number of the changes affect assets in a divorce.

ESTATE PLANNING DURING AND AFTER DIVORCE

Many women feel that they don't really need a will since they only have a few assets—a home, a car, and some personal effects. Regardless of your personal assets, you do need a will. If you do not have a will when you pass on, you die *intestate*, which means without testamentary evidence of your wishes as to the division of your estate. In this situation, a *probate* court appoints an administrator to handle your affairs, and your property is distributed to your heirs based on a formula fixed by state law. There are significant variations from one state to another, so it is important for you to understand the laws in your own state. After the payment of taxes, debts, funeral expenses, and administrative costs, the property goes to the surviving spouse, children, and/or other relatives. The laws are very specific about how property is to be distributed, including which relatives have priority and how the inheritance is divided.

You might say to yourself, "I will wait until the divorce is final to change my will." Please understand this: regardless of your intentions about changing your will, if the will you signed while married is in effect at the time of your death and it still names your surviving spouse as your beneficiary, any assets designated to him as a surviving spouse become his property.

A will controls only the disposition of an individual's separate property at death and one-half of any community property owned by the deceased and his or her spouse. It does not control the disposition of *nonprobate* assets, which include pension benefits, life insurance, or assets held mutually with right of survivorship.

I have worked with several clients whose husbands have died during the divorce process. In all of the cases, the male spouses had changed their wills to govern how these assets were to be shared at their death. Trusts, outright gifts, and special bequests were included in their wills. The pension and survivor benefits, as well as the beneficiaries on life insurance policies, have stayed as they were when the spouse filed for divorce and these assets passed directly to the wife at the husband's death.

In one recent case, more than two million dollars in nonprobate assets passed to the spouse, including the family residence, vacation home, life insurance proceeds, a pension, a profit-sharing plan, deferred compensation, and company stock. The husband tried to have the beneficiary changed but was unable to do this lawfully until divorced. He died first.

During the divorce process, check the owner registration of all of your marital assets. Based on how the assets are registered, think about what would happen if you or your husband died while in the process of getting a divorce.

You do not need to have a large estate to plan and prepare a will. Anyone who owns property, whether personal or real property, should plan and prepare a will. If you are separated or in the process of getting a divorce, I still recommend revising your will for the time of separation. For your postdivorce estate, I would recommend additional revisions where appropriate.

Name an executor or personal representative in your will to fulfill your directions and requirements. Choose someone who is competent and willing to serve on your behalf. In addition, name an alternate representative in the event that this person is unable or unwilling to serve as your personal representative.

The personal representative is responsible for settling your financial affairs and disposing of property according to the provisions of your will. This will mean assembling and inventorying assets as well as paying any debts, expenses, and taxes. If required, the executor will submit a final accounting to the beneficiaries and to the probate court.

I have been involved in situations in which the heirs and the wife leveled serious disagreements against the decisions of the personal representative, particularly if the deceased was the father or mother of the representative, a potential heir. A father who wishes to bypass his wife in favor of the children may leave his family with fuel for resentments and anger, as well as legal costs to satisfy the will. In one particular case, the adult children argued back and forth regarding the issues facing the mother, whose husband died prior to his divorce. The mother had legal rights to marital assets as well as to the nonprobate assets.

If you find yourself in this situation, you will need to start working with an estate-planning attorney immediately. A financial planner can be invaluable in helping you take inventory of the assets and work with the heirs in creating a win-win strategy for the family estate. This is the time to inform all the parties about what legal rights belong to whom, as a beneficiary, personal representative, and spouse. There are several legal terms used in estate planning that will help you to become informed about your rights.

Durable Power of Attorney

I believe everyone needs to have this document filed safely with other personal papers. The durable power of attorney provides an individual of your choice with the power to act on your behalf to handle your legal and financial affairs upon your incapacitation or incompetence. This document becomes effective only if there is sufficient evidence and two doctors' signatures to support a claim of incompetence. Name someone you trust to handle your financial affairs and name a successor in case the first person is unable to perform these duties.

Directive to Physicians

This is a document signed by a competent individual stating her wishes regarding medical care should she become incapacitated. In addition to specifying acceptable forms of treatment, it provides for the withdrawal of life-sustaining procedures in terminal cases. Be sure that the language of your living will conforms to the laws of the state in which you reside. A copy of the directive must be filed with the patient's doctor and it can be revoked by its maker at any time.

ELEVEN OF THE MOST COMMON MISTAKES I SEE AMONG MY CLIENTS IN ESTATE PLANNING ARE:

1. Failure to have a will.
2. Failure to coordinate other estate planning techniques with the will (for example, registration of assets).
3. Failure to deal with business succession.
4. Failure to deal with incapacity or incompetence.
5. Illiquidity—lack of cash to pay estate taxes.
6. Leaving everything to a spouse.
7. Wrong choice of three key players (executor, trustee, and guardian).
8. Treating all beneficiaries the same.
9. Failure to educate the would-be survivors.
10. Failure to review and update the estate plan.
11. Failure to deal with noncitizenship issues.

See an attorney who specializes in estate planning to determine which documents are most appropriate for your circumstances.

Prenuptial Agreements as a Component of Retirement Plans

Marriage and divorce are the most important financial transactions in anyone's lifetime. A contemporary woman needs to be informed about both of them. Divorce is the one business deal that puts everything that a couple owns on the table.

Planning for the contingency that a marriage may end in divorce is not romantic, but if the statisticians are correct, approximately 50 percent of all present marriages will end that way. If a woman were in any other business enterprise with a failure rate that high, she would certainly protect herself. If you have sizable wealth, own a business, or are entering into a second marriage with significant personal assets, you will probably want a prenuptial agreement. The number of second marriages ending in divorce is greater than 50 percent.

In a prenuptial agreement, you will negotiate the financial terms of your marriage and each partner's role before saying the vows. Financial issues include: bill paying, earnings, career goals, short- and long-term financial goals, estate planning in the event of death or divorce, and disability. Other issues include:

- How will income taxes be paid?
- Who will pay to defend a tax audit?
- Who will pay for specific expenses and obligations in a divorce? Certain levels of support may be promised after a certain number of years of marriage, or perhaps a percentage of income may be shared per an agreed-upon formula.
- How will a pension be shared? You can't waive rights to pension benefits if you are not married, so this may require a postnuptial agreement in which you waive the pension rights in lieu of some other asset.

I recommend that couples allow six months to complete the prenuptial agreement.

There are several useful purposes for a prenuptial agreement other than planning for dissolution. These could include the following:

- Establishing a written record of each party's separate property and its value and determining the procedures to assist you in maintaining it as separate property.
- Defining each person's debts and protecting the other person's property and earnings from liability.
- Reducing the fear that one spouse is marrying the other for money.
- You may be giving up alimony/maintenance from a former spouse when remarrying and want some financial security for this action.
- Planning for the disposition of property upon death, including preserving an existing estate plan and ensuring that each party's children are provided for and that certain family assets, especially family business interests, remain in the bloodlines.
- Many remarrying senior citizens are using the prenuptial agreement to address the possibility of future disability. They want to protect the way their financial affairs are handled if one spouse suffers a stroke or develops Alzheimer's or is struck by another disabling health condition. This agreement determines who pays for health care on the incapacity of one spouse, whether inside the home or in a convalescent home. Whether to sell the primary residence to cover the costs of care, as well as the use, possession, and disposition of personal assets can be covered in the agreement. If there are adult children or children from prior marriages, the prenuptial agreement can be used to minimize the threat of litigation or interference by these children, who may believe they are protecting their parent or inheritance rights.

Prenuptial agreements can have some unusual clauses:

- A "sunset" clause making some or all of the provisions ineffective after a number of years.
- The stay-at-home spouse negotiates for a monthly dollar amount for leaving her job to travel and be with her husband or becoming a stay-at-home mother, or asks for a lump sum to compensate for lost career time and/or lost retirement savings.
- A "signing bonus" can be awarded to one spouse immediately after the wedding and is hers to keep even if the marriage doesn't outlast the honeymoon.
- An "escalator clause" is used to provide the less affluent spouse with increasing amounts of money the longer the marriage lasts. Donald Trump's divorce from Marla Maples was just before the five-year mark, and Tom Cruise split from Nicole Kidman just before their tenth wedding anniversary. The timing on these divorces may have been less a matter of coincidence than avoiding a key condition in their prenuptial agreements.
- There should be a clause that states that if any provision of the agreement is invalidated, the rest of the agreement remains valid.
- Some agreements include a clause ensuring the laws of the state in which the couple were married prevail if they get a divorce in another state.
- A business valuation formula or method of valuation may be included to be used in the event of divorce.

Donald Trump used a prenuptial agreement in all three of his marriages:

1. **Ivana:** Ivana Zelnicek was a former competitive skier and model when she married Donald Trump on April 7, 1977. They were divorced on December 11, 1990. Ivana unsuccessfully challenged her prenuptial agreement and in the end agreed to a divorce settlement not greater than $25 million as originally dictated in the prenuptial agreement. She received $14 million in cash, $350,000 in annual alimony, and $300,000 per year for the support of her three children. She also got their forty-five-room mansion in Greenwich, Connecticut, an apartment in the Trump Plaza, and a 1987 Mercedes.
2. **Marla:** Marla Maples was an actress who married Donald on December 20, 1993, and was divorced from him in 1999. Her prenup had a minimum duration marriage clause, and she was served a

notice for divorce a few weeks before the clause would have been satisfied. She received $1 million in property and child support. Had she made it past the specified deadline, she would have received much more.

3. **Melania:** For Melania Knauss, the specifics of her prenuptial are unknown.

Just because there is a prenuptial agreement does not mean that it is enforceable. I see judges rule against prenuptial agreements regularly. The issue of separate property is taken into account directly or indirectly when a property settlement is reached. Some of the reasons a prenup may not be enforceable include:

- The agreement is interpreted to be unfair to one spouse.
- Both parties did not enter into the agreement voluntarily with independent legal advice and with full knowledge and understanding of the document's content.
- There was not full disclosure of all the assets and liabilities at the time the prenuptial agreement was signed.
- The timing of the signing of the prenuptial agreement did not allow for an informed decision. Allow plenty of time to create the prenuptial agreement, time for all of the factors to fall into place, and time for a thorough investigation of all assets and liabilities.

Your attorney will work with you to determine whether he believes your prenuptial agreement is enforceable. Some clients prefer not to sign a prenuptial agreement at the time of marriage or remarriage, but they attempt to maintain separate property through the registration of the assets and through their estate plan.

If you want a prenuptial agreement and the other party is reluctant to comply, consider revising your estate plan to include new wills, a buy-sell agreement, powers of attorney, or a Qualified Terminable Interest Property Trust (QTIP) to accompany the prenuptial agreement. Remember that with or without a prenuptial, you should use some care in how you title your assets. Changing a title to joint ownership can create marital property, subject to a property settlement in much the same way that commingling assets in a bank account or brokerage account may jeopardize the separate property characteristics of the assets. Regardless of how you handle these financial affairs, keep careful and accurate records. I have several clients who maintain these and other similar records in their safety-deposit box.

Your divorce decree and property settlement will summarize the assets you are to receive. If there are pension and retirement assets, these will be

STATUS OF ASSET TRANSFERS

Asset Description	Old Acct. # New Acct. #	Decree Value Transfer Value	Former Contact New Contact	Old Phone New Phone	Amount of Transfer	Payment Received	Notes
EXAMPLE	1234567	11,215	John Doe	444-5555	(5,855)	☐	Joe called to confirm receipt of
	2345678	11,710	Joe Smith	555-7777	5,855	7/14/2005	funds at Great Northwest
						☐	
						☐	
						☐	
						☐	
						☐	
						☐	
						☐	
						☐	
						☐	
						☐	

Assets to include: Bank Accounts, Mutual Funds, Brokerage Accounts, Insurance and Annuities, Partnerships, Retirement Accounts, and other assets.

© Copyright Miller Advisors, Inc. 2005

FIGURE 11.4   Asset Transfer Record

transferred by a QDRO, by the divorce decree, or by special paperwork provided by the plan. Once your decree is final, create a spreadsheet for yourself that chronicles the transfer of all of these assets. These transfers can take several weeks to complete before the account and funds are reregistered in your name.

Let me give you an example of how delaying the transfer and reregistration of assets can be costly. Recently I had a client who asked me to help her transfer 401(k) funds from her husband's account into a local bank. The divorce decree specified that the transfer would be authorized via a QDRO. There was no QDRO with the final divorce papers, so we had to have one drawn up that met the legal requirements and would be accepted by the administrator of the bank plan.

This took two weeks. We then sent the request for transfer of these funds on the form from her new IRA custodian to the bank custodian. Remember, you do not want to have these funds sent directly to you, because there are adverse tax consequences. The bank did not accept the wording of the first QDRO, and it had to be revised by the attorney's office. It took four months for these funds to be transferred and several phone calls from me to accomplish the transfer.

The divorce decree stated a dollar amount that was to be transferred from my client's ex-husband's account to her IRA. It did not state that this was a minimum dollar amount to which any appreciation on the assets since the valuation date would be added. This couple had been separated nearly a year before the divorce was final, and then another five months had passed. The original value in the decree was as of the date of separation. During this sixteen-month period, the husband had control of how the funds were invested in the plan. He had the funds invested 30 percent in a bond account and 70 percent in an aggressive stock fund. The market was down at the end of March when she finally was able to transfer the funds to her account. There was a 16 percent decrease in the value of her account from the date of separation.

If we had been able to accomplish this transfer sooner, she probably would not have experienced the loss. We would have worked together to create an investment strategy that fit her risk tolerance and then gradually invested the money. Some of this could have been avoided if the attorney had prepared the QDRO in a timely manner. The QDRO also should have stated that there would be a minimum dollar amount transferred plus a *pro rata* share of any increase since the date of separation.

I always meet with my clients after the divorce to discuss transfers and their income tax liability as soon as they have a decree and property settlement in writing. I have found that what is written and what the woman thinks she is getting are sometimes quite different. I consult for a number of attorneys who ask me to review the wording in the property settlement and to suggest changes or clarifications as appropriate. Your attorney is your legal advisor and may not have a practical understanding of all the money issues.

Long-term financial independence is something we all strive for. Understanding the comprehensive pension, retirement, and Social Security benefits of both parties in the marriage is essential when dividing the marital assets. Women who have not had a career outside marriage or who have interrupted their careers to stay home and raise a family need to be objective when looking at benefits and how they can be shared.

Determining the proper division of retirement benefits can be difficult in mid-term marriages when one spouse is returning to work or entering the job force for the first time. There is a disparity of earnings between the spouses, the wife is going back to school to upgrade her skills, she has teenage children at home, and she is in direct competition with her children for college funds. Typically, these families have a good start on their retirement funding, but the maximum funding years typically come when the clients are fifty or older.

You can find additional information and help from AARP, the Pension Rights Center, and the Older Woman's League. You will find contact information in Resources at the end of this book.

12

Women and Investing

Go confidently in the direction of your dreams! Live the life
you've imagined. As you simplify your life, the laws of the universe
will be simpler.

—Henry David Thoreau

As a result of divorce, many women find themselves "on their own" for the first time, responsible for not only their own financial well-being but their children's as well. It is important that you understand the basics of financial planning, feel comfortable maintaining your finances, and manage the money you receive as a settlement to help you live now and retire comfortably later.

You now are faced with managing your financial future after your divorce.

Women demonstrate many qualities investors need to be able to reach their financial goals. On the whole, we are goal-oriented, less inclined to take ill-advised risks and more inclined to stick with our strategy in volatile times. These qualities lead us to achieve better returns in our investment portfolios over the long term. According to a study by economists at the University of California, Davis, men turn over their investment portfolio 45 percent more often than women. This excess activity leads to a reduction in their portfolio returns by 94 basis points annually compared to portfolios of the women in the study.[1] Since changes in the values of securities are often small, the financial industry uses the term "basis point" instead of "percent." One basis point equals one one-hundredth of one percent, so 94 basis points is equivalent to 0.94 percent. Although women tend to invest more conservatively than men, by taking lower risks and receiving lower potential returns, women can become more comfortable with an investment strategy that includes assets with a history of higher potential gain with the encouragement of a good advisor.

A research study by Oppenheimer Funds indicates that women are more likely to recognize their lack of investment knowledge than men and be willing to ask for assistance. This is important because demographic trends indicate that 90 percent of all women will be responsible for their own finances at some point during their lives.[2]

Women need to be prepared to take charge of their financial lives. Although women's lack of cultural role models has been a psychological barrier to achieving this goal, another challenge has been that most women have not had financial independence until relatively recently. There is strong evidence that the challenges facing women in achieving their financial goals have become less of an obstacle as women break through other barriers in life.

- In 2004, women represented 46 percent of the total United States labor force.[3]
- The number of women-owned businesses is growing at twice the rate of all U.S. businesses.[4]
- Women control 51.3 percent of the nation's investment wealth.[5]
- American women occupy 13.6 percent of all board seats and five chief executive positions in Fortune 500 companies, and they also occupy 7.1 percent of CFO and 1.6 percent of CEO positions at the 500 largest companies.[6]
- Women's wealth is expected to reach $22 trillion in the next decade.[7]
- Women make up 40 percent of all Americans with gross investable assets of more than $600,000.[8]
- The number of wealthy women in America increased by 68 percent from 1996 to 1998, compared with a 36 percent increase for men.[9]
- In the United States, more than one-third of baby boomer women are likely to be single when they retire.[10]
- Every eleven seconds a woman opens a new business.[11]
- Today, women business owners employ almost 28 million people— 35 percent more than all the Fortune 500 companies combined.[12]

Yet:

- Women are less likely to receive a pension, and those who do receive a pension collect about half as much as men.[13]
- Only 35 percent of single women have a retirement account.[14]

- Women can expect to live six years longer on average than men, which means they'll need to plan to have more money for their retirement years.

WHAT DOES MONEY MEAN TO YOU?

For many of us, money is never just money. It can represent love, power, happiness, security, and self-esteem. As a result, we have intense feelings about money, feelings we often hide from, which prevent us from dealing with it productively.

Just as our feelings about money can vary, so too, can our behaviors. Some people hoard money while others spend it freely. Some are responsible about attending to daily financial management tasks, while others avoid these tasks and responsibilities as much as possible. Some people don't invest their money at all, others very conservatively, and still others take great financial risks.

It is important for each of us to know our issues surrounding money so that we are more aware of how a specific investment strategy may affect us emotionally, before we invest in it. **Regardless of the potential gain expected from an investment strategy, it is not a good strategy for you if it makes you uncomfortable.**

In the initial data-gathering sessions with my clients, we go through a series of exercises designed to help assess their feelings about money. In one of these exercises, the client describes what she perceives to be her strengths and weaknesses in dealing with money. I ask that my clients refer to this list periodically during and after their divorce process to help them understand what they are feeling about their finances and how these emotions may affect progress toward their financial goals.

Another exercise I ask my clients to complete is the Moneymax© questionnaire. This tool is a financial personality profiling system available at *www.financialpsychology.com*. The questionnaire was developed by Kathleen Gurney, Ph.D., founder and CEO of Financial Psychology Corporation, and a pioneering expert in the study of psychology and money. The aim of the questionnaire is to help people identify, understand, and work within the boundaries of their unique money-management styles. Each profile will fall into one of nine money-management styles: Achievers, Entrepreneurs, High Rollers, Hunters, Money Masters, Perfectionists, Producers, Optimists, and Safety Players. Analyzing each client's style helps me show the client which of their traits are assets and which traits could actually block their success and peace of mind in dealing with money and investing.

Comparing this analysis with a thorough evaluation of the family's spending habits provides an incentive for women to examine their strengths and weaknesses and to deal honestly with what they see.

Some questions to ask yourself are:

- How did you deal with money as a couple during your marriage?
- What was your role and that of your husband?
- What attitudes do your children have about money?
- How are you similar or dissimilar to the example your parents displayed about money?
- How would people close to you describe you and your money habits (a hoarder or spendthrift, careless or disciplined)?

Olivia Mellan has written an excellent book entitled *Money Harmony: Resolving Money Conflicts in Your Life and Your Relationships.* In her book she gives readers a money personality quiz that goes even further with this concept than the exercises I use in my planning sessions. I recommend that each of my clients take this personality quiz and share their results with me. Mellan talks about common money myths, which include:

- Money equals happiness
- Money equals love
- Money equals power
- Money equals freedom
- Money equals self-worth
- Money equals security

She believes, as I do, that first we need to identify those money myths that have been important in our lives and our marriages and see how they are affecting us. Next, we must spend some time debunking these money myths. Only then will we be free to use money and make decisions about our money in a way that enhances our life rather than constrains it.

Here are some practical tips to help you get started:

- Believe in yourself (Master a task that will build your confidence, such as learning how to program your DVD or VCR to time-record or changing the oil in your car.)
- Make your finances a priority
- Invest as early and as much as you can
- Set, plan, and prioritize realistic short- and long-term goals
- Develop a strong relationship with your financial advisor
- Do your homework
- Ask a lot of questions—and get the answers

- Learn some investment and financial jargon
- Conquer your feelings of inadequacy about money decisions
- Be enthusiastic, outgoing, and visible in your research process
- Learn how to say "No"

At this point in your life, you are the decision-maker, the one determining how your money will be invested. Here is some basic information you will need to help you get started on the right path.

Bonds Versus Stocks—To "Loan" or to "Own"?

When you invest, you are essentially either a loaner or an owner. When you buy a bond, you are making a loan. Buy a stock, and you become an owner.

Bonds

Being a loaner is a more conservative approach than being an owner. When you buy a bond, you are loaning money to the government or a corporation. A bond is basically an IOU for the money loaned. The issuer of the bond promises to return the original amount loaned, referred to as "principal" or "capital," plus, in most cases, will pay you interest. Investors who are interested in current income and preservation of capital or principal are often attracted to bonds.

Bond returns are subject to three main types of risk: *interest rate risk*, *credit risk*, and *inflation risk.*

Interest rate risk occurs when interest rates fluctuate. When interest rates move higher, the prices of bonds generally move lower. When interest rates decline, bond prices usually rise. Generally, the shorter the maturity of the bond, the less the price will fluctuate because of interest rate changes.

The credit risk of bonds reflects the ability of the issuer to repay the face amount of the bond as promised. The underlying risk is that if the business fails, bondholders can lose part or all of their investment. Bonds from lower-quality issuers will generally pay a higher rate of interest, since bondholders must be compensated for assuming additional risk. Such bonds are often referred to as "junk bonds."

Inflation risk is also a factor in holding bonds, since the investor is locked in at a fixed rate of return over the life of the bond, which may be lower than the inflation rate. In this situation, the income from the bond loses purchasing power. The principal is subject to the same risk if the bond's total return does not exceed the rate of inflation.

Stocks

When you buy a stock, you become a part-owner in the company that has issued the stock. Stocks can pay investors in two ways. Companies that issue stock can distribute income by paying dividends. If the company prospers, the shares themselves can increase in price. Investors seeking this type of return are interested in growth of capital, sometimes referred to as capital appreciation. If the company does poorly, of course, the shares may decrease in value.

Mutual Funds

Mutual funds are one of the most popular ways to invest. With a mutual fund, your money is pooled with that of other investors to purchase a variety of securities that are professionally managed as a single investment account. Mutual fund portfolios may contain dozens, or even hundreds, of different securities. Many mutual funds even reach beyond the borders of the United States to include global opportunities. When you buy a share of a stock mutual fund, you are actually buying an investment in the stocks of many different companies. Mutual funds allow people with similar goals to pool their resources to get professional management and greater diversification than they could as individual investors. If your resources were such that you were able to buy only one or two individual stocks or bonds, you would need to place all your faith in just one or two companies. It's better to spread your risk by buying stock in a wide variety of companies, but only a few individuals can afford to do that by investing in individual securities. Investing in a single share of a common stock mutual fund provides partial ownership in dozens of companies—often a hundred or more—resulting in a diversification of the investor's assets. Someone who invests $1,000 in a mutual fund owns a piece of the same securities as a person who invests $1 million in the same mutual fund.

Mutual Funds Offer Various Investment Objectives

Some people want to make money gradually and are unwilling to put up with significant bumps along the way. Others are willing to accept significant fluctuations in hopes of greater returns for the risk they undertake. Mutual funds invest in different types of securities to help meet many specific objectives. You can choose from thousands of stock, bond, balanced, and money market mutual funds. Money market securities are essentially short-term IOUs issued by corporations and governments, typically for large values. Since they are large investments, most investors can only invest in them through pooled purchases of mutual funds. One exception to this is government treasury bills. Each fund is managed toward a particular investment objective, specifically growth, income, or asset preservation. The mutual fund's prospectus will explain the fund's investment objective and tell you what securities the fund holds.

Advantages of mutual funds include:

- Diversification: When people talk about using diversification as a means of reducing investment risk, what they are really saying is "Don't put all your eggs in one basket." That's one reason mutual funds are included in most company retirement plans. They are the essence of diversification.
- Professional management: Managing investments requires a commitment of time, resources, and expertise, which most individuals don't have. A mutual fund's investment advisor determines which securities should be bought or sold to best serve the fund's objectives. These decisions are based on extensive, ongoing research.

Is It Better to Be a Loaner, an Owner, or a Combination of Both?

The answer to this question depends on a variety of factors, including how many years will pass before you need your money and how much risk you are willing to bear in exchange for the potential rewards.

You can start to make your decision by looking at some examples from the past. History is the only experience on which investors can draw. Keep in mind that history may not repeat itself and can only serve as a guide.

Figure 12.1 gives you a look at how $1,000 has grown in various investment and savings vehicles over the past ten and twenty years.

As you can see, an investment in stocks would have done best in three of the four time periods. If you have a low tolerance for even short-term losses, a significant portion of your investment dollars placed in bonds or other short-term savings may make more sense for you than a 100 percent investment in stocks. These figures are historical. In the future, of course, there may be periods—even long periods—when bonds or savings accounts outperform stocks.

RISK VERSUS RETURN

As we look at the historical returns of different investment categories, an important pattern emerges. There is a fundamental relationship between risk and return. In exchange for more risk, you should expect

How $1,000 Has Grown							
Over the Past	Stocks	Average Annual Return	Bonds	Average Annual Return	Savings	Average Annual Return
5 YEARS	$890	-2.30%	$1,416	7.21%	$1,127	2.42%
10 YEARS	$3,126	12.07%	$1,995	7.15%	$1,440	3.72%
15 YEARS	$4,743	10.94%	$2,854	7.24%	$1,808	4.03%
20 YEARS	$11,983	13.22%	$4,754	8.11%	$2,560	4.81%

All figures through 12/31/2004 with dividends reinvested or interest compounded.

Stocks: Standard and Poor's 500 Composite Index
Bonds: Lehman Brothers Intermediate Government/Credit Bond Index
Savings: 30 Day Money Market Index - All Taxable

All Data Provided by Thomson Financial Company. All Rights Reserved.

FIGURE 12.1   The Growth of $1,000 in Various Investment Vehicles

greater returns. How much risk you can or should tolerate will depend on your personal circumstances, the amount of time you can leave your investment untouched, and the stamina it takes to watch the value of your investments go up and down with the markets.

Risk Tolerance

Your comfort level with risk is an important consideration in any investment decision. As I have discussed, increased return is almost always accompanied by additional risk. Increased knowledge about risk and an objective evaluation of your individual situation will allow you to determine how much risk is acceptable to you.

To help assess your tolerance for risk, consider these questions:

- Are you comfortable with the possibility that your investment may decline in value tomorrow or a week or a year from now?

- Would you find it easy to add to your investment as it was declining in value?
- Do you feel you could insulate yourself from the emotional reactions caused by volatile markets that lead so many investors to buy and sell at the wrong times?
- If your account value declined 10 percent six months after starting your long-term investment program, would you be able to retain your original, long-term perspective and hold on to the investment?

If you answered yes to most or all of the questions above, you are well positioned to assume some risk in your investment program in pursuit of higher returns. If you answered no to most or all of the questions, it does not mean you should not invest. You may want to choose lower-risk investments and be willing to accept the resulting lower returns.

How Much Risk Are You Taking When You Invest? Can You Reduce Risk?

Risk is a scary word. Experienced investors know that risk and potential reward go hand-in-hand. That's why they are willing to put up with the fluctuations they experience when investing. They try to reduce risk by following two key guidelines:

1. Invest for the long term
2. Diversify holdings

Diversification as a Risk Reducer

In three of the last five years, and in three of the last ten years, bonds have had higher annual total returns than stocks. Over the past thirty calendar years, bonds beat stocks eleven times and international stocks beat U.S. stocks thirteen times.[15] There are similar comparisons to be made between small and large company stocks, as well as short- and long-term bonds. Since you cannot predict which asset class, company size, or sector of the U.S. economy or foreign markets will do better year by year, it makes sense to consider a diversified portfolio of all investment assets available. You can take advantage of the long-term growth potential of stocks in various markets while benefiting from the relative long-term stability that can be provided by bonds.

Measuring Your Return

Investment returns can be the combination of dividends, interest income, and the gain or loss in the investment. It is important to note that until you actually sell the investment, changes in value are just on paper or unrealized.

RETIREMENT FUNDS: HOW MUCH IS ENOUGH?

If you have been counting on monthly Social Security checks as the basis for your retirement income, you'll probably discover that they won't be enough. Experts on retirement planning vary in their estimates of how much income will be needed at retirement to maintain your lifestyle. A common estimate is 85 percent of what you earn immediately before retirement. According to the Employee Benefits Research Institute, Social Security and traditional pension plans are likely to provide less than half of that amount.

In theory, many of your expenses should decrease once you are no longer working. The expectation that you will have fewer dry-cleaning bills and won't need to pay for transportation to and parking at your workplace help lead to this notion that you won't need as much money during retirement. Additional leisure activities, travel, or the purchase of a second home can dramatically alter this assumption.

Figure 12.2 shows a simple example of someone who earns $40,000 per year, then retires and receives $14,000 in Social Security. As you can see, retirement planning fills an important need.

Up to this point, you may have shared with your spouse in investing for your retirement. Now you will need to create a new investment plan toward your retirement, using the assets you have received under the QDRO. Do you have a retirement savings plan available at work? Does your employer contribute an amount into the plan for you? Can you contribute to the plan with pretax dollars (before taxes are calculated on your pay)? If so, this might be a good way to begin to achieve your retirement saving goals. Ask your financial advisor to help you determine whether investing in your employer's plan would be a good option for you.

Studies have shown that going through the process of determining how much a person needs to save toward specific retirement goals leads to an increased awareness and focus on doing what it will take to achieve those goals. When asked, many people believe they have sufficient savings and investments to keep them comfortable during their retirement years. Unfortunately, when asked how they came to this conclusion, many people say they guessed. Though estimating your retirement needs is not a

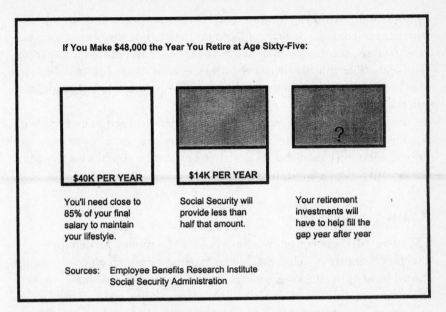

If You Make $48,000 the Year You Retire at Age Sixty-Five:

$40K PER YEAR	$14K PER YEAR	?
You'll need close to 85% of your final salary to maintain your lifestyle.	Social Security will provide less than half that amount.	Your retirement investments will have to help fill the gap year after year

Sources: Employee Benefits Research Institute
Social Security Administration

FIGURE 12.2   Sources of Retirement Income

perfect science, your financial advisor can help you determine the current contributions toward your investments necessary to provide for those needs. Setting reasonable expectations of investment returns, inflation, health care costs, Social Security, part-time income, and living expenses is a big step toward being able to achieve your retirement goals.

When setting your future expectations, please do not underestimate the impact inflation can have on your retirement savings and lifestyle. It's important to keep in mind that the cumulative effect of rising prices can erode the long-term buying power of a dollar. If your savings are not gaining at least as much as the rate of inflation over time, you are losing purchasing power!

WHEN TO CHANGE INVESTMENT OPTIONS

Monitor your needs on an ongoing basis. If your needs change, maybe your investment and asset allocation strategies should, too. Regularly track the performance of your investments to make sure your strategies continue to meet your needs.

Investments in stocks and bonds provide an opportunity for individuals to participate in the growth and development of the nation's businesses, as well as to earn income and build assets for the future. A professional investment advisor can help you answer such questions as whether it is appropriate to participate in those markets at a particular time in your life, whether funds might be better placed in one kind of investment over another or some combination, or what kind of securities products might suit your goals. Selecting an advisor requires the same careful examination, research, and comparison you would make as when you select your attorney and tax advisor.

Investment decisions are not easy, but they don't need to be as difficult as some people would have you believe. Below are some investment tips for you. Develop a plan and stick with it, and you can build a comfortable, secure, and independent retirement.

READY TO INVEST?

The money designated for investing shouldn't be money needed for everyday living expenses. Current living expenses and emergency savings should be kept in checking, savings, or money market accounts or in very short-term certificates of deposit (CDs). If you know you will need a certain amount of money within the next twelve to twenty-four months, either for living expenses or a down payment on a home or a new car, keep this money in one or more of these safer, short-term deposit accounts. Any investment in the stock market or bond market could fluctuate enough in value during a short term to derail your spending plans. Investment in the stock market could reward you with profits, but investors must be prepared to accept the financial risk of declines, even for relatively safe investments. No investment is totally protected from these risks.

One of the first steps is to determine what is wanted from an investment. This determination should be based on four elements: age, lifestyle, cash needs, and the amount of risk you are willing to absorb.

CHOOSING A FINANCIAL ADVISOR

The best source for choosing an advisor has proven to be a personal reference—friends, relatives, or colleagues who have had experience with a particular advisor or advisory firm. You might also ask your attorney or tax professional whether either of them has a relationship with a specific financial advisor or advisory firm. A good working relationship can be important when there is a need to coordinate information and strategies among these professional disciplines. For example, my planning firm, Miller Advisors, Inc., has a division that offers ongoing investment advice and investment monitoring services in addition to the pre- and postdivorce financial planning. For many of our clients, we offer a central point of contact regarding their investments, tax planning, estate planning, and wealth management services, and we coordinate with our clients' attorney(s) and CPA as well as other professionals.

A financial advisor may be an employee or an independent contractor with a brokerage firm that is a member of the National Association of Securities Dealers (NASD). The firm also may be a member of one or more securities exchanges. The Securities Exchange Commission, along with the various exchanges and with the NASD, function as regulators of the securities marketplaces. To qualify for a license, potential advisors must acquire knowledge of the marketplace and pass a demanding exam given by the NASD on behalf of the securities industry.

The First Step

You should interview any potential financial advisor candidate face-to-face. If convenient, visit the firm to be sure it is what it claims to be. Legitimate securities firms work closely with federal and state regulators to rid the marketplace of unscrupulous operators. Be wary of brokers, investment advisors, or financial advisors promising quick and large returns on risk-free investments. The phrase "if it sounds too good to be true, it probably is" has a strong base in reality.

During the interview, ask these questions:

- How long have you been involved in the securities business and in what capacity?
- How long have you been an advisor and what qualifying exams given by the NASD have you passed? (There are many different exams advisors may take, depending upon the kinds of investments in which they are involved.)
- Do you specialize in a particular product or type of client?
- Can you explain your fee and sales charge policies, including how you are compensated on the different products you offer?
- What do you consider your firm's area of expertise?
- How are client-advisor problems and disputes resolved at your firm?
- What additional services do you supply, such as estate planning or tax planning, and at what extra cost?
- How often (how many times a day/week/month) do you talk to your clients?
- Do you generally call your clients or do you expect them to call you?
- Are you easily accessible to answer questions?
- Is there a certain type of client you find difficult to work with?
- Who will handle my needs for information or transactions when you are away?

- What is your general approach: long-term investment or short-term gains?
- Do you have written material about your firm and the investment products you sell? How can they be obtained so I can review them before I make a decision?
- Tell me about your firm: its history and marketplace memberships.
- Where is the nearest office? Where is the firm's headquarters?
- What kind of research reports will I receive and how frequently?
- What other resources and research services do you provide or are available, and at what cost?
- Do you provide a personal investment portfolio report to your clients? How often do they receive this report? May I see an example of one of your reports?

At the end of the interview, ask the advisor for client references, then check them. Contact the references and ask the following questions:

- How long have you used this advisor/firm?
- Why did you select this firm or advisor?
- Are you happy with the performance you've received on your portfolio?
- If anything, what would you change about your relationship with this advisor?
- What makes your partnership work so well?

After Selecting an Advisor

Once you have selected an advisor, schedule another meeting to define investment terms that will be used frequently in conducting transactions. It isn't enough to understand the basics of investing; you need to be sure you and the advisor mean the same when using industry terms. Annually, or semiannually, you should review investment decisions and be sure your advisor is doing a satisfactory job. If there is a problem, discuss it with the advisor or his or her manager.

SUMMARY OF BASIC INVESTMENT TIPS FOR WOMEN

- *Get started now!* It's impossible to stress this point too much! Despite other financial pressures, this can often make the difference in reaching your goal. Stock values appreciate in the long run, so investing over longer periods can help your appreciation potential with managed risk.

- Establish a regular investment program. Even experts cannot predict when prices are low and on the rise. The best strategy is to invest a set amount every month. This approach cannot protect you from loss or guarantee a profit, but it may help lower the average cost of your investment purchases. Buying a security with regularly scheduled purchases will change the price you pay. Over time the average cost of the security may be lower than if you had made a one-time purchase of the entire asset at a single price. This is known as dollar-cost averaging.
- Reinvest returns. By reinvesting distributions from investments, you may be able to increase your account balance over the long term. Assuming a positive return on your investment, you will realize greater benefits from the power of compounding.
- Choose an advisor carefully. Find someone with whom you feel comfortable talking and who answers your questions in a way that you understand.
- Determine your financial needs, such as capital preservation, current income, tax-free income, and growth of capital. Realize your money needs will change as your life changes and as the economy fluctuates.
- Assess your spending habits; make up a budget and follow it. Living within a budget you have set for yourself can help increase your self-confidence with money and keep you on track with your savings plan.
- Decide what your investment goals are before you spend any money. Determine what you will need for college education(s), retirement, and so on.
- Get educated about financial and investment issues. It is not as difficult as you might expect. You probably already know a lot more than you think.
- Assess your risk tolerance. Regardless of the potential return of an investment, you want to be able to sleep at night.
- Don't put all your money in supersafe investments such as savings accounts and certificates of deposits. If you do, inflation will reduce your purchasing power over time.
- Diversify your investments to reduce risk. Compare performance histories, risk factors, and management styles. Focus on the long term.
- Monitor your investments on an ongoing basis. If your needs change, make changes in your investment plan. Ask your advisor for regular reporting.
- Trust your own instincts. If an investment makes you uncomfortable, don't do it.
- Teach your children what you have learned about investing!

Taking control of your postdivorce finances may seem overwhelming. As with the divorce process itself, take it one step at a time. Develop a solid relationship with someone whose advice you trust. Ask questions until you are comfortable with the answers and have confidence in your financial plan. You do not need to become a financial expert to invest successfully—you just need common sense, an open mind, the commitment to stick to a plan, and good advice.

When you have put your postdivorce financial strategy in motion, you will have walked off that escalator I described in chapter 1 on your own power. You will have a new independence and a fresh start in life. Don't forget to enjoy it!

As I close this chapter on fair share divorce, I leave you with one last checklist. If you have followed the suggestions in earlier chapters, the postdivorce checklist should be easy to complete. Use it to keep your new life on track.

POSTDIVORCE CHECKLIST

- Request a written document from your attorney and other experts showing the portion of their fees that is deductible under IRS Code Section 212.

- If your former spouse intends to work with the accountant and financial advisor you had worked with together, ask your friends or business associates if they know of someone else they might recommend for you to work with.

- Prepare income tax estimates with your accountant so that you can begin making quarterly tax payments. Bypassing this important step could cost you IRS fines and penalties when you file your return.

- Create your cash-control system for income and expenses. Try to use the guidelines offered in chapter 7. Follow the program for at least a year in order to make sure that it is appropriate for your situation.

- If the settlement has not addressed the issue of paying the costs of divorce, you should establish a payment plan, included in your budget, which is agreeable with your creditors.

- Use figure 11.4 (see page 240) to make sure that your retirement assets are being transferred in accordance per any Qualified Domestic Relations Orders (QDROs).

- You should also use the worksheet to track the reregistration on retirement and investment assets, including partnerships. You want only your name on the accounts as soon as possible after the divorce documents are signed.

- Redo estate-planning documents, including your personal will, trusts, Durable Power of Attorney, and your Directive to Physicians.

- Hire a financial advisor to help you with your investment allocation, implementation, and monitoring system.

- Request tax cost basis records on any investment or other asset you receive in your settlement. Contact either your former spouse or the appropriate investment advisor for the information. This should really be handled before the divorce is final, but if the information is not collected very soon after the divorce, the tax consequences could be frustrating.

- Assemble your tax returns and the supporting documentation and keep them in a safe place for at least three years.

- As with your tax returns, you should be sure to have all tax cost basis information on your residence. In addition, you should find the last IRS Form 2119 filed with your name on it since it will show whether any gain from the sale of a previous home was postponed.

- Keep good financial records on your children's expenses. Remember that child support may change over time, and you will be asked to provide this information at some point in the future.

- Monitor your career plan, including education and/or subsequent employment, with your career advisor.

Some Final Thoughts

*Learn to get in touch with the silence within yourself and
know that everything in this life has a purpose.*

—Elisabeth Kubler-Ross

This book is filled with information, insight, and advice to help you create
a postdivorce life that is not only livable, but enjoyable and productive.
Not everything in these pages will pertain to you and your situation, but
there are a few things that are universal in each divorce case. The following are some points I hope you will take away with you after reading this
book:

- **Divorce will change your life, but it does not have to destroy your
  life.** A major change such as divorce often brings with it difficulties
  that lead to depression or resentment, especially when you were not the
  one to initiate that change. Although having to rearrange your life can
  present challenges, it can also bring about opportunities. Be open to
  the positive effects of change. You may be surprised as to what comes
  your way.

- **Don't rush through your divorce process.** It took you years to come to
  this point of dissolution. Don't feel pressured to complete the process
  before you're ready. For your own future and that of your children, research options, talk to professional advisors, and even ask the advice of
  friends and family who have been there. You won't know what's best
  for you until you have some real-life information and the opportunity
  to consider the choices you face.

- **Recognize the complexity of divorce.** When you divorce, you are dissolving a relationship that has many facets—physical, emotional, and
  financial. Take time to understand all of these components and especially how they affect one another. Reevaluate what is most important

for you in the future, and then create a plan that helps you work toward creating that reality. Don't dwell on what has gone wrong—that won't help you. Focus your attention on goals that are positive and possible, and then work on moving toward attaining those goals.

- **Don't let yourself become a victim.** Even if you are the "wronged" party in a divorce, don't fall prey to the victim mentality. That kind of thinking can either paralyze you or send you into a downward spiral from which you may never recover. Keep in mind that you are your best advocate. You can help yourself by seeking the advice of such experts as attorneys, financial planners, career advisors, and therapists, learning as much as you can on your own, being organized and proactive, and keeping emotion out of the negotiations. You want to come from a position of confidence and power in your divorce proceedings. Being prepared and savvy are your best tools for securing an equitable divorce settlement.

Remember, no matter where you are in this process, it is never too late to take charge. By following the guidelines found in this book, you will make your divorce—and your postdivorce life—run more smoothly.

I would enjoy your sharing your divorce experience with me—the good and the bad. Please contact me at KMiller@FairShareDivorce.com, or visit either of my Web sites: www.FairShareDivorce.com or www .MillerAdvisors.com. I encourage you to share this book with others facing divorce, so that postdivorce life becomes more financially equitable for everyone involved—women, men, and, most important, the children. We can work together to promote a win-win marital settlement or a fair share divorce.

Appendix A

The Economically Disadvantaged Spouse

In the middle of difficulty lies opportunity.
—Albert Einstein

Case Study—Jake and Judith Jessup

The Jessup case follows the dissolution of a mid-term marriage in which the wife faces financial difficulties as a result of the divorce. It illustrates the importance of documentation, research, and attention to detail in building a case for an equitable settlement.

The following is a summary of my work, including some of the documents used in the negotiations for a property settlement. You will find a great many details in the presentation, some of which may seem irrelevant. I have included them for two reasons:

- They accurately reflect the thoroughness needed in collecting your own family history and financial information.
- If you or your attorney choose to analyze the case in-depth, these details will be needed to understand how the final proposal was developed.

I have used the Jessup case on numerous occasions to demonstrate to my own clients' attorneys the methods I use in completing an analysis. Understanding how the models show the economic impact of various settlement proposals will help you evaluate the choices you face in creating your divorce strategy.

Time Line for Jake and Judith Jessup's Premarital and Married Life

1985   Jake and Judith move in together.

1988   Jake and Judith are married.

1989   Their first son, Sam, is born. Jake agrees that Judith should stop teaching to take care of Sam.

1989   Jake buys the family business from his father. Annual revenues are less than $750,000.

1991   Jacob is born. Late in the year, Judith begins part-time volunteer work for the school district.

1995   Judith decides to work part time as an aerobics instructor. In 1996, she opens J&W Aerobics with a partner.

1998   Frances is born.

1999   Jake pays off the balance of his debt on the business.

2001   Judith's business partner moves away; Judith closes the business and takes on part-time work teaching aerobics.

2003   Judith and Jake separate.

2003   Jake files for divorce.

2003   Temporary alimony and child support orders are issued. Judith receives $3,000 in alimony and $1,500 in child support.

2004   Judith and Jake list the house for sale.

2004   The house sells on June 30, 2004. Judith and Jake decide to rent until the divorce is final and a property settlement is agreed upon.

2004   Judith starts her course of study at the university full time in the fall.

2004   The divorce is finalized in October and the property settlement agreed upon.

2005   Jake and Judith each buy a house. Jake begins settlement note payments.

Summary of Jessup Family	
Husband: **Occupation:** **Education:** **Age:** **Salary:**	Jake Jessup Self-employed owner of family business BA in Business Management Forty-six $156,000 including $15,000 bonus in 2005
Wife: **Occupation:** **Education:** **Age:** **Salary:**	Judith Jessup Homemaker - Teacher for five years after marriage BA in Physical Education, 5th - year certificate Forty-three $8,500 in 2005
Children:	Sam, age fifteen - 10th Grade Jacob, age thirteen - 8th Grade Frances, age six - 1st Grade
Duration of Marriage:	16 years, plus 3 years of cohabitation premarriage
Retirement Contributions:	Jake contributes the maximum in his 401(k) plan Judith contributes the maximum in her IRA
Issues:	▶ Sale of family residence ▶ Purchase of two new residences ▶ Judith's career and education plan ▶ College funding ▶ Retirement funding ▶ Valuation of Northwest Systems, Inc. ▶ Disparity of earnings ▶ Sharing of bonus ▶ Maintenance ▶ Income tax filing status ▶ Five-year cash flow and tax analysis ▶ Five-year general living expenses ▶ Five-year net worth comparison

Copyright © 2005 Miller Advisors, Inc.

FIGURE A.1   Summary of Jessup Family

Characteristics of This Divorce

- Mid-term marriage (sixteen years)
- Judith and Jake are each in their primary working years, with twenty-plus years to retirement
- Judith and the children are competing for future education costs
- Judith wants to be the primary caretaker of the children, working part time outside the home while the children live at home. Her divorce circumstances make delaying her move into the workforce unrealistic.
- Disparity of earnings between Jake and Judith
- Increasing erosion of Judith's married standard of living

The summary on p. 265 serves as a quick reference to the facts regarding the Jessups' income, work skills, ages, and financial issues.

For the first two months of the separation Jake gave Judith $3,000 per month for living expenses and paid the home mortgage. Jake wanted to settle the divorce in ninety days. He proposed that Judith take the house and he would keep the business. They would split the retirement fifty-fifty, and he would pay her three years of alimony at $2,000 per month plus $1,000 per month of child support. (It is not unusual for the person who is planning the divorce to have a settlement plan in mind when he files for divorce.) Judith was not in agreement with Jake and experienced emotional trauma about facing the economic responsibilities of raising the family and finding full-time employment. She needed time to evaluate her position and to create a career and financial plan. She was not willing to be rushed into a divorce settlement.

Judith filed her financial declaration that resulted in $3,000 per month in alimony and $1,500 per month in child support under a temporary order. Realizing Judith had understated many of her budgeted expenses, her attorney recommended she come to see me. We worked together to show how the family of five had historically spent money. From this information, I created the historical budget analysis you saw in chapter 7. From my report, we were able to initiate a motion for reconsideration that resulted in an increase in Judith's support payments to $4,500 per month for alimony while keeping the same $1,500 per month for child support. Judith was to pay the mortgage out of these funds. Over the next six months Judith and Jake worked on the other financial issues in their divorce settlement, including the parenting plan.

By August of 2004 they had each been provided valuations on the marital assets from their experts. Jake made an initial property settlement offer, Judith countered, and the dialogue went back and forth for more than a month. They were scheduled for trial in November of 2004. What follows is their final property settlement agreement. The economic impact of this settlement is analyzed for both parties for a five-year period. There were several areas of disagreement between Judith and Jake; however, through negotiation and mediation they were able to come to an agreement.

The cash flow, living expense detail, income tax analysis, and net worth spreadsheets were used to help them come to a final settlement. I was able to model both of their proposals and help them compromise on the various financial issues. This modeling consists of using the spreadsheets in conjunction with other financial tools to produce a series of "what-if" projections by changing the various assumptions about interest rates, alimony and support payments, wages, expenses, taxes, and investment returns.

Financial Issues

1. Sale of Family Residence

Initially Jake wanted Judith to take the house, and he would keep the business. Once they had gone through the initial phase of the budgeting, the temporary alimony and child-support levels were set by the court, and a careful analysis of the family's historical spending was completed, they both agreed that the current home was too costly for either of them to maintain individually.

They listed the house for sale in January of 2004. The house sold more quickly than they had anticipated and the transaction closed in June of 2004. Judith and Jake were still in disagreement about their overall property settlement and decided to put the house sales proceeds into a *blocked account* until they had finalized the entire property settlement and parenting plan. (It is common to create accounts that require both parties to agree to any withdrawal during divorce proceedings.) They each moved into a rental house and signed six-month leases. Jake paid $1,100 per month while Judith, with the children, had rental payments of $1,375.

2. Purchase of Two New Residences Coordinated with Parenting Plan

In the final property settlement they agreed to purchase two homes. Each would look for a home valued at $250,000. Jake would take out a mortgage for $200,000 and Judith $160,000. Both chose fixed mortgages at

6.5 percent. Given the housing conditions in the areas they chose, and with coordinated timing in the closing terms, both were able to move into their new homes on January 1, 2005.

Throughout the duration of the Jessups' marriage, Judith's role had primarily been that of a homemaker. Although she had been both a business owner and an employee at several area health clubs, she had no significant employment history, which was borne out by the vocational report on her career assets.

Jake requested joint custody of the children, asking that they live with him at least 50 percent of the time. He was willing to hire a driver-housekeeper to assist him in sharing the responsibilities of the children. Judith reacted angrily to this request, feeling that her mothering skills were being questioned, that Jake was "hiring a wife" to replace her, and that he was more concerned about money than the children. Jake, Judith, and the children did see a court-appointed child evaluator, who gave her report to the attorneys just as the certified financial planner, business valuator, and career advisor had done in this case. In the end, Judith retained primary custody, and Jake had generous visitation and shared rights and responsibilities. Once the intense emotions were diffused, everyone was satisfied with the outcome.

Judith and Jake purchased homes in the same school district so that the children would have fewer disruptions when going back and forth between the two homes. They agreed to reevaluate their parenting plan in another year and to have family meetings with the children through counseling to discuss the workability of the parenting plan.

3. Judith's Career and Education Plan

For the three years prior to the divorce Judith worked part time as an aerobics instructor at a local health club. Knowing this would not provide enough income as a career, Judith started working with a career advisor. Judith realized she would have to invest in her future by paying for additional education and by adapting her lifestyle to the realities of a new career (for example, less independence and free time, and more responsibilities for financial management). The career evaluator, Janice E. Reha, summarized Judith in the following manner:

"Ms. Jessup is a competent, energetic woman who is entering the job market at mid-age. Typical of women in her age group, she lacks consistent paid work experience. In addition, many employers are currently hiring part-time and temporary workers to avoid paying expensive benefits and retirement. Ms. Jessup's present employment symbolizes this trend.

"Since the job market is extremely competitive, Judith would benefit greatly by obtaining additional skills and knowledge to sell to an employer. If she were to teach physical education in the high school, her age would likely be a handicap. Also, Judith is concerned about her ability to cope with the physical stamina needed in this position. For this reason, Ms. Jessup is seeking an occupation more suitable to her present and future financial needs.

"According to the results from the inventories, Judith shows strong inclinations toward more enterprising occupations, including sales. Because she has not thoroughly researched this option, Judith intends to gather more information about this broad field and simultaneously begin to take business-related classes to gain a more theoretical basis as well.

"I believe that Judith has the determination and motivation to achieve her goals. In the past she has performed well in her educational endeavors. Once she has reached more resolution emotionally about this divorce, I think that Judith will be ready to achieve her goals of economic self-sufficiency. In the interim, she will need financial support to help her overcome both the internal and external obstacles that impede this process. I strongly encourage her to seek counseling to help facilitate her in bridging the transition from marital to single status."

The vocational report completed by Judith's career advisor was used by attorneys and by Judith as a guideline for her anticipated college expenses, her reentry into the job market, and as a basis to determine her future earnings.

4. College Funding

Jake and Judith agreed to share in the funding of their children's college education based on a pro rata (proportional) share of their adjusted gross income. Each of the children has $10,000 in a college fund provided by their grandparents. Jake and Judith have agreed to fund up to $10,000 per year in today's dollars for each child's undergraduate education. This funding includes tuition, books, lab fees, travel, an allowance, and miscellaneous expenses. Both Jake and Judith want the children to pay for part of their own education.

5. Retirement Funding

Jake sees funding for his retirement coming from the following sources:

- The company funds up to 15 percent of employee compensation in a profit-sharing plan. This contribution is voluntary and is paid only if there are profits in the company and management. Jake, as the owner, makes that determination.

- Northwest Systems, Inc., also started a 401(k) plan five years ago and Jake has been contributing the maximum allowed into this plan.
- As an executive, Jake expects to receive a cash bonus from Northwest Systems, Inc.
- Jake hopes to sell the business to his son in a few years or to an outside person when he retires.

Judith will make the maximum contribution each year to her Individual Retirement Account (IRA) and will participate in whatever form of pension or retirement benefits is available once she obtains employment.

Jake and Judith recognized that Judith's ability to fund her retirement from her earnings would be limited; therefore, she received their current retirement assets in the property settlement.

6. *Valuation of Northwest Systems, Inc.*

Jake and Judith each hired their own expert to value the family-owned business. The valuations differed by $75,000. They agreed to settle on a price halfway between the amount of the two valuations.

7. *Disparity of Earnings*

Jake and Judith are aware of the difference in their future earning power. The disproportionate share of assets to Judith and five years of alimony were given as consideration for this disparity.

8. *Sharing of the Bonus*

Jake did not wish to share his bonus with Judith. He insisted there was no guarantee the company could afford a bonus each year given the time he spent away from the business during the divorce, his desire to work less in the future, and an unpredictable economy.

Although Jake's argument is a common one when a couple divorces, many judges are skeptical of this line of reasoning. If the divorcing couple can come up with a formula for sharing the bonus, these arguments typically go away.

Judith wanted to share in the growth of Northwest Systems, Inc, as she had shared in the building of the company during the marriage. They finally agreed to assume that Jake's cash bonus would be $15,000 per year for the next five years for purposes of calculating their individual cash flow, taxes, and net worth. Jake would keep the entirety of his bonus, but agreed to pay alimony for five years (the first three years are nonmodifiable, meaning that neither party can request changes to the amount set in the agreement) and 75 percent of Judith's college expenses as outlined in her vocational report.

9. Alimony

Alimony is a part of the Jessup settlement. Jake will pay this alimony as follows:

- 2 years at $4,500 per month ($54,000 per year)
- 1 year at $4,000 per month ($48,000 per year)
- 1 year at $3,000 per month ($36,000 per year)
- 1 year at $2,000 per month ($24,000 per year)

This income is taxable to Judith and tax-deductible to Jake.

10. 2004 Income Tax Filing Status

The Jessups did not file jointly in 2004 because there was a cost savings in finalizing the divorce in 2004 and filing separate returns. The income tax savings comes from utilizing the lower tax brackets twice, and, since Jake has deductible alimony payments, his marginal tax bracket drops. Judith's marginal tax bracket increases, but not enough to offset the benefits of filing separately.

11. Five-Year Income Tax and Cash-Flow Analysis

A five-year income tax and cash-flow analysis was completed for the Jessups based on assumptions that were discussed in the property settlement negotiations. See the assumptions for this analysis on pp. 277–80 for more detailed information.

12. Five-Year General Living Expense Detail

In chapter 7, I showed you how to complete a comprehensive analysis of your historical spending and used the Jessup family as our example. We then created a temporary budget for Judith Jessup, which was used as a basis for her revised alimony and child support request. Finally, we created a postdivorce budget for Judith based on her changing economic circumstances.

We provided Jake and Judith with a proposed postdivorce budget that included other new living expenses. These budgets serve as a guideline by both Jake and Judith in their postdivorce budget planning and are designed to create a fair and equitable postdivorce lifestyle for each of them. Having gone through this process, both realize life is going to be different for each of them in the long-term, although Judith's adjustments are likely to be greater than Jake's.

13. Five-Year Net Worth Comparison

The purpose of this analysis is to project realistic estimates of the future net worth of both Jake and Judith in five years. The assumptions used in this analysis are conservative. They represent a "what-if" scenario, incorporating all the financial information prepared throughout the financial analytical process. The goal is to create a win-win strategy for both spouses.

Judith has time to complete her education and find full-time employment. We believe a five-year projection is realistic for a sixteen-year (or mid-term) marriage, plus their three years of living together prior to marrying. By the time the divorce is final, Judith and Jake have been together financially for more than twenty years, nearly all of their adult lives.

Contents for Spreadsheet Analysis on Jessups

- Reallocation of Assets
- Historical and Projected Wages
- General Living Expense Detail (Postdivorce Budget)
- Income Tax Analysis
- Cash-Flow Analysis
- Net Worth Estimates

Reallocation of Assets

Assumptions: A list of the Jessup assets is shown in figure A.2. They agreed upon an overall fifty-five–forty-five split. Jake would owe Judith $72,520 in a settlement note. He would pay no interest on this note in year one and thereafter pay only 7 percent interest each year. The remaining note principal will be due at the end of the sixth year.

| Jake & Judith Jessup — Summary of Assets and Liabilities | | | | | | Wife: 43 Years Old / Husband: 46 Years Old / 16 Year Marriage | |

COMMUNITY PROPERTY							
Assets	JT W/H	Value Date	Present Position	Debt	Net Equity	Judith	Jake
Real Estate							
1 Home Value	JT		475,000	(320,000)	155,000	125,000	30,000
2 Expense of Home Sale	JT			(33,250)	(33,250)	(33,250)	0
Total Real Estate					121,750	91,750	30,000
Retirement Assets							
3 Company Profit Sharing Plan	H		104,000		104,000	104,000	0
4 Company 401(k) Plan	H		60,000		60,000	60,000	0
5 IRA - Jake	H		4,380		4,380	0	4,380
6 IRA - Judith	W		5,670		5,670	5,670	0
Total Retirement Assets					174,050	169,670	4,380
Investment Assets							
7 Checking and Savings	JT		4,500		4,500	4,500	0
8 Money Market Fund	JT		41,000		41,000	21,750	19,250
9 Investment Account	JT		50,000		50,000	27,500	22,500
10 Tax Loss Carry Forward 2005	JT					50%	50%
Total Investment Assets					95,500	53,751	41,751
Business							
11 Northwest Systems, Inc	JT		315,000		315,000	0	315,000
Total Business Assets					315,000	0	315,000
Personal Property							
12 SUV	JT		18,000	(12,000)	6,000	6,000	0
13 Mirage Ski Boat	JT		22,000	(10,500)	11,500	0	11,500
14 Personal Property	JT		32,000		32,000	22,000	10,000
Total Personal Property					49,500	28,000	21,500
15 Settlement Note - Jake to Judith						72,520	(72,520)
TOTAL			1,131,550	(375,750)	755,800	$ 415,691	$ 340,111
Percentage Allocation					100%	55.00%	45.00%

For settlement purposes only.   Copyright © 2005 Miller Advisors, Inc.

FIGURE A.2   Summary of Assets and Liabilities

Historical and Projected Wages

Assumptions: The only assumption for this model is in the projection of income. Both parties have an assumed wage growth rate equal to our assumed inflation rate, or 3.5 percent.

Jake and Judith Jessup
Historical and Projected Wages

Assumed Wage Growth = 3.5 percent

				GROSS WAGES			
Year	Jake's Salary	Jake's Bonus	Judith's Salary	Total	Jake's % of Total	Judith's % of Total
2001	$ 86,000	$ 14,000	$ 3,000	$ 103,000	97%	3%
2002	112,000	18,000	4,000	134,000	97	3
2003	140,000	10,000	8,500	158,500	95	5
2004	150,000	15,000	8,500	173,500	95	5
2005	156,000	15,000	3,000	174,000	98	2
2006	161,460	15,000	3,000	179,460	98	2
2007	167,111	15,000	3,000	185,111	98	2
2008	172,960	15,000	3,000	190,960	98	2
2009	179,014	15,000	48,000	242,014	80	20
2010	185,279		49,680	234,959	79	21
2011	191,764		51,419	243,183	79	21
2012	198,476		53,218	251,694	79	21

SUMMARY OF HISTORICAL & PROJECTED WAGES

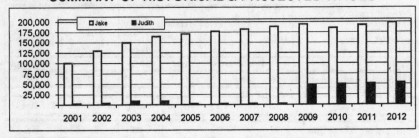

Notes
- ▶ Both parties have agreed to an estimated annual bonus of $15,000 per year for the next 5 years.
- ▶ Judith has agreed to give up any share of future bonus compensation in exchange for Jake paying her college expenses, tuition, books and lab fees.

For settlement purposes only.   Copyright © 2005 Miller Advisors, Inc.

FIGURE A.3   Historical and Projected Wages

General Living Expense Detail

Assumptions: Judith and Jake have agreed on the figures as proposed for their postdivorce general living expenses. As you compare the temporary budget to the postdivorce budget, note that the mortgage payment is now included only in the income tax and cash-flow analysis. In addition, I have

Post Divorce Annual Living Expenses for
Jake and Judith Jessup

5.1 HOUSING	Judith	Jake		5.5 TRANSPORTATION	Judith	Jake
1. Rent, 1st Mortgage/Line of Credit	*(See Cash Flow)*			1. Vehicle Payments or Leases		Company Pays
2. Improvements - Repairs				2. Insurance & License	1,206	
3. Real Estate Taxes	2,250	2,250		3. Gas, Oil, Ordinary Maint.	2,600	
4. Insurance	500	500		4. Parking	420	120
5. Installment Payments for Furniture	500	1,200		5. Repairs	720	
6. Yard Care and House Repair	600	600		**Total 5.5 TRANSPORTATION**	**4,946**	**120**
Total 5.1 HOUSING	**3,850**	**4,550**		**5.6 HEALTH CARE**		
5.2 UTILITIES				1. Insurance	2,100	
1. Heat (Gas and Oil)	1,600	960		2. Unins. Dental, Ortho, Med., Eye Car	480	3,000
2. Electricity	900	900		3. Counseling after Copay	2,880	
3. Water, Sewer, Garbage	600	500		4. Prescriptive Drugs	600	600
4. Telephone/Cell Phone	1,200	900		**5.6 HEALTH CARE**	**6,060**	**3,600**
5. Cable	500	500		**5.7 PERSONAL EXPENSES**		
Total 5.2 UTILITIES	**4,800**	**3,760**		1. Clothing/Accessories	2,400	2,400
5.3 FOOD & SUPPLIES				2. Personal Care, Cosmetics, Hair Care	1,200	600
1. Food	9,600	6,000		3. Clubs, Recreation	1,380	1,200
2. Supplies (Paper, Tobacco)	1,200	600		4. Education *(See Cash Flow Report)*		
3. Meals Eaten Out	2,000	3,600		5. Books, Newspapers, Magazines	480	300
4. Pet Care	720			6. Gifts	1,200	600
Total 5.3 FOOD AND SUPPLIES	**13,520**	**10,200**		7. Entertainment, Vacations	1,800	900
5.4 CHILDREN				**Total 5.7 PERSONAL EXPENSES**	**8,460**	**6,000**
1. Child Care				**5.8 MISCELLANEOUS**		
2. Clothing	3,600			1. Life and Disability Insurance		720
3. Other Child Related Expenses				2. Bank and Credit Card Fees	120	120
4. Health Care				3. Federal Taxes	Incl. in Cash Flow	
5. School Expenses				4. Donations	500	
6. Tuition				5. Professional Fees	1,000	
7. Personal Expenses	12,000	6,000		**Total 5.8 MISCELLANEOUS**	**1,620**	**840**
8. Gifts for Friends						
9. Transportation						
Total 5.4 CHILDREN	**15,600**	**6,000**		**TOTAL EXPENSES**	**56,780**	**35,070**

For settlement purposes only.   Copyright © 2005 Miller Advisors, Inc.

FIGURE A.4   Postdivorce General Living Expenses

included expenses for items for which Jake and Judith are assuming responsibility, such as Judith's future anticipated health insurance expenses. Note also that both Jake and Judith have adjusted their expenses to reflect their current requirements based on their estimates in their new living environments. For instance, Judith has adjusted her budget for her gas heat from $100 per month down to $75 per month, based on an estimate obtained for her new residence.

In each subsequent year, most living expenses increased by an assumed inflation rate of 3.5 percent. However, it is assumed that medical expenses increase by 8 percent per year to reflect current trends in the industry. Since Judith and Jake have agreed that all other expenses grow with inflation, I made no additional rate assumptions. I could also vary the growth rate for real estate taxes, which tend to vary differently from inflation, should there be a need for multiple projections.

Jake and Judith Jessup
Income Tax Analysis

AGE:	Year 1		Year 2		Year 3		Year 4		Year 5	
	46	43	47	44	48	45	49	46	50	47
INCOME SOURCES by Year	Husband	Wife	Husband	Wife	Husband	Wife	Husband	Wife	Husband	Wife
1 Gross Corporate Income/Wages	156,000	3,000	161,460	3,000	167,111	3,000	172,960	3,000	179,014	48,000
2 Bonus Income	15,000	0	15,000	0	15,000	0	15,000	0	15,000	0
3 Pension(Contribution)	(15,000)	(4,000)	(15,000)	(4,000)	(15,000)	(5,000)	(15,000)	(5,000)	(15,000)	(5,000)
4 Maintenance(Payment)/Income	(54,000)	54,000	(54,000)	54,000	(48,000)	48,000	(36,000)	36,000	(24,000)	24,000
5 Investment Income - Interest - Dividends	544	1,344	770	1,312	943	1,353	993	1,071	1,504	272
6 Long Term Capital Gains	0	0	0	0	0	0	0	0	0	0
7 Taxable Social Security Income	0	0	0	0	0	0	0	0	0	0
8 **Adjusted Gross Income:**	102,544	54,344	108,230	54,312	120,054	47,353	137,953	35,071	156,518	67,272
PERSONAL EXEMPTIONS:	(3)	(2)	(3)	(2)	(3)	(2)	(3)	(2)	(3)	(2)
9 Personal Exemptions	(9,600)	(6,400)	(9,600)	(6,400)	(9,600)	(6,400)	(9,600)	(6,400)	(9,600)	(6,400)
10 Personal Exempt Adjustment	0	0	0	0	0	0	0	0	(768)	0
DEDUCTIONS:										
11 Deductible Real Estate Taxes	2,250	2,250	2,329	2,329	2,410	2,410	2,495	2,495	2,582	2,582
12 Home Interest Expenses	12,934	10,347	12,784	10,228	12,625	10,100	12,454	9,963	12,272	9,818
13 Deductible Medical Expenses	0	0	0	0	0	0	0	0	0	0
14 Misc. Deductible Expenses	0	0	0	0	0	0	0	0	0	0
15 High Income Adjustment	0	0	0	0	0	0	0	0	(317)	0
16 Itemized Deductions (or)	(15,184)	(12,597)	(15,113)	(12,556)	(15,035)	(12,510)	(14,949)	(12,458)	(14,537)	(12,400)
17 Standard Deductions (if greater)	0	0	0	0	0	0	0	0	0	0
18 **TAXABLE INCOME:**	77,760	35,346	83,517	35,356	95,419	28,443	113,404	16,213	133,148	48,472
19 Federal Income Tax:	16,279	6,347	17,891	6,348	21,224	5,311	26,260	3,477	31,788	7,615
20 Capital Gains Tax:	0	0	0	0	0	0	0	0	0	0
21 **NET FEDERAL INCOME TAX:**	16,279	6,347	17,891	6,348	21,224	5,311	26,260	3,477	31,788	7,615
22 *Filing Status:*	S	H/H	S	H/H	S	H/H	S	H/H	S	H/H

For Settlement Purposes Only.   Copyright © 2005   Miller Advisors, Inc.

For illustrative purposes only.

This schedule is an approximation intended for planning purposes only. It is not a substitute for your tax return. Please review with your tax advisor.

FIGURE A.5   Income Tax Analysis

The sum of all general living expenses for each year is carried into the cash-flow analysis presented in figure A.6. Therefore, the growth rate on general living expenses may differ from that of other income and expense items.

Income Tax Analysis

Assumptions:

1. Jake files as a single taxpayer and Judith as head of household.
2. Jake earns $165,000 in total wages and Judith $3,000.
3. Jake pays Judith $54,000 in alimony starting in 2004, the year of their separation, and continues to pay alimony on a declining schedule for the next five years.
4. Jake and Judith have minimal interest income.
5. Jake continues to fund his 401(k) plan with his maximum contribution allowed and Judith funds a $2,000-per-year contribution to her IRA.
6. Jake claims two children and Judith one child.
7. In 2004, Jake takes the interest deduction for the boat and Judith takes the deductions for the house and car.
8. Minimal charitable contributions are made by Judith and Jake. Jake contributes through his corporation.
9. Future itemized deductions are based on the appropriate mortgage interest and taxes for their individual residences and vehicles.
10. Income tax savings come from utilizing the lower tax brackets twice, and since Jake has deductible alimony income, his marginal tax bracket drops. Judith's marginal tax bracket increases, but this not enough to offset the benefits of filing separately.

Cash-Flow Analysis

Assumptions:

1. Jake and Judith each have their base wages increasing at 3.5 percent annually, the assumed rate of inflation for these reports.
2. Judith works part time as an aerobics instructor while going to school. She earns $3,000 per year for four years.
3. Judith starts working full time in year three. Based on the vocational report above, we assume that Judith will be able to find employment with an entry-level salary of $48,000.

Jake and Judith Jessup
Cash Flow Analysis

	Year 1		Year 2		Year 3		Year 4		Year 5	
AGE:	46	43	47	44	48	45	49	46	50	47
CASH INFLOW — Source by Year	Husband	Wife	Husband	Wife	Husband	Wife	Husband	Wife	Husband	Wife
23 Gross Corporate Income/Wages	156,000	3,000	161,460	3,000	167,111	3,000	172,960	3,000	179,014	48,000
24 Bonus Income	15,000	0	15,000	0	15,000	0	15,000	0	15,000	0
25 Pension (Contribution)	(15,000)	(4,000)	(15,000)	(4,000)	(15,000)	(5,000)	(15,000)	(5,000)	(15,000)	(5,000)
26 Maintenance (Payment) / Income	(54,000)	54,000	(54,000)	54,000	(48,000)	48,000	(36,000)	36,000	(24,000)	24,000
27 Investment Income - Interest - Dividends	544	1,344	770	1,312	943	1,353	993	1,071	1,504	272
28 Social Security Income	0	0	0	0	0	0	0	0	0	0
29 **TOTAL CASH INFLOW**	102,544	54,344	108,230	54,312	120,054	47,353	137,953	35,071	156,518	67,272
CASH OUTFLOW	Year 1		Year 2		Year 3		Year 4		Year 5	
30 Federal Income Taxes	16,279	6,347	17,891	6,348	21,224	5,311	26,260	3,477	31,788	7,615
31 Social Security Tax (6.2%)	5,580	186	5,580	186	5,580	186	5,580	186	5,580	2,976
32 Medicare Tax (1.45%)	2,480	44	2,559	44	2,641	44	2,725	44	2,813	696
33 Mortgage Payments	15,170	12,136	15,170	12,136	15,170	12,136	15,170	12,136	15,170	12,136
34 Child Support Payment -/(Income)	18,000	(18,000)	18,000	(18,000)	18,000	(18,000)	18,000	(18,000)	18,000	(11,880)
35 Real Estate Taxes	2,250	2,250	2,329	2,329	2,410	2,410	2,495	2,495	2,582	2,582
36 Post Divorce Living Expenses	29,220	48,970	30,243	50,684	31,301	52,458	32,397	54,294	33,531	56,194
37 Estimated Medical Insurance Payments	3,600	6,080	3,888	6,566	4,199	7,092	4,535	7,659	4,898	8,272
38 Settlement Note Interest Only			5,076	(5,076)	5,076	(5,076)	5,076	(5,076)	5,076	(5,076)
39 Judith - Education Expenses	7,080		7,080							
40 Reduction in spending when children are in college									(2,000)	(4,000)
41 Personal Line of Credit										
42 College Funding as a % of Joint AGI									6,994	3,006
43 **TOTAL CASH OUTFLOW**	99,658	58,012	107,815	55,216	105,601	56,560	106,117	63,333	118,311	72,521
44 **DISCRETIONARY CASH FLOW:**	2,886	(3,668)	415	(904)	14,453	(9,207)	31,836	(28,262)	38,206	(5,249)

For settlement purposes only.   Copyright © 2005 Miller Advisors, Inc.

For illustrative purposes only.

This schedule is an approximation intended for planning purposes only. It is not a substitute for your tax return. Please review with your tax advisor.

FIGURE A.6   Cash-Flow Analysis

ASSUMPTIONS

Real Estate / Other Asset Growth Rate	3.50%	Investment Asset Income (Dividend/Interest)	3.50%	Medical Services Inflation	2.50%	Social Security Increase	5.00%

Real Estate / Other Asset Growth Rate	3.50%	Investment Asset Income (Dividend/Interest)	3.50%	Medical Services Inflation	2.50%	8.00%
Retirement Asset Growth Rate	8.00%	Business Interest Growth Rate	5.00%	Social Security Increase	5.00%	2.00%
Investment Assets Growth (Capital Gain)	5.50%	Inflation Rate	3.50%		

NET WORTH ESTIMATES

AGE:	46	43	47	44	48	45	49	46	50	47
	Year 1		Year 2		Year 3		Year 4		Year 5	
Asset: by Year	Husband	Wife	Husband	Wife	Husband	Wife	Husband	Wife	Husband	Wife
45 Real Estate/Other Assets	250,000	250,000	258,750	258,750	267,806	267,806	277,179	277,179	286,881	286,881
46 Mortgage Balance	(200,000)	(160,000)	(197,765)	(158,212)	(195,379)	(156,304)	(192,834)	(154,268)	(190,119)	(152,095)
47 Retirement Assets	19,380	173,670	35,930	191,564	53,805	211,889	73,109	233,840	93,958	257,547
48 Taxable Investment Assets	21,751	53,751	30,798	52,497	37,737	54,112	39,732	42,852	60,174	10,891
49 Business Assets	315,000	0	330,750	0	347,288	0	364,652	0	382,884	0
50 ADJUSTED ASSETS	406,131	317,421	458,464	344,599	511,256	377,503	561,838	399,604	633,778	403,223
51 Settlement Note	(72,520)	72,520	(72,520)	72,520	(72,520)	72,520	(72,520)	72,520	(72,520)	72,520
52 **Total Assets**	333,611	389,941	385,944	417,119	438,736	450,023	489,318	472,124	561,258	475,743

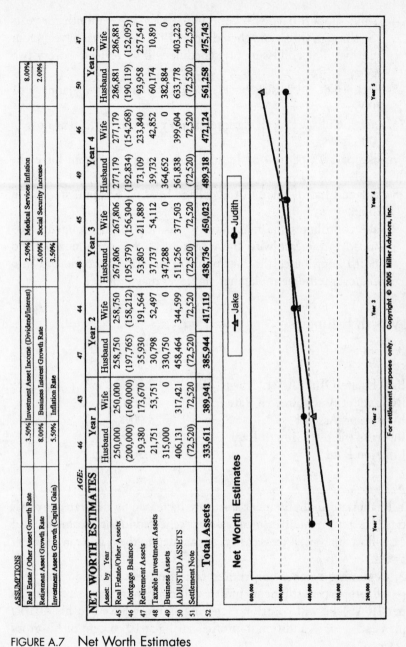

Net Worth Estimates

Legend: Jake, Judith

For settlement purposes only. Copyright © 2005 Miller Advisors, Inc.

For illustrative purposes only.

This schedule is an approximation intended for planning purposes only. It is not a substitute for your tax return. Please review with your tax advisor.

FIGURE A.7 Net Worth Estimates

4. Child-support payments continue at $1,500 per month for years one through three, and then drop to $983 per month in years four and five. The child-support schedule will be reviewed every two years.

5. Both Jake and Judith have mortgages that start in January of 2005.

6. Judith will start receiving interest only on the settlement note in 2006.

7. Jake pays 75 percent of Judith's college expenses from his earnings.

8. Jake and Judith share in the college funding for Sam starting in 2009.

9. Jake contributes the maximum to his 401(k) plan annually (assumed to increase with the wages at 3.5 percent annually), and Judith contributes the maximum to her IRA account and into whatever retirement plan her employer may provide.

Net Worth Estimates

Assumptions:

Real Estate/Other Asset Growth Rate	3.50%
Retirement Asset Growth Rate	8.00%
Investment Assets	8.00%
Business Interest Growth Rate	5.00%
Inflation Rate	3.50%

Notes to Net Worth Estimates:

1. Real estate and retirement assets are increased by the stated growth rate. The return on investment assets is reflected in the income tax and cash-flow analysis. Excess cash flow is added to the taxable investment assets.

2. Beginning balances on retirement assets are based on the proposed property settlement. Judith will contribute the maximum to her IRA; Jake will contribute the maximum allowed to his 401(k) plan each year in addition to profit-sharing at 10 percent of his gross wages.

Conclusion

The net worth analysis is the summary of all of the assumptions made in these reports for the five-year projections for the Jessups. The results of my analysis, while limited to the assumptions we made, show that it is possible, given current and potential earnings, to divide the assets to allow for the economic growth of both parties. The Jessups agreed to the terms of my settlement proposal in the final mediation session.

These terms provide for a reallocation of the assets that favors Judith in the very short term, allocating 55 percent of marital assets to Judith, along with five years of alimony on a declining scale. We feel this level of alimony is fair and compensates her for lost career opportunities. Another adjustment to the net worth of both parties will occur when Jake must pay the principal balance on the judgment note at the end of the fifth year. The 2009 net worth for both parties, adjusted by the principal on the note, is $561,258 for Jake and $475,743 for Judith.

The payment of the settlement note will be absorbed so that Jake's net worth will still have increased over the five-year period. In addition, due to Judith's income level beyond the five years—it is likely that it will never equal or exceed Jake's income—Jake will once again begin quickly to increase his net worth.

If Judith does not go to an accredited school and earn her master's in business administration or a comparable degree, Jake does not pay for her educational expenses. Jake can earn unlimited income in his business and Judith can take on more clients for personal training. The children intend to live with Judith; however, that could change over time. Child support will be reviewed every two years.

Life is not static. Future projections are a "what-if" blueprint based on reasonable assumptions that both parties and their attorneys can agree upon.

VOCATIONAL REPORT

for

MS. JUDITH JESSUP

August 31, 2005

FIGURE A.8   Vocational Report for Judith Jessup

NAME: Judith (Judy) Jessup

ADDRESS: 20925 N.E. 142nd St.
                Woodinville, Washington 98072

PERSONAL HISTORY

Sessions: 6

Education:

2005	Computer-related classes, Bellevue Community College, Bellevue, WA
1995	Aerobics National Test Certification, ACE
1985	Teaching Certification, Washington State University, Pullman, WA
1984	Bachelor of Arts degree in Physical Education and Health, Washington State University, Pullman, WA
1980	High School Diploma, Wenatchee High School, Wenatchee, WA

Behavioral Observations:

Judy presented herself as an outgoing, slender, slightly harried middle-aged woman who indicated that she was quite apprehensive about becoming a single parent. As a parent of three children she reported feeling hesitant about returning to the workplace or school on a full-time basis. She still wants time to remain involved in her children's activities. Therefore she feels conflicted about having to incorporate the role of financial wage earner along with roles of primary parent and homemaker. She proved to be responsible and diligent about completing her assignments and appeared at each session on a timely basis. She asked appropriate questions and for guidance as needed.

Social History:

Judy was born on May 15, 1962, and is forty-three years old. Judy and Jake Jessup were married on January 28, 1989, and have been married sixteen years. Jake is Owner/President of Northwest Systems, Inc., which is a distributor of forklifts and other heavy machinery. He nets approximately $156,000 yearly. He has his Bachelor of Arts degree in Business Management from Seattle University. They have three children: Sam, who is fifteen; Jacob, who is thirteen; and Frances, who is six. The children currently reside with their mother in the family home.

Emotional Status:

Judy has been experiencing some depression and anxiety resulting from the transition. She has sought counseling and would benefit from more in-depth therapy to assist her with coping with her new single status. She also is taking an antidepressant prescribed by her physician.

FIGURE A.8   *(continued)*

Physical Status:

Judy reports being in generally good health. She had to undergo knee surgery in 2002 and now cannot stand for extended periods of time. Also, she will have to limit her engagement in vigorous physical activities.

Work History:

Paid:	2000–2002	Aerobics Instructor, Bellevue Community College, part time, $33 an hour.
	1998–1999	Aerobics Instructor, Seattle Athletic Club, part time, $25 an hour.
	1996–2001	Owner/Instructor, J&W Aerobics (part time).
	1993–1998	Aerobics Instructor, King County Parks & Recreation, part time, $25 an hour.
	1985–1990	Junior High Teacher and coach of three sports, Bellevue Schools, full time.
Unpaid:	1995–2005	Volunteer in PTA—has held treasurer and secretarial positions for this organization
	1997–2002	Coached volleyball for fifth and sixth graders.

Judy was born in Wenatchee, Washington, and is the oldest of three children. Her father recently sold a sporting goods store he owned in Wenatchee. Her mother taught elementary school and is now retired. One of her siblings is a computer programmer. Her other sibling owns a pet shop.

As a young child, Judy was quite active and enjoyed playing out-of-doors. She recalls being more interested in physical activities than dolls. She also tended to be the ringleader in her neighborhood. Her parents called her a "live wire."

Upon entering elementary school, Judy indicated that she liked both learning and the social aspects of school. She had no difficulty comprehending reading or math and was an excellent student. She also participated in Blue Birds and played soccer as well as started skiing. In addition, she engaged in an after-school gymnastics program and competed in various events.

During junior high school, Judy started feeling more self-conscious. She gained weight during this period and was shorter than her classmates. She still performed well academically and particularly enjoyed her math and English classes. Between eighth and ninth grade, Judy grew several inches without gaining weight. She continued her involvement with gymnastics, skiing, and swim meets, excelling in each of these sport activities. During this period her self-confidence improved.

FIGURE A.8   (continued)

In high school, Judy decided to try out for cheerleading and actually was selected due to her athleticism. She stated that she enjoyed her math classes, but found calculus more challenging. She also completed several business classes that she enjoyed. She started working in the family retail store and then became a waitress during the summers. Her family encouraged her to attend college and assisted her with college applications. Judy was interested in attending a college that was within proximity of her home so she chose to attend Washington State University. She graduated from high school in 1980.

While attending Washington State University, Judy participated in the cheerleading squad. As a result, she decided to major in Physical Education, since she had no clear educational objective in mind. While she was involved with cheerleading, Judy became connected with the coaches, who encouraged her to teach all the gymnastic classes. Through this effort, she earned money to pay for some of her education. She also was a vice-president of her class and received payment for this office. In addition she worked for a private organization teaching gymnastic classes. Her industriousness led her to pay off her school loans, as well as to recognition in *Who's Who in American Colleges*. She reports that it is her tendency to overachieve and strive to "get things right." After graduation, she completed her fifth-year certification in teaching. During this period Judy completed her internship in the Bellevue, Washington, school system, where she was subsequently hired as a full-time Physical Education instructor in 1985.

Judy met her spouse in 1985, and they married in 1988. She quit working for the school district when her first child was born in 1989. In 1991, Judith decided to start teaching part time to retain her skills and health. She taught night classes while focusing on her main job of raising her family. The couple's second child was born in 1991 and their third child was born in 1998. In 1994, Judy became involved in aerobics classes and then completed the aerobics certification in 1995. She attempted to develop her own aerobics business, but did not have the time to devote to it. She obtained a position instructing aerobics at a local health club and then for Bellevue Community College. Judy continued working on a part-time basis approximately six to twelve hours a week until 2002, when she had knee surgery for an Achilles tendon. She engaged in physical therapy for one year following the surgery. Consequently she was forced to quit this part-time position.

Since 1995, Judy has been very involved in her children's schools. She also held secretary and treasurer offices in their school's PTAs for several years. In 1997, Judy became involved in an investment club and discovered that she enjoyed researching and successfully selecting various investments. In 2001 the couple started to experience marital difficulties after which they sought counseling. In 2003, they separated briefly. They returned to counseling and continued for six months, at which time they agreed to separate. In August of 2003, Mr. Jessup left the family home. In January of 2005, Judy started taking courses in Microsoft Office at Bellevue Community College.

Some of Judy's personal interests include golfing, participating in an investment club, and attending cultural events. She also enjoys engaging in family activities including hiking and camping.

FIGURE A.8   *(continued)*

PRESENT EARNING CAPACITY, SKILLS, AND FINANCIAL CONSIDERATION

Judy encounters the following obstacles in entering the current job market:

1. Sporadic work history.
2. Concern about her ability to be able to handle both home and work responsibilities.
3. Some physical limitations due to knee surgery.
4. Lack of opportunity to earn an income level equivalent to her spouse's earning and potential.

Judy has only worked on a part-time basis for the last fifteen years. She followed the traditional role of women who remained in the home to provide for the emotional and social support for their families while their spouses provided the family's major financial support. During this period, she was active in volunteering in her children's schools and other community-related activities. Also Judy worked part time to supplement the family income. According to research by Christopher L Hayes, executive director of the National Center for Women and Retirement Research at Long Island University, for every year a person is out of the job market, she loses five years of income potential. Now at the time of divorce, Judy confronts the reality of having lost many years of income and retirement earnings.

As indicated in our sessions, Judy has no desire to return to teaching in the K-12 school system. She prefers teaching adults, however she cannot obtain a full-time position in the college system due to her lack of a Master's in Education. In addition, she has limitation of movement due to her knee surgery, therefore she cannot engage in the level of activity she previously pursued. Finally, her physical stamina may wane as she matures; consequently, a career change is inevitable.

Recently, a new analysis of Census Bureau data released in 2004 by the Institute for Women's Policy Research reflects that the workplace pay gap between men and women has only been getting worse. Women make only 75.5 cents for every dollar that men earn. The General Accounting Office attempts to explain this discrepancy by stating that women are more likely to leave the labor force for longer periods of time than men, further suppressing women's wages. Men with children appear to get an earnings boost, whereas women with children lose earnings. Women have fewer years of work experience. This difference can be demonstrated by comparing Judy's length of full-time work experience with her spouse's.

Having lost some of the most productive years of her career life, from twenty-five to forty, Judy will have a much shorter span of time for either earning an income commensurate with her spouse's or achieving his earning capacity. She will also obtain a lower Social Security benefit so the disparity gap continues well into her retirement years. Note the disparity in benefits at sixty-six for Judy and her spouse based upon earnings of each at this time. His benefit would be $2,300 a month, whereas Judy's would be $1,113. At that time, his benefit would twice as much as Judy's.

FIGURE A.8   *(continued)*

DISCUSSION OF ASSESSMENT RESULTS

The following career instruments were administered to Judy: the Strong Interest Inventory, the Jackson Vocational Interest Survey, the Campbell Interest and Skill Survey, the 16 PF, and the Myers-Briggs Type Indicator.

STRONG INTEREST INVENTORY

Judy scored highest on the Conventional-Enterprising General Occupational Themes. People with interests in these themes enjoy:

- Supporting the work of others, usually in business settings
- Structured, results-oriented work environments
- Being close to the center of power

She scores **Very Similar** and **Similar** Interests to people on the following occupational themes:

Investments managers	Life Insurance Agent
Banker	Small Business Owner
Housekeeping and Maintenance Supervisor	Accountant
Business Education Teacher	Athletic trainer
Physical Education Teacher	Community Services Organization Director

Her **Work Style Scale** score suggests that she may enjoy a balance of working alone and with others working on teams, committees, or group projects.

Her **Learning Environment Scale** score suggests that she is interested in applied or practical problems. She may be interested in short-term training that can teach her practical skills that will help her prepare for a particular job.

Her **Leadership-Style Scale** score suggests that she is interested in assuming a directive leadership style. She is probably outspoken about her opinions and enjoys motivating people toward meeting goals that she has set.

Her **Risk-Taking Adventure Scale** score suggests that she enjoys some risks or adventures now and then. Before jumping into something new, however, she probably wants some time to think about it and to prepare adequately.

FIGURE A.8   (*continued*)

JACKSON VOCATIONAL INTEREST INVENTORY

Judy scored above **85 percent** on the following Basic Interest Scales:

    (94%)   **Business.** Interested in the day-to-day functioning of business and commercial organizations.

    (90%)   **Human Relations Management.** Enjoys acting as "the person in the middle" between people in conflict; enjoys resolving interpersonal situations, including those that are difficult or emotionally charged.

    (88%)   **Planfulness.** Is organized in work habits and prefers working in an environment in which activities occur in an expected sequence.

    (88%)   **Finance.** Interested in meeting the financial needs of the public, in solving financial problems, and in investment and trade.

    (86%)   **Mathematics.** Enjoys working with mathematical formulas and quantitative concepts; interested in performing computations and in planning and applying mathematical methods to the solutions of problems.

    (85%)   **Adventure.** Enjoys novel situations; seeks out the unusual or dangerous.

Judy scored **Similar** and **Moderately Similar** to university students who were enrolled in the following major fields:

Business
Health, Physical Education, and Recreation

She scored **Similar** and **Moderately Similar** to people in the following job groups:

Occupations in Accounting, Banking, and Finance
Personnel and Human Management
Clerical Services
Sales Occupations

FIGURE A.8   *(continued)*

CAMPBELL INTEREST AND SKILL SURVEY

Judy scored **High** interest on the following Orientations:

> **Organizing.** Organizing the work of others, managing and monitoring financial performance.
> **Adventuring**. Adventuring, competing, and risk-taking through athletic, police, and military activities.
> **Influencing.** Influencing others through leadership, politics, public speaking, sales, and marketing.

In consecutive order, Judy scored **Very High** to **High in Interest** compared to people in the following occupations:

Hospital Administrator	Banker	Financial Planner
Insurance Agent	Accountant	Athletic Trainer
Fitness Instructor	Hotel Manager	Marketing Director ,

Her Academic Focus interest score is moderately high and her skill score is moderate. People who have this pattern of scores typically report strong interest and moderate confidence in academic activities, such as studying, conducting research, and writing scientific papers.

Her Extraversion interest score and skill scores are moderately high. People who have scores like hers report moderately strong interest and confidence in work situations requiring a great deal of personal contact with others. Careers with some emphasis on people-oriented activities would be satisfying for her.

16 PERSONALITY FACTORS (PF)

This report reflects the scores on the following scales:

SELF-ESTEEM AND ADJUSTMENT

At the present time, Judy's self-esteem is typical of most adults. Although she is often self-assured and confident, there are other times when she may question her competence and feel insecure.

The degree of emotional stability shown by Judy is typical of most adults. That is most of the time, she tends to be calm and relaxed, but in demanding situations, she may be reactive or upset.

Judy generally feels at ease in social gatherings and may take the initiative in making contracts. Social Adjustment is high-average.

FIGURE A.8   *(continued)*

LEADERSHIP AND CREATIVITY

In a group of peers, Judy's potential for leadership is predicted to be above average. She may possess the pragmatism and self-discipline that characterizes effective leaders.

At the client's own level of abilities, potential for creative functioning is predicted to be average. This does not necessarily indicate a lack of creative ability but may reflect some aspect of motivation, flexibility, or resources.

Judy's personality characteristics differ from those of persons who invest a lot of personal time producing novel or original works. She may be more oriented to quality rather than quantity of output.

VOCATIONAL ACTIVITIES

Judy shows personality characteristics similar to **Conventional** persons, who tend to be methodical, systematic, and extremely precise. Conventional persons focus on practical issues and do not get lost in the world of fanciful ideation.

Occupations Fields: Accounting
                       Clerical Occupations
                       Finances
                       Administrative Occupations

Judy also shows personality characteristics similar to **Social** persons, who indicate a preference for associating with other people. Such interactions are distinguished by a nurturing, sympathetic quality. She may find it easy to relate to all kinds of people.

Occupational Fields: Teaching
                       Counseling
                       Psychology
                       Social Work
                       Health Services

MYERS-BRIGGS TYPE INDICATOR

Judy reflects an **Extroverted Thinking with Introverted Sensing Type (ESTJ).** According to the Introduction to Type description by Isabel Briggs Myers, ESTJ's like to organize projects, operations, procedures, and people, and then act to get things done. They value competence, efficiency, and results. ESTJ's are excellent administrators because they understand systems and logistics. They can project the steps needed to accomplish a task, foresee potential problems, assign responsibilities, and marshal resources. Their orientation is to tasks, action, and the bottom line.

FIGURE A.8   (*continued*)

Occupations that are compatible with ESTJs are the following:

Insurance agent	Budget analyst	Cost estimator
Real estate appraiser	Credit analyst	Project manager
Treasurer, controller, and chief financial officer		

COMPILATION OF ASSESSMENT RESULTS

A major theme that surfaces in the assessment results and Judy's background is the **Conventional** theme. These types of people like activities that require attention to organization, data systems, detail, and accuracy. They often enjoy mathematics and data-management activities such as accounting and investment management. Judy's present and past work experience fits this theme. However, she has indicated that she would prefer a more challenging career and one that offers her greater salary potential. Clerical and personal service jobs tend to pay lower and often do not offer adequate compensation for short-term and more important long-term financial security. Therefore, Judy wants to obtain more specialized education in a career that offers her a greater financial reward.

Another lesser reoccurring pattern in Judy's assessments and work history is the **Enterprising** theme. These types of people enjoy working with other people and leading them toward organizational goals and economic success. Judy's scores reflect some management and sales inclinations. Enterprising people are generally confident of their ability to persuade others and they usually enjoy the give-and-take of debating or negotiating.

A third less distinct theme that emerges in her assessments is Judy's **Social** theme. These types of people like to work with people; they enjoy working in groups, and sharing responsibilities. Central characteristics are helping, nurturing, and caring for others, and teaching and instructing. Judy's choice pursuing education reflects this orientation.

After discussing career options, Judy explored two areas more fully. She researched the human resource field and some areas of finance. After more exploration, Judy decided to pursue the finance field that offered more job opportunity. Since Judy has an undergraduate degree, she decided to obtain a Master's in Business Administration. This degree will offer her greater access into the financial field. She is specifically interested in becoming a financial analyst.

To enter a MBA program, Judy will need to complete prerequisites in accounting, economics, and math. She will complete these classes at Bellevue Community College. Then she intends to transfer to University of Washington, Bothell Branch. If she attends college full time, she will enter a new career direction during her forties, which will be more advantageous for her. It is her desire to enter the workplace as soon as possible to begin advancement in a new field and to fund her retirement.

A more detailed description of her educational and college plans follows in the next section.

FIGURE A.8   *(continued)*

RECOMMENDATION

<u>Career Goal</u>

To become a Financial Analyst.

<u>Educational Goal</u>

To complete a Master's in Business Administration with an emphasis on finance at University of Washington, Bothell Branch.

<u>Plan of Action</u>

Phase One: **Fall 2005 to Spring 2007**

Provide primary parenting for three children
Complete prerequisite classes at Bellevue Community College (eight classes)
Prepare for and complete Graduate Management Admission Test (GMAT)
Continue to participate in counseling to assist with transition

Phase Two: **Fall 2007 to Spring 2010**

Complete Masters in Business Administration degree
Start becoming involved with affiliations and community organizations to develop job contacts

Phase Three: **2010 and beyond**

Obtain a full-time position—may have to start at a lower salary to gain work experience

<u>Educational Costs</u>

Tuition for six quarters at Bellevue Community College	$ 4,728.00
Books and supplies	$ 2,000.00
Tuition at U of W for six quarters	$30,348.00
Books and supplies	$ 6,000.00
New computer and software programs	$ 2,500.00
Total Educational Costs	**$45,576.00**

FIGURE A.8   *(continued)*

Job Outlook and Wages

According to the Washington Occupation Information Service, between 2002 and 2007 the financial analyst occupation is expected to grow about as fast as the average for all occupations in Washington. Employment is projected to increase 10.3 percent during this period.

In Washington, the average entry-level wage for financial analysts is $42,000. Half of all financial analysts earn between $38,598 and $47,823. If the woman is older, the starting salary is normally in the lower range.

CONCLUSION

Judy entered this office overwhelmed and stressed about the prospect of managing the additional role of becoming a primary financial wage earner along with her parenting and homemaking responsibilities. However, in the past seven months she has gained some equilibrium with the benefit of counseling. She appears more ready to cope with her new single parent status.

In the past few months Judy has entered college, completing some computer-related courses, and demonstrating her desire to prepare for additional training. I believe that Judy possesses the characteristics of someone who has leadership and organizational qualities. While attending college, she would benefit from completing an internship in some area of finance to gain experience and a foothold in the job market. She would also benefit immensely from obtaining a minimum of a Master's in Business Administration, thereby increasing her income potential. This degree will also help her overcome some of obstacles to reemployment due to her interrupted career. By doing so, she will demonstrate to an employer that she has the persistence and motivation to enhance her skills. I also suggest that Judy attend college full time so that she can expedite her reentry into the job market.

Financial support during the educational and reentry phase of this career plan will alleviate Judy's financial concerns and increase her chances for achieving financial independence.

I certify, under penalty of perjury, under the laws of the State of Washington that the preceding information is true and correct.

Janice E. Reha, M.A.
Licensed Mental Health Counselor
Bellevue, Washington

FIGURE A.8   (continued)

Appendix B

Long-Term Marriage and Divorce

*The events in our lives happen in a sequence in time,
but in their significance to ourselves, they find their own order . . .
the continuous thread of revelation.*

—EUDORA WELTY

The strategies used to create a win-win settlement in the dissolution of a long-term marriage differ significantly from those used for a mid-term marriage. There are a number of changes in the assumptions used in the calculations. One of the most important considerations is the division of various pensions.

Before we look at this case I want to comment briefly on the software used to create the figures presented in this and the Jessup case in appendix A. I do not use an off-the-shelf packaged program as do many financial planners. While I have tested a number of the programs on the market, none of them provided the depth and flexibility required for my work. Instead, I have developed my own proprietary package, which is augmented by several specialized commercial utility programs. Many of the spreadsheets I use are rather complex and are not designed to be used by someone interested in a do-it-yourself approach to dissolution. Without a background in financial planning for divorce, it would be of little value to most users, so it is not available as a self-help kit. Even after nearly two decades of refinements and thousands of cases, I still find opportunities to "tweak" the system.

The following case study takes you through the complete process for distributing marital assets equitably in a long-term marriage.

Case Study—Gerald and Barbara Hudson

Gerald and Barbara Hudson, fifty-seven and fifty-two, respectively, are divorcing after thirty years of marriage. The following time line summarizes
the events of their marriage:

Time Line for the Hudson Marriage

1972   Gerald and Barbara marry. Gerald works for Boeing and Bar-
        bara is still a student.

1975   Barbara graduates with a B.A. in English and Gerald completes
        his M.B.A. Barbara begins teaching English at a private high
        school.

1977   Son Jason is born. Barbara resigns from her teaching position to
        be the stay-at-home parent.

1978   Son James is born.

1986   Daughter Jennifer is born.

1992   Barbara does substitute teaching at her son's school.

1993   Barbara does substitute teaching part time at her daughter's
        school.

1994   Gerald and Barbara move to Brussels, where Gerald takes a
        three-year assignment.

1996   Barbara teaches English as a second language to Belgian busi-
        nessmen and -women part time.

1997   Barbara works as a substitute teacher after returning to the
        United States.

1998   Barbara teaches three-quarter time at her daughter's school.

2002   Barbara starts teaching full time.

2003   Gerald and Barbara separate in June. They reconcile in October
        for three months.

2004   Gerald moves out in the first week in January. He files for di-
        vorce in February.

Barbara Hudson's Professional Team During Her Divorce Process

- Attorney
- Financial Planner
- Career Advisor
- Actuary
- Appraisers
- Therapist

As Barbara's financial advisor, I have counseled Barbara and her attorney through the financial stages of her divorce as follows:

Initiation Phase

1. Create the historical budget for one year prior to separation.
2. Prepare Barbara's budget to establish need for temporary support, including child support until Jennifer, the only child still living at home, starts college.
3. Select a career advisor.

Analysis and Planning Phase

1. Make an evaluation of marital and separate property assets, including the pension, as of date of separation.
2. Assist Barbara in finding a replacement home.
3. Assist in creating Barbara's postdivorce budget.

With both parties in agreement on the above issues, the next step is to make settlement offers and to respond to those presented by Gerald's attorney.

Negotiation-Settlement Phase

1. Create a written report and a property settlement proposal.
2. Determine how Gerald and Barbara will share additional college funding costs beyond the education trust already set up for their daughter.
3. Analyze the economic impact of the divorce property settlement for Gerald and Barbara.

The following is a sample report prepared by my firm, to be presented by Barbara and her attorney to Gerald and his attorney. I have highlighted those areas of the report that I will explain in detail. Throughout the report, my observations and comments for you, the reader, will be in italics.

Contents

Summary of Hudson Family
Gerald and Barbara—Chronological Summary

Current Status of Hudson Dissolution Negotiations

House Sale Income Tax Calculation—**figure B.1**
Reallocation of Assets—**figure B.2**

Footnotes to Reallocation of Assets and House Sale

Boeing Pension Benefit Analysis

- Methods of Sharing Defined Benefit Pension
- Summary of Pension Income
- Summary of Our Recommendation

Long-Term Cash-Flow Analysis

- Introduction
- Categorization of Assets Assumptions
- Income Sources
  - Retirement Assets
  - Barbara's Income Potential
  - Social Security
  - College Funding
- Cash-Flow Analysis
- Conclusions on Long-Term Cash-Flow Analysis

Need for Life Insurance

Current Status of Hudson Dissolution Negotiations

At the time this report was prepared, Gerald and Barbara had agreed to the following:

1. The house is to be sold and has been listed for three months. Since Barbara will need substantial cash to purchase a replacement residence, she will receive the first $252,025 and the balance

House Sale Income Tax Calculation Gerald and Barbara Hudson		
Gross Sales Price		475,000
Cost of Sale	6.00%	(28,500)
Fix Up Expenses		0
Adjusted Sales Price		446,500
Purchase Price		(205,853)
Remodels		(15,132)
Capital Gains		225,515
Joint Gain Exclusion		(500,000)
Taxable Gain		0
Capital Gains Tax	15.00%	0
Net Proceeds After-Tax		446,500
First Mortgage Balance		(150,000)
Second Mortgage - LOC Balance		0
Net Cash Proceeds		296,500
Net Cash to Wife	85.00%	252,025
Net Cash to Husband	15.00%	44,475

For illustrative purposes only.

This schedule is an approximation intended for planning purposes only.

It is not a substitute for your tax return. Please review with your tax advisor.

Copyright © 2005 Miller Advisors, Inc.

FIGURE B.1   House Sale Income Tax Calculation

of the sales proceeds will be allocated to Gerald to effectuate an agreed-upon property distribution.

2. With the exception of the Boeing pension benefit, all the marital asset values have been agreed upon. The assets are listed in figure B.2.

3. The amount and duration of alimony has to be determined.

<table>
<tr><td colspan="2">Gerald and Barbara Hudson
Summary of Assets and Liabilities</td><td colspan="8">Wife 52 Years Old
Husband 57 Years Old
30 Year Marriage</td></tr>
</table>

COMMUNITY PROPERTY

Assets	JT W/H	Value Date	Present Position	Debt	Net Equity	Barbara	Gerald
Real Estate							
1 Family Home	JT	9/04	475,000	(178,500)	296,500	252,025	44,475
2 Camano Island Log Cabin	JT	9/04	165,000	(50,000)	115,000		115,000
			Total Real Estate		411,500	252,025	159,475
Retirement Assets							
3 IRA - Gerald - US Bank CD	H	9/04	6,100		6,100		6,100
4 IRA - Barbara - Mutual Fund	W	9/04	9,487		9,487	9,487	
5 Boeing VIP - Gerald	H	9/04	348,620		348,620	190,714	157,906
6 Boeing FSP - Gerald	H	9/04	49,855		49,855		49,855
7 Boeing Pension	H	9/04			0	50%	50%
			Total Retirement Assets		414,062	200,201	213,861
Investment Assets							
8 Boeing Credit Union	JT	9/04	50,300		50,300	30,300	20,000
9 Investment Account	JT	9/04	32,426		32,426	21,111	11,315
10 Limited Partnerships at cost	JT	9/04	25,000		25,000	12,500	12,500
			Total Investment Assets		107,726	63,911	43,815
Personal Property							
11 Boston Whaler	JT	9/04	12,000		12,000		12,000
12 Nissan Pathfinder	H	9/04	8,325		8,325		8,325
13 SUV	W	9/04	21,000	(9,832)	11,168	11,168	
14 Gun Collection	H	9/04	8,500		8,500		8,500
15 Antique Doll Collection	W	9/04	5,000		5,000	5,000	
16 Personal Property	JT	9/04	35,000		35,000	25,000	10,000
			Total Personal Property		79,993	41,168	38,825
TOTAL			1,251,613	(238,332)	1,013,281	**$557,305**	**$455,976**
Percentage Allocation					100%	**55.00%**	**45.00%**

SEPARATE PROPERTY

Assets		Value Date	Present Position	Encumbrances	Net Equity	Barbara SEPARATE	Gerald SEPARATE
Real Estate							
17 1/4 Interest in Farm		9/04	80,000		80,000	80,000	
Investment Assets							
18 Bank of America CD		9/04	20,000		20,000	20,000	
19 Washington Mutual Fund		9/04	28,000		28,000		28,000
Separate Property TOTAL			128,000		128,000	**$100,000**	**$ 28,000**

For settlement purposes only.   Copyright © 2005 Miller Advisors, Inc.

FIGURE B.2   Summary of Assets and Liabilities

4. Gerald and Barbara have agreed to go to mediation. One week prior to the meeting, each of their attorneys will submit a written property settlement proposal to the mediator. A six-hour meeting has been scheduled. If an agreement cannot be reached through mediation, the attorneys will prepare for a specified trial date.

(**Note:** Gerald agrees to pay Barbara $3,000 per month in alimony until his retirement (projected at age sixty-five), but this figure will not be finalized until Barbara's concerns are addressed at the mediation.)

Footnotes to Reallocation of Assets

Unless otherwise stated on the "Valuation Date" column in the analysis, property values are as of September 30, 2004.

Item 1: Personal Residence

(Refer to figure B.1, "House Sale Income Tax Calculation.")

The primary residence is to be sold. The gross sales price is expected to be $475,000. Please note that the $150,000 mortgage balance and $28,500 estimated sales expenses are to be deducted from the sales proceeds of the home. Since the actual sales price of the property is unknown, the ultimate distribution of the sales proceeds will be determined upon the sale of the home. Barbara proposes that when the house is sold, the first $252,025 of the proceeds will go to her, and the balance will be allocated in such a way as to effectuate the agreed-upon property settlement percentages.

Item 2: Camano Island Cabin

Gerald and Barbara have jointly hired a real estate appraiser from Camano Island and have agreed on a property value of $165,000. The current mortgage balance is approximately $50,000. Gerald has been living at the cabin since their separation and staying in the city in a hotel an average of two nights a month. He intends to make the cabin his personal residence after some extensive remodeling. This remodeling is estimated to cost approximately $85,000 and will be financed through a home equity loan.

Items 3 and 4: Individual Retirement Accounts (IRAs)

For simplicity in the property allocation, Barbara proposes that they each keep their own Individual Retirement Accounts.

Item 5: 401(k) or Voluntary Investment Plan (VIP)

Since the date of separation, Gerald has continued to make contributions to his 401(k) plan. These contributions are considered his separate property and the values listed in figure B. 2 reflect the current value, minus the postseparation contributions.

Item 6: Financial Security Plan (FSP)

Both parties have agreed to use the account value as of an agreed-upon date.

Item 7: Boeing Pension

Due to the length of marriage, a present value calculation has not been prepared on the Boeing pension plan. We recommend that Gerald and Barbara share the pension income at retirement. (See figure B.6.)

Item 8: Boeing Credit Union

Since their separation, Gerald and Barbara have each withdrawn $10,000 from this account. They have agreed that they do not have to account for the withdrawn funds and that these funds will not be included in the allocation of assets. The account value is the amount left after these withdrawals.

Item 9: Investment Account

With the help of a financial planner, Gerald has historically selected and managed the mutual fund investments. There have been no distributions or changes in mutual fund investments since separation.

Item 10: Limited Partnerships

The Hudsons have invested in three limited partnerships during their marriage. With no active market to establish the actual value of the investments, it is proposed that the ownership be divided between the parties. The partnerships should be notified of the Hudsons' divorce and the ownership reregistered into separate ownership interests.

> OBSERVATION: *If the partnership investment is of questionable value, you may want to consider giving the asset to your spouse. The accounting costs of reporting the partnership activity, the generally nominal cash flow, and*

the potential income tax liability on the partnership may be greater than the economic value of the asset.

If you do split or keep the asset, be sure to obtain copies of the initial subscription paperwork, prior year income tax returns with complete partnership K-1s, and a report of "suspended passive activity losses" relating to prior unallowed partnership losses. This information will be needed at some point in the future, and it is surely easier to get the information incident to divorce rather than several years down the road.

Often there is a nominal cost for this reregistration and the actual reregistration can take months. It is best to contact the partnership to see if there are specific forms to make the name change, but generally you will be required to send a letter of instructions to the general partners with a copy of the section of your divorce decree discussing the division of the partnership. Be sure to start early so you will be getting the partnership information and tax reports the year the divorce is final. I recommend that you send your reregistration request by certified mail.

Items 11–16:

Gerald and Barbara have agreed on the values and allocation of these assets.

Items 18–20: Separate Property

Barbara and Gerald have each received inheritances during their marriage. The inherited funds have been maintained in separate accounts and each party recognized the other's separate ownership of the assets.

> OBSERVATION: *In a community property state, gifts and inheritances are deemed to be the separate property of the person receiving the gift or inheritance. However, in a dissolution, the judge has the discretion to consider separate property in the allocation of assets. Since Gerald and Barbara came to mutual consent to leave the separate assets out of the settlement, only the community assets are being divided.*

BOEING PENSION BENEFIT ANALYSIS

In addition to the 401(k) Voluntary Investment Plan and the Financial Security Plan, Boeing provides for a monthly pension income at retirement. Since this benefit is not received until retirement or death, a method of valuation or allocation must be agreed upon. The two primary methods of allocating pension income benefits include preparing a present value calculation and allocating the future pension benefit as either a fixed-dollar amount or as a percentage of the ultimate benefit.

We feel that the present value method does not fairly address the issues regarding the allocation of pension income. Present value calculations tend to be most beneficial when spouses divorce after retirement so that the benefits are already fixed. Present value calculations are least valuable when retirement is still several years away, especially since earlier retirement, death, disability, and any other number of unforeseen factors can significantly alter the result.

Methods of Sharing Defined Benefit Pension

In the allocation of future pension benefits, there can be an allocation of either a fixed dollar amount or an allocation of a percentage of the ultimate pension benefit. Traditionally, a fixed-dollar amount is allocated to the nonemployee spouse. There has more recently been a trend toward the participatory allocation method. (There are several names for the "participatory" allocation method, but the theories and calculations are nearly always the same).

Fixed-Dollar Amount Allocation

Under the normal defined benefit pension plan, the final pension benefit is calculated by multiplying the average annual compensation by the average annual final salary that is multiplied by a certain percentage. If the fixed dollar amount method is used in allocating the pension, the nonemployee spouse is not fully compensated for the years that the parties were married.

This method assumes that Gerald and Barbara share the retirement income from Gerald's Boeing pension under a Qualified Domestic Relations Order (QDRO) when he retires at sixty-five. Barbara will be sixty years old when Gerald retires at sixty-five. Figure B.3 shows what each would receive under this "flat" method calculation.

Remember, his total estimated pension from Boeing at age sixty-five is $6,140 per month from Boeing's retirement projection and based on Boeing's calculation method.

Barbara's Pension	$1,670 / Month at her age 60
Gerald's Pension	$4,470 / Month at his age 65

FIGURE B.3   Barbara and Gerald's Pensions

Wife's % of Retirement Benefit	X	Community Years of Service / Total Years of Service	X	Final Pension Benefit	=	Wife's Part of Husband's Retirement Benefit

FIGURE B.4   The Coverture Fraction Formula

Participatory Allocation

Under the participatory allocation method, the formula used in calculating the allocation of benefit is shown in figure B.4.

> **OBSERVATION:** *The community interest in the pension could have been based solely on the years of marriage. Instead, the courts are now beginning to recognize a community interest in the additional pension benefits obtained after the marriage. The formula shares the pension benefit based on the ratio of community years of service (years of the marriage) to the total years of service for the company paying the pension. This figure will decline over time, since the employee will continue to work, but the community years of service remain unchanged. The wife would be allocated an agreed-upon percentage of the final benefit, multiplied by this ratio. The result is that the husband begins accruing separate benefits immediately after the divorce, but there is still a community interest in the pension benefits that are shared.*

The calculation is summarized in figure B.5 and is based on the ratio of the number of years married (from date of marriage to date of separation) to the total number of years of service (from the date employment began to the projected retirement date). Please refer to the calculation and to figures B.6, B.7, B.8, and B.9 in reference to our results and discussion.

The balance of the projected benefit, or $3,763 ($6,140 minus $2,377), will be Gerald's portion of the benefits.

Barbara's Projected Pension Benefit

$$50\% \quad X \quad \frac{30.9}{39.9} \quad X \quad \$6,140 \quad = \quad \$2,377$$

FIGURE B.5   Barbara's Projected Pension Benefit

Summary of Pension Income
Gerald and Barbara Hudson

Year	Estimated Total Pension	Flat Method			Participatory Method		
		Community Pension	Gerald's Pension	Barbara's Pension	Community Pension	Gerald's Penson	Barbara's Pension
2005	3,340	3,340	1,670	1,670	3,340	1,670	1,670
2006	3,586	3,340	1,916	1,670	3,473	1,849	1,737
2007	3,846	3,340	2,177	1,670	3,612	2,040	1,806
2008	4,122	3,340	2,452	1,670	3,757	2,244	1,878
2009	4,414	3,340	2,744	1,670	3,907	2,460	1,954
2010	4,722	3,340	3,052	1,670	4,063	2,690	2,032
2011	5,048	3,340	3,378	1,670	4,226	2,935	2,113
2012	5,392	3,340	3,722	1,670	4,395	3,194	2,197
2013	5,756	3,340	4,086	1,670	4,571	3,470	2,285
2014	6,140	3,340	4,470	1,670	4,753	3,763	2,377

For illustrative purposes only.
This schedule is an approximation intended for planning purposes only.
It is not a substitute for your tax return. Please review with your tax advisor.
Copyright © 2005 Miller Advisors, Inc.

FIGURE B.6   Summary of Pension Income

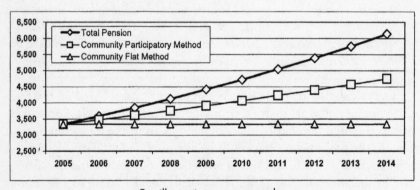

For illustrative purposes only.
This schedule is an approximation intended for planning purposes only.
It is not a substitute for your tax return. Please review with your tax advisor.
Copyright © 2005 Miller Advisors, Inc.

FIGURE B.7   Summary of Pension Income

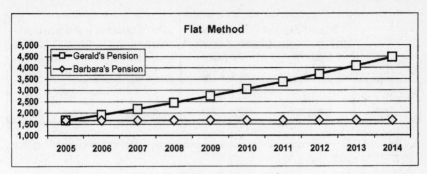

For illustrative purposes only.
This schedule is an approximation intended for planning purposes only.
It is not a substitute for your tax return. Please review with your tax advisor.
Copyright © 2005 Miller Advisors, Inc.

FIGURE B.8   Flat Pension Allocation Method

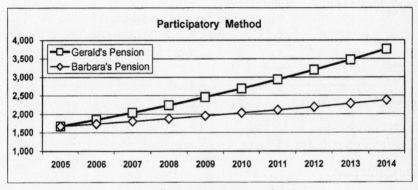

For illustrative purposes only.
This schedule is an approximation intended for planning purposes only.
It is not a substitute for your tax return. Please review with your tax advisor.
Copyright © 2005 Miller Advisors, Inc.

FIGURE B.9   Participatory Pension Allocation Method

Summary of Our Recommendation

We believe the fair and equitable method to divide this pension is the participatory allocation method. This is because it not only recognizes Barbara's community interest in Gerald's thirty-three years at Boeing, but it allows her to share in the continued growth of the pension benefit to retirement, based on her community interest at the date of separation. All defined benefit

	Fixed Dollar Allocation		Participatory Allocation	
	Monthly Income	Annual Income	Monthly Income	Annual Income
Barbara	$1,670	$20,040	$2,377	$28,524
Gerald	$4,470	$53,640	$3,763	$45,156

FIGURE B.10   Comparison of Incomes Under Fixed Dollar and Participatory Allocation

formulas recognize the last few years of the employee's earnings when calculating this retirement benefit. Barbara helped Gerald and was a partner with him in the thirty years prior to divorce and was in the marriage in the low-earning years. It is fair that she should participate in the "fruit of these labors" in his final high-earning years at Boeing.

Since we are not recommending a current present value, no dollar amount is shown in figure B.2. There will be an allocation of the retirement income benefit that will be used in our long-term cash-flow analysis in the next section of the report.

A comparison of the two methods helps to clarify the significant differences in the pension to be received by each party.

Long-Term Cash-Flow Analysis

Introduction

> **OBSERVATION:** *One of the elements we have found grossly missing from the work of many attorneys is to project the future financial positions of each party after the dissolution. In a mid-term marriage, looking out five to seven years may be sufficient. In a long-term marriage, it is our opinion that the future should be projected out much farther.*

As is typical in many long-term marriages, and in the case of Gerald and Barbara, Gerald has a substantially greater earnings capacity than does Barbara. This is referred to as "disparity of earnings." When there is a large disparity of earnings in a long-term marriage, an unequal division of assets is often awarded in addition to alimony payments because the person with the larger earning capacity is able to replace assets in the future. For the Hudsons, we propose that Gerald should receive 45 percent of the community assets and Barbara should receive 55 percent.

Categorization of Assets Assumptions

In this section of the report, we have attempted to illustrate the future financial position of each of the divorcing parties. To prepare a long-term cash-flow analysis, it is necessary to categorize the assets. We have summarized these categories as follows:

1. Residence: The residence is an asset, but the equity is not available to supplement living expenses.
2. Retirement Assets: These assets are designed for retirement and would be fully taxable if withdrawn. Assets listed here would include 401(k), profit-sharing, pension, annuities, and any other tax-deferred investments.
3. Investment Assets: These assets would include bank accounts, mutual funds, stocks, bonds, and essentially any asset not designated as one of the other asset classifications. These assets can be designated as income or growth assets.
4. Personal Assets: These assets are those that produce no income. Included in this category would be personal automobiles and checking account balances.

In the reallocation of assets analysis, we have listed the assets by category. The personal residence is listed first. The residence is assumed to appreciate in value over time, but this increase in value is not readily available as a means of funding the living expenses of either person. Therefore, only after other assets have been depleted would the residence be sold to provide for living expenses.

Retirement assets are assumed to grow at the stated rate of return with additional retirement contributions added to the account value. Until the earlier of age 70½ or the need for additional income for living expenses, the retirement assets are assumed to remain in this category. Retirement assets are used for living expenses only after all personal investment assets are depleted.

Income and growth on personal investment assets are assumed to be available for living expenses each year and to be subject to income taxes each year. These are the first assets to be used to supplement other sources of income should the need arise. Where total income needs exceed income sources, the shortage is taken from the personal investment assets. If income sources exceed living expenses, the excess is added to the following year's beginning asset balance.

Living expenses are generally composed of fixed and variable expenses. Mortgage payments are fixed in nature and will not increase with inflation. Other living expenses will increase with inflation. In the analysis, we have kept the mortgage payments constant until paid, and increased the other living expenses by the stated rate of inflation.

The income less expenses column in the cash-flow analyses is the difference between the total income and the gross living expenses. If this number is negative, the difference must be taken from assets. If the number is positive, the excess is added to the investment assets.

Income Sources

Retirement Assets

In allocating retirement funds, there are several factors to consider. First, after a dissolution, the accumulation of retirement funds may be inconsequential because of lower wages earned by one spouse. Retirement funds received by this individual in the dissolution may be the major retirement funds used to provide for retirement. On the other hand, when ultimately paid out, money received from a retirement account will generally be fully taxable to the recipient. If you are able to receive assets that do not have a pending income tax liability, and they are then invested and managed for future retirement, you may have a better settlement.

Barbara's Income Potential

After meeting with a career counselor, Barbara determined that she would need to have additional schooling to pursue her interest in teaching English as a second language. She intends to complete this schooling over the next two summers and through evening classes at a language school. After completing the necessary education, Barbara would eventually like to work in a language school and lessen her teaching commitments with the public school system. Part of Barbara's maintenance is deemed to be "compensatory."

While there may be an "equitable" distribution of the assets at the time of the dissolution, particularly in the case of a large disparity of earnings dissolution, the higher-income spouse is able to set aside considerably more money for the future than the lower-income spouse. This will make for a considerably more comfortable retirement for the higher-earning spouse. Many ex-spouses will continue to accrue larger and larger pension benefits, as was discussed earlier.

Social Security

Social Security is yet another area for debate. Based on the best available information, Gerald's accrued monthly Social Security benefit at age sixty-five will be approximately $2,000, while at age sixty-two Barbara will be entitled to a spousal benefit of only $1,000 per month based on his contributions. Given Barbara's anticipated work history, her personal Social Security benefit would be substantially less than the spousal benefit. Even if Barbara waited until age sixty-five to draw on Gerald's spousal benefit, she would receive far less than he will. You can see that the disparity of earnings issue does not lessen over time for women. Over the years the economic inequity only gets greater.

> **OBSERVATION:** *Part of the "Social Security—Personal Earnings and Benefits Statement" received for Barbara was used to provide the mentioned value. We did not receive a copy of this summary for Gerald; however, his company benefits statements provided us with the estimated age sixty, sixty-two, and sixty-five Social Security benefits used in our analysis. Keep in mind the numbers in this analysis are based on assuming Gerald retires at age sixty-five. They also depend upon the total value of his available benefits, and are subject to changes in the Social Security rates, which are adjusted annually, but not by a fixed formula. The "Social Security—Personal Earnings and Benefits Statement" shows a person's work history laid out in black and white and is available to anyone who requests it. I always recommend that you order this form at the very beginning of your divorce proceedings as it can be a very effective tool in your negotiations for longer-term maintenance. At the end of the earnings report, an estimate of your individual level of anticipated Social Security income at retirement is provided. The report can be ordered online at www.ssa.gov.*

In addition, as a wife who has stayed home to raise the children, Barbara does not have a significant earnings history with the Social Security Administration. After Gerald retires she will be entitled to either her own accrued Social Security benefits or one-half of the former spouse's, whichever is greater. While the spousal benefit may provide the greater income, it is still only one-half of what he receives.

Where we are involved in the dissolution process, we attempt to ensure that everyone involved is aware of **all** the financial long-term effects of the marriage to foster a "fair share" settlement.

> **OBSERVATION:** *You do not automatically receive Social Security benefits but need to qualify for them based on your "work credits" or those of your*

Long Term Cash Flow Analysis
for Barbara Hudson

Real Estate Growth Rate:	4.5%	
Retirement Asset Growth Rate:	8.0%	
Personal Investment Growth Rate:	7.0%	
Social Security Growth Rate:	2.5%	
Inflation Rate:	3.5%	
Monthly Living Exps (not incl taxes or Mtg Pmts):		$4,000
Monthly Mortgage Pmts (Added to Living Exps):		$632
Total Beginning Monthly Living Expenses (Plus Taxes):		$4,632
Total Beginning Annual Living Expenses (Plus Taxes):		$55,585

Beginning of Year	Age	Real Estate Equity	Retirement Assets	Personal Investment Assets	Tot. Return Personal Investments	Social Security	Maintenance Income	Boeing Pension	Teacher Pension	IRA Cont.	Wages	Total Return/ Income	IRA Payout	Living Expenses Incl. Taxes	Income Less Exps	TOTAL ASSETS
2005	52	$105,000	$200,000	$220,000	$15,400	$0	$36,000	$0	($804)	($4,500)	$28,000	$74,096	$0	$69,986	$4,110	$525,200
2006	53	115,343	220,716	224,110	15,688	0	36,000	0	(874)	(5,000)	28,980	74,794	0	71,883	2,910	560,168
2007	54	126,175	243,373	227,020	15,891	0	36,000	0	(909)	(5,000)	29,994	75,977	0	73,962	2,014	596,569
2008	55	137,522	267,843	229,034	16,032	0	36,000	0	(945)	(6,000)	31,044	76,132	0	75,847	284	634,399
2009	56	149,407	295,271	229,319	16,052	0	36,000	0	(983)	(6,000)	32,131	77,200	0	78,025	(825)	673,996
2010	57	161,856	324,892	228,493	15,995	0	36,000	0	(1,022)	(6,000)	33,255	78,228	0	80,261	(2,033)	715,242
2011	58	174,898	356,884	226,460	15,852	0	36,000	0	(1,063)	(6,000)	34,419	79,208	0	82,554	(3,346)	758,242
2012	59	188,560	391,434	223,114	15,618	0	36,000	0	(1,105)	(6,000)	35,624	80,137	0	84,907	(4,770)	803,109
2013	60	202,874	428,749	218,344	15,284	0	0	28,524	3,600	(6,000)	36,871	78,279	0	86,638	(8,359)	849,967
2014	61	217,870	469,049	209,985	14,699	0	0	28,524	3,600	(6,000)	38,161	78,984	0	89,087	(10,103)	896,905
2015	62	233,583	512,573	199,883	13,992	12,084	0	28,524	3,600			58,200	0	81,712	(23,512)	946,038
2016	63	250,046	553,579	176,371	12,346	12,386	0	28,524	3,600			56,856	0	83,668	(26,812)	979,996
2017	64	267,297	597,865	149,559	10,469	12,696	0	28,524	3,600			55,289	0	85,650	(30,361)	1,014,722
2018	65	285,375	645,694	119,198	8,344	13,013	0	28,524	3,600			53,481	0	87,525	(34,044)	1,050,267
2019	66	304,320	697,350	85,154	5,961	13,338	0	28,524	3,600			51,423	0	89,473	(38,050)	1,086,824

For illustrative purposes only.

This schedule is an approximation intended for planning purposes only.
It is not a substitute for your tax return. Please review with your tax advisor.

Copyright © 2005 Miller Advisors, Inc.

FIGURE B.11   Long-Term Cash-Flow Analysis for Barbara Hudson

Living Expense Summary
Barbara Hudson

Beginning of Year		Variable Living Expenses	Fixed Housing Expenses	Other Expenses	Medicare & FICA	Estimated Income Tax	Premature Distribution Penalty	Total Living Expenses
Year	Age							
2005	52	$48,000	$7,585	$0	$2,142	$13,384	$0	$71,111
2006	53	49,680	7,585	0	2,217	13,711	0	73,192
2007	54	51,419	7,585	0	2,295	14,042	0	75,340
2008	55	53,218	7,585	0	2,375	14,369	0	77,547
2009	56	55,081	7,585	0	2,458	14,695	0	79,819
2010	57	57,009	7,585	0	2,544	15,049		82,187
2011	58	59,004	7,585	0	2,633	15,393		84,615
2012	59	61,069	7,585	0	2,725	15,726		87,106
2013	60	63,207	7,585	0	2,821	15,284		88,897
2014	61	65,419	7,585	0	2,919	15,567		91,490
2015	62	67,709	7,585	0	0	7,343	0	82,636
2016	63	70,079	7,585	0	0	6,978	0	84,641
2017	64	72,531	7,585	0	0	6,558	0	86,674
2018	65	75,070	7,585	0	0	5,948	0	88,603
2019	66	77,697	7,585	0	0	5,326	0	90,608

For illustrative purposes only.

This schedule is an approximation intended for planning purposes only. It is not a substitute for your tax return. Please review with your tax advisor.

Copyright © 2005 Miller Advisors, Inc.

FIGURE B.12   Living Expense Summary for Barbara Hudson

Long Term Cash Flow Analysis
for Gerald Hudson

Real Estate Growth Rate: 4.5%
Retirement Asset Growth Rate: 8.0%
Personal Investment Growth Rate: 7.0%
Social Security Growth Rate: 2.5%
Inflation Rate: 3.5%

Monthly Living Exps (not incl taxes or Mtg Pmts): $4,000
Monthly Mortgage Pmts (Added to Living Exps): $853
Total Beginning Monthly Living Expenses (Plus Taxes): $4,853
Total Beginning Annual Living Expenses (Plus Taxes): $58,240

Beginning of Year	Age	Real Estate Equity	Retirement Assets	Personal Investment Assets	Tot. Return Personal Investments +	Social Security +	Maintenance Payments	Boeing Pension +	Boeing VIP +	Wages +	Total Return/ Income +	IRA Payout +	Living Expenses incl. Taxes =	Income Less Exps =	TOTAL ASSETS
2005	57	$115,000	$213,800	$116,290	$8,140	$0	($36,000)		($15,000)	$125,000	$82,140	$0	$79,224	$2,916	$445,090
2006	58	127,759	253,404	119,206	8,344	0	(36,000)		(15,000)	129,375	86,719	0	82,088	4,631	500,369
2007	59	141,125	296,176	123,838	8,669	0	(36,000)		(15,000)	133,903	91,572	0	85,216	6,356	561,139
2008	60	155,128	342,370	130,193	9,114	0	(36,000)		(15,000)	138,590	96,703	0	88,485	8,219	627,692
2009	61	169,799	392,260	138,412	9,689	0	(36,000)		(15,000)	143,440	102,129	0	91,900	10,229	700,471
2010	62	185,171	446,141	148,641	10,405	0	(36,000)		(15,000)	148,461	107,866	0	95,470	12,395	779,952
2011	63	201,277	504,332	161,036	11,273	0	(36,000)		(15,000)	153,657	113,929	0	99,202	14,728	866,645
2012	64	218,154	567,179	175,764	12,303	0	(36,000)		(15,000)	159,035	120,338	0	103,101	17,237	961,096
2013	65	235,839	635,053	193,001	13,510	24,000	0	45,156	0	0	82,666	0	83,909	(1,243)	1,063,893
2014	66	254,372	685,857	191,758	13,423	24,600	0	45,156	0	0	83,179	0	86,140	(2,961)	1,131,987
2015	67	273,795	740,726	188,797	13,216	25,215	0	45,156	0	0	83,587	0	88,420	(4,833)	1,203,317
2016	68	294,151	799,984	183,964	12,877	25,845	0	45,156	0	0	83,879	0	90,749	(6,871)	1,278,098
2017	69	315,487	863,983	177,093	12,397	26,492	0	45,156	0	0	84,044	0	93,128	(9,084)	1,356,562
2018	70	337,850	933,101	168,009	11,761	27,154	0	45,156	0	0	84,070	58,319	111,356	31,034	1,438,961
2019	71	361,292	944,765	199,043	13,933	27,833	0	45,156	0	0	86,922	61,749	115,608	33,063	1,505,100

For illustrative purposes only.

This schedule is an approximation intended for planning purposes only.
It is not a substitute for your tax return. Please review with your tax advisor.

Copyright © 2005 Miller Advisors, Inc.

FIGURE B.13 Long-Term Cash-Flow Analysis for Gerald Hudson

Living Expense Summary
Gerald Hudson

Beginning of Year		Variable Living Expenses	Fixed Housing Expenses	Other Expenses	Medicare & FICA	Estimated Income Tax	Premature Distribution Penalty	Total Living Expenses
Year	Age							
2005	57	$48,000	$10,240	$0	$7,393	$13,592	$0	$79,224
2006	58	49,680	10,240	0	7,456	14,713	0	82,088
2007	59	51,419	10,240	0	7,522	16,036	0	85,216
2008	60	53,218	10,240	0	7,590	17,437	0	88,485
2009	61	55,081	10,240	0	7,660	18,920	0	91,900
2010	62	57,009	10,240	0	7,733	20,489	0	95,470
2011	63	59,004	10,240	0	7,808	22,150	0	99,202
2012	64	61,069	10,240	0	7,886	23,906	0	103,101
2013	65	63,207	10,240	0	0	10,463	0	83,909
2014	66	65,419	10,240	0	0	10,482	0	86,140
2015	67	67,709	10,240	0	0	10,472	0	88,420
2016	68	70,079	10,240	0	0	10,431	0	90,749
2017	69	72,531	10,240	0	0	10,357	0	93,128
2018	70	75,070	10,240	0	0	26,046	0	111,356
2019	71	77,697	10,240	0	0	27,671	0	115,608

For illustrative purposes only.

This schedule is an approximation intended for planning purposes only.
It is not a substitute for your tax return. Please review with your tax advisor.

Copyright © 2005 Miller Advisors, Inc.

FIGURE B.14   Living Expense Summary for Gerald Hudson

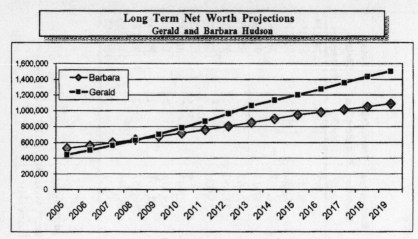

For Illustrative Purposes Only.
This schedule is an approximation intended for planning purposes only.
It is not a substitute for your tax return. Please review with your tax advisor.
Copyright © 2005 Miller Advisors, Inc.

FIGURE B.15   Estimated Net Worth Projection

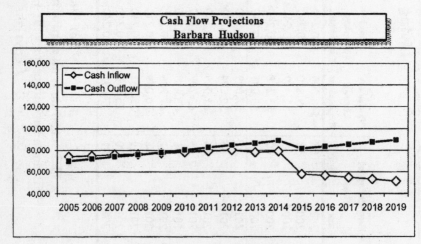

For Illustrative Purposes Only.
This schedule is an approximation intended for planning purposes only.
It is not a substitute for your tax return. Please review with your tax advisor.
Copyright © 2005 Miller Advisors, Inc.

FIGURE B.16   Barbara's Estimated Cash-Flow Projection

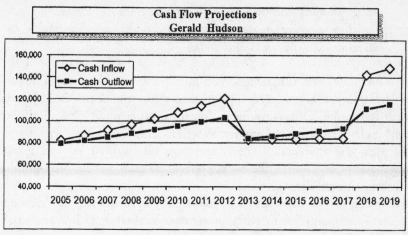

For Illustrative Purposes Only.
This schedule is an approximation intended for planning purposes only.
It is not a substitute for your tax return. Please review with your tax advisor.
Copyright © 2005 Miller Advisors, Inc.

FIGURE B.17 Gerald's Estimated Cash-Flow Projection

spouse acquired during your working years. Request this earnings record every three years to ensure that your W-2 information has been accurately reflected in your Social Security benefit calculation.

College Funding

Although the Hudsons have planned ahead for their daughter's education expenses, there are not sufficient funds available to provide for four years of college expenses. The $20,000 that is currently set aside for their daughter will be used to pay for the first two years of college. The remaining two years of college will be shared by Gerald and Barbara in proportion to their earned income.

OBSERVATION: *These calculations work by using several aspects of long-term cash flow and income tax planning. It incorporates current tax law based on the assumptions used in our proposal and performs a pro forma (projected) calculation of the tax implications of our proposed settlement. For instance, the model will calculate not only the payment for our proposed postdivorce mortgage amounts, but it will calculate the income tax deduction for home mortgage interest and incorporate the amount into the tax and cash-flow projections. It also determines the point at which various assets must be utilized in maintaining the household and the applicable* *penalties for early distributions of IRA funds when this becomes necessary. As mentioned earlier, the investment assets are depleted first and the personal residence is the last to be depleted.*

The model uses various assumed rates for expected increases in variable living expenses, wages, real estate assets, investment assets, and Social Security income. This allows us to control a rather significant number of variables in presenting our analysis as well as simplifying the revision process when one or several of the assumptions are disputed. We can change each assumption and see the overall effects on each person, both graphically and numerically.

Note, however, that these are projections and reality will vary depending on the economy, job markets, investment markets, inflation, and so on. The individual also has a lot to do with the similarity of our projections to their actual financial picture, since he or she controls the ultimate disposition of the assets.

Conclusions on Long-Term Cash-Flow Analysis

Refer to figure B.15, entitled "Long-Term Net Worth Projections for Gerald and Barbara Hudson." Our goal was to achieve an equitable long-term financial outlook for both Gerald and Barbara. Our proposal suggests a disproportionate allocation of the marital assets, leaving Barbara better off than Gerald. This may be true in the short term, but based on our analysis and Gerald's potential income, both Barbara and Gerald end up approximately equal in the fourth year after their divorce, after which Gerald begins to build his net worth steadily through his retirement years. Note that both parties have an increasing net worth, even after fifteen years.

The culmination of our analysis work is that both Gerald and Barbara are able to meet their financial needs with the allocation of assets and future income presented here. Gerald will eventually exceed Barbara in total net worth. However, the purpose is not to achieve an exact parity, but to allow for Gerald and Barbara to maximize their postdivorce net worth and lifestyle without leaving either party financially indigent. We believe that our proposal meets this criterion.

Need for Life Insurance

Gerald has agreed to maintain Barbara as 50 percent beneficiary on his group term life insurance coverage at Boeing until his retirement. The children are beneficiaries for the other half. He currently has $250,000 in death benefit coverage through his employment.

The Role of the Career Specialist in Divorce

When a couple divorces, one spouse—usually the wife—finds herself at a financial disadvantage. The most common reason for this postdivorce disparity is that the woman has spent her years in the marriage as a stay-at-home parent and homemaker, supporting her husband in his career advancement instead of pursuing a career of her own. The divorced woman is suddenly faced with the prospect of having to enter the workforce with neither the training nor experience to get a job that will suit her needs.

Seeking the help of a career specialist can ensure that you do not fall victim to this decline in economic resources. The career specialist can help you in two ways: by presenting information to the court so that your alimony needs are clear and by developing an effective plan to prepare you for economic self-sufficiency.

THE CASE FOR POSTDIVORCE MAINTENANCE

Since many divorcing women cannot immediately find a job that will allow them to maintain their previous lifestyle, they will need some form of maintenance as they seek training or education that will make them marketable to prospective employers. The career specialist can assist you in negotiating a fair maintenance agreement by:

- Giving a financial appraisal of your income potential
- Assessing your loss of income potential resulting from the years you did not work
- Establishing your current employability, long-range financial prospects, and other factors to determine what type of maintenance is required

- Providing accurate testimony as to the likelihood of your finding future employment
- Substantiating your case for rehabilitative and/or long-term alimony

SELECTING A CAREER SPECIALIST

You will want a career specialist who is able to guide you toward training and education that matches your abilities and fulfills your financial requirements. This specialist should:

- Possess at least a master's degree in counseling or psychology
- Have acquired enough experience to adequately determine your aptitudes, interests, and values
- Use standardized, well-researched career and psychological tests and counseling techniques
- Understand the local employment market and available training program options, including the costs, duration, employment outlook, and expected wages of program graduates
- Be sensitive to your psychological and physical requirements
- Make appropriate referrals to other specialists when additional assessment and/or therapy is needed

LOCATING THE RIGHT CAREER SPECIALIST

Referrals are a great way to find a professional in any area of expertise. Ask your attorney, friends or relatives, the Better Business Bureau, or local community college for referrals. You should interview at least three qualified experts to ensure you are compatible with the person and confident in his ability to provide expert witness testimony.

Notes

1. What Should You Do First?

1. Suzanne M. Bianchi, "The Gender Gap in the Economic Well-Being of Non-resident Fathers and Custodial Mothers," *Demography* 36, no. 2 (May 1999): 195–203.

2. Janet Wilmoth, "Does Marital History Matter? Marital Status and Wealth Outcomes Among Preretirement Adults," *Journal of Marriage and Family* 64 (February 2002): 254–68.

3. The term *alpha earner* was popularized in a May 12, 2003, *Newsweek* article entitled "She Works, He Doesn't," by Peg Tyre and Daniel McGinn. The authors cite statistics from a study by University of Maryland demographer Suzanne Bianchi suggesting that as of 2001, in more than 30 percent of households with a working wife, the wife earns more than her husband, and 11 percent of marriages feature a woman whose income represents at least 60 percent of the family income. These women are referred to as alpha earners.

2. The Five Emotional Stages of Divorce

1. Lois Brenner and Robert Stein, *Getting Your Share: A Woman's Guide to Successful Divorce Strategies* (Lincoln, Nebr.: Authors Choice Press, 2001).

2. In legal terms, the divorce process discussed in this book is often called an *absolute divorce (divorce a vinculo matrimonii)*. It legally terminates the marital status and separates the parties' property. Don't confuse this with the legal term *limited divorce (divorce a mensa et thoro)*, which is also referred to as a *legal separation*. A legal separation terminates rights of cohabitation, but leaves all other aspects of the marriage in place (for example, the parties are not free to marry other people).

3. If you represent yourself in court, you are called a pro se litigant, a term meaning "on one's own behalf."

4. Many writers have mistakenly cited California as the first state to pass no-fault divorce statutes. In fact, Oklahoma was the first, in 1953. Governor Ronald Reagan signed the California bill into law in 1970. Now every state has some provision for no-fault divorce.

4. The Financial Implications of Contemporary Relationships

1. This material is reprinted with permission of Segue Esprit, Inc., which credits the sources as: the U.S. Census Bureau; National Center for Health Statistics; Americans for Divorce Reform; Centers for Disease Control and Prevention; Institute for Equality in Marriage; American Association for Single People; Ameristat; and Public Agenda.

2. The details included in these examples are all a matter of public record and do not reveal any information that was not widely available in newspapers or magazines.

7. The Budget Process

1. Portions of this section are quoted with permission from the October 2003 ICFE press release, "Protecting Your Credit During a Divorce: How Making the Wrong Decisions Harms Your Credit." Copyright © 2003, Paul Richard and ICFE.

8. Closing In on Disparity: A New Era Deserves a New Divorce Model

1. Joan C. Williams, *Unbending Gender: Why Family and Work Conflict and What to Do About It.* (New York: Oxford University Press, 2001).

2. Jacknowitz Hiader and May Schoeni, *The Economic Status of Elderly Divorced Women* (Ann Arbor: University of Michigan, Michigan Retirement Research Center, 2003).

3. Williams, op. cit.

9. Financial and Tax Checkpoints Along the Way to the Property Settlement

1. *George v. United States,* 434F2d 1336 (1970), Regs. 1-211-1(k)(n).

11. Preparing for Life After Divorce: Restricted Securities, Insurance, Housing, Debt, and Estate Planning

1. P. Kemper and C. M. Murtaugh, "Lifetime Use of Nursing Home Care," *The New England Journal of Medicine* 324, no. 9 (February 28, 1991): 595–600.

2. Ibid.

3. Data provided by the Agency for Health Care Policy Research, Harvard University, 1987–89.

12. Women and Investing

1. Terrance Odean and Brad M. Barber, "Boys Will Be Boys: Gender, Overconfidence, and Common Stock Investment" (University of California at Davis, September 1999).

2. Data provided by the National Center for Women and Retirement Research.

3. Data provided by the Department of Labor, www.dol.gov.

4. Hannah Shaw Grove and Russ Alan Prince, "Women of Wealth," *Financial Advisor Magazine,* July 2003.

5. Data provided by the Federal Reserve (2000).

6. *WOW! Facts 2004: U.S. Multicultural and Global Markets* (Washington, D.C.: Diversity Best Practices and Business Women's Network, 2004), 47.

7. Grove and Prince, op. cit.

8. New Research Report Release, "Women: The Largest Consumer Market," (North Granby, Conn.: Capital Reflections, Inc., February 1999).

9. Grove and Prince, op. cit.

10. Mary Duenwald and Bernard Stamler, "On Their Own, in the Same Boat," *The New York Times,* April 13, 2004.

11. Data provided by the Center for Women's Business Research, www.nfwbo.org (May 2000).

12. Ibid.

13. Data provided by the National Center for Women and Retirement Research Web site (NCWRR)

14. Duenwald and Stamler, op. cit.

15. Data taken from Ibbotson Analyst. Copyright © 2004, version 8.6.

Glossary

Alpha earner. A wife who makes more than her husband. Based on the original usage, it applies to wives who make at least 60 percent of the total household income.

Amortization. The process of paying off a debt (such as a home mortgage) over time through a fixed schedule of installment payments.

Annuity. An investment contract between you and an insurance company for a specific amount of time. You purchase an annuity by giving the company a set amount of cash that they invest. When you commit to take money out of the contract over a set period of time, you have agreed to annuitize the contract. The aftertax dollars invested in an annuity are tax-deferred and are only taxed when the money comes out of the contract.

Arbitration. A process in which an impartial third party acts as a judge and makes binding decisions about contested issues between disputing parties.

Blocked account. An account that restrains either party regarding transactions in the account. It is normally used to prevent one account owner from withdrawing funds unless both owners agree.

Bond. A type of investment where the investor loans money to the issuer (a municipality, government, or corporation) in return for a specified amount of interest. The "loan" becomes due at a specified date (that is, it "matures"). It is a form of debt instrument and is subject to credit risk, inflation risk, and interest rate risk.

Collaborative law. A cooperative approach to divorce used by attorneys, clients, and professionals providing support services, where all work together to resolve the problems that result from the breakdown of the relationship. All parties agree in writing to refrain from resorting to the court system (that is, going to trial) to resolve the issues.

Community property. Assets and debts considered to be owned and shared equally by both spouses.

Consolidated Omnibus Budget Reconciliation Act of 1985 (COBRA). A federal law that enables a spouse to continue health care coverage under an existing policy for up to thirty-six months following a divorce.

Cooling-off period. The required time between filing (the complaint date) and the date the divorce decree is granted.

Cost basis. The amount paid for an asset or the purchase amount remaining, adjusted for stock splits, dividends, and return of capital distributions, after deducting depreciation claimed for tax purposes. Also called tax basis.

Credit risk. The risk of loss of an investment in a bond due to the issuer defaulting on their contract to pay the investor the stated interest (coupon or principal) in the specified time period.

Deposition. Information or testimony taken under oath by either party's attorney (for example, spouse, experts, and witnesses).

Discovery. A process of gathering information about the nature, scope, and credibility of the opposing party's claim. The procedures used include depositions, written interrogatories, and notices to produce case-related documentation.

Equitable distribution. A system whereby courts are given the discretionary power to divide marital property in a fair and equitable manner.

Financial affidavit. The document filed in court that provides detailed information on a divorcing spouse's financial circumstances.

Front-loading. The practice of making very large alimony payments during the first few years of divorce, often disguised as child support.

Income stream. A series of payments received as income.

Inflation risk. The risk associated with the return from an investment not covering the loss in purchasing power caused by inflation.

Intangible personal property. Assets such as bank accounts, stocks and bonds, vested pensions, life insurance, annuities, money market accounts, and retirement accounts.

Interest-rate risk. The risk that the relative value of a bond or stock will fall due to an interest-rate increase.

Interrogatory. Written questions sent by a lawyer to the other party that are answered under oath within a certain prescribed period of time and which are admissible in court.

Intestate. Dying without a will to dispose of one's assets. When this is the case, the deceased person's assets will be divided and distributed following state statutes by a representative named by the court. If the deceased has small children, the court will also name a legal guardian for those children.

Joint tenancy. Ownership in which both spouses own half, but neither spouse can will his or her half to anyone other than the other spouse. When one spouse dies, the surviving spouse automatically inherits the half owned by the deceased spouse.

Keogh. A tax-deferred retirement plan specifically designed for self-employed workers. Its major advantage is the high pretax contributions the employee can make compared to other forms of IRAs.

Lien. The legal right to take and hold or sell the property of another to satisfy an obligation or debt.

Litigation. Formal legal proceedings to settle a dispute.

Maintenance. Temporary financial payments specified by a court order to "rehabilitate" or "compensate" the nonworking spouse so he or she can enter the job market and earn a living. In most cases the term is interchangeable with *alimony*.

Marital estate. The assets or property and accumulated income acquired by both spouses during the marriage.

Mediation. A voluntary and confidential process in which an impartial third party (a trained mediator) helps disputing parties reach a mutually agreeable settlement. Unlike an arbitrator, a mediator cannot issue a legal decision that binds both parties to the agreement.

No-fault divorce. A divorce in which neither spouse blames the other for the breakdown of the marriage. Both spouses agree that *irreconcilable differences* have arisen and that neither time nor counseling will save the marriage.

Nonprobate. A method to divide assets that do not pass per the will or within an estate that is probated. Retirement plans, life insurance policies, and annuities are paid to survivors according to beneficiary designations.

Petition. A written document requesting some kind of action (relief) from the court.

Phantom stock.   A promise to pay the employee the monetary equivalent of a fixed number of shares at a specified future date, without the employee or the company having to own the stock. Unlike a stock-appreciation right, this form of compensation may include the effects of dividends and stock splits.

Private pension plan.   A retirement plan not regulated by the federal government.

Probate.   The legal method by which an individual's estate is divided and the validity of the will is established under the jurisdiction of a court (usually called a *probate court*).

Promissory note.   A written, signed promise to pay money to another party under specific conditions.

Property settlement.   That portion of the divorce decree that specifies which party receives which assets, including furniture, stocks, insurance policies, and cars, and which party must assume which liabilities, including credit-card debt, policy premiums, and loan payments.

Pro rata.   To divide or distribute based on a proportion.

Pro se divorce.   The dissolution of a marriage without the use of attorneys.

Qualified Domestic Relations Order (QDRO).   A written agreement between a divorcing couple that spells out who gets what when it comes to retirement money held in a company pension plan such as a 401(k) plan, a 403(b), and most pensions in private companies. QDROs were created and are governed by the Employment Retirement Income Security Act of 1974 (ERISA) and control pensions and company-sponsored retirement accounts.

Rabbi trust.   A nonqualified, deferred compensation plan, usually for key executives of a company, also called a *grantor trust*. It provides more protection of the assets in the trust than some other deferred benefits, but is still subject to the company's creditors in the case of bankruptcy.

Real property.   Land and the buildings (that is, improvements) on that land.

Restraining order.   An order by the court that limits or restricts certain actions by either or both spouses.

Restricted stock.   In general terms, restricted or controlled stock is any unregistered stock that is limited by the Securities and Exchange Commission Rule 144. There are also restricted stock awards and restricted stock units that are part of a company's benefit plan. Awards involve the issuance of shares according to a vesting schedule, while units are based on an equivalent monetary amount, with no shares being issued.

Retainer.   An advance payment to be applied against future fees. An attorney and experts may have a retainer letter for clients to sign at the start of the engagement that outlines the basics of the working relationship.

Roth IRA.   A retirement plan that does not provide tax deductions for contributions, but for which all earnings are tax-free when you withdraw them. It also has the double benefit of not requiring you to start withdrawing at age seventy and a half and the minimum distribution rules for other IRAs do not apply. You can contribute to regular IRAs as well as to a Roth.

Secular trust.   A key employee benefit similar to the **rabbi trust,** but with more protection of the assets in case the company files bankruptcy. Unlike under the rabbi trust, an employee must pay taxes on contributions to the plan as they are deposited, rather than when the employee withdraws them.

Separate property.   Property owned before marriage or property acquired during marriage by gift or inheritance. Also called *nonmarital property*.

Separation agreement.   A contract between a husband and a wife in which they agree to resolve such matters as property division, debts, custody, and support when they separate from each other, prior to the granting of the final divorce decree.

SEP-IRA.   A form of tax-deferred retirement plan, the Simplified Employee Pension is provided by small businesses that do not have other plans, such as a 401(k). Only the employer contributes to this type of plan, which has a higher maximum contribution than other IRAs. The employee can also have other types of personal retirement plans.

Settlement agreement.   The written version of the agreement reached by the divorcing parties with terms on how the property is being divided or the terms of child custody that becomes part of the final divorce decree.

SIMPLE-IRA.   Unlike a SEP plan, the Savings Incentive Match Plan for Employees allows both the employee and employer to contribute pretax dollars in a firm with fewer than 100 employees. The employer can contribute up to 100 percent of the amount contributed by the employee (up to a maximum of 3 percent of the employee's salary), or a straight 2 percent of salary for all employees, even if they do not contribute themselves. You can also participate in other IRA plans simultaneously.

Split dollar plan. A method of buying insurance whereby a company splits the premiums, cash value, death benefit, and ownership of the policy. When the employee dies, his beneficiaries receive the principal death benefit and the employer receives the portion of the premiums that it contributed. Both this and the reverse split dollar, which reverses what each party receives, are used as key employee incentives.

Stock appreciation rights. A very flexible benefit under which the employee does not own stock, but rather the employer agrees to pay him the equivalent of any increase in stock value over a specified period of time. These are usually allocated under a fixed vesting schedule.

Stock option. A right granted by an employer allowing the recipient to purchase shares of its stock at a favorable (below market) price at some future date. Options normally have a vesting schedule, and a price fixed at some discount from the market value on a specific date. The tax consequences of exercising (that is, buying the stock) and reselling it depend on whether the option is nonqualified, or an incentive option.

Tangible property. Items such as cars, jewelry, furniture, and antiques. These assets do not include **real property.**

Temporary order. An order handed down by a judge that directs one spouse to pay support to the other until the divorce trial begins or a settlement is reached.

Temporary orders trial. A formal legal proceeding to determine how financial issues will be resolved during the time of separation, such as a review of temporary maintenance and of child support.

Tenancy by entirety. In separate property states only, this form of ownership works like a **joint tenancy,** but is reserved for married people exclusively.

Tenancy in common. Ownership by which both spouses own half, and each can will their portion to whomever they like.

Total return. The full amount of return an investor receives from an investment—including dividends, interest, and capital gains—to give a complete picture of how an investment has performed over time.

Trial. A formal court hearing in which all outstanding issues can be decided by a judge.

Waiting period. The minimum state residency required of one spouse to be eligible to file for divorce.

Resources

Web Sites

There are many Web sites you can refer to when learning about divorce. However, I suggest you check any information you find on a Web site with your local attorney before making any major decisions.

The following resources are grouped by topic.

Legal

Check the Web sites of local law schools in your area. You may find a Women's Center as part of one of these sites. Most attorneys now maintain their own individual sites.

www.aaml.org

www.findlaw.com

www.lawinfo.com

www.nolo.com

www.westlaw.com. Subscription-based research site.

www.abanet.org/family/home.html. Family law site for the American Bar Association.

www.martindale.com. Gives information on lawyers and their firms across the United States.

www.collaborativefamilylawassociation.com. Presents questions and answers about using collaborative law as an approach to divorce.

Divorce

These sites contain comprehensive financial information and tools devoted to divorce issues that can help you calculate various divorce obligations. Verify with your attorney that the information you find on the Web site is applicable to your situation. These sites will link you to other helpful resources. Many times your spouse will be reading the information on these sites and then "telling you the law." Trust, but verify!

www.divorcesource.com

www.divorcenet.com

www.divorcetopics.com

www.divorceinfo.com

www.preciousheart.net. A compendium of many divorce Web sites.

www.divorcecentral.com

www.womansdivorce.com

www.equalityinmarriage.org

www.smartdivorce.com

www.divorcemag.com. Subscription focusing on pre- and postdivorce issues.

www.fairsharedivorce.com

Child Support

State child-support guidelines on the Web:

www.supportguidelines.com. Gives state child-support guidelines.

www.divorcelawinfo.com. Calculations for child support.

www.collegeboard.com. Costs of college tuition and other expenses.

Financial Resources

www.nfcc.org. National Foundation for Credit Counseling (NFCC). The NFCC is a national nonprofit network that provides free or low-cost counseling and education on budgeting, credit, and debt resolution, including bankruptcy options. Visit their Web site to find a location near you or call 1-800-388-2227 for assistance.

www.irs.gov. To request copies of past income tax returns, visit the Internal Revenue Service's Web site or call 1-800-829-1040.

www.irs.gov/taxpros/lists/0,,id=98042,00.html. You can find the most recent Applicable Federal Rates at this link on the IRS Web site.

Expert Advice

www.collaborativepractice.com. International Academy of Collaborative Professionals.

Actuaries

To get information about actuaries:

www.actuary.org. American Academy of Actuaries.

www.soa.org. Society of Actuaries.

Appraisers

If you need an accredited appraiser in your area:

www.appraisers.org. American Society of Appraisers. Herndon, Virginia. 1-800-272-8258.

www.nacva.com. National Association of Certified Valuation Analysts. Salt Lake City, Utah. 1-801-486-0600.

Career Services

www.careerdiscoveryinc.com. Janice E. Reha, CMHC, M.A., provides career services to companies, colleges, and career changers from her office in Bellevue, Washington.

www.salary.com

www.bls.gov/cpi. Consumer Price Indexes (CPI).

Financial Planners

To find a financial planner in your area:

www.fpanet.org/plannersearch/plannersearch.cfm. You can locate a planner with the CFP designation in your area on this site, or call 1-800-647-6340.

www.institutedfa.com. This is the home site for the Institute for Certified Divorce Financial Analysts where you can locate a CDFA in your area.

www.nasd.com/InvestorInformation/index.htm. National Association of Securities Dealers, Inc. (NASD). 1-800-289-9999. You can request a copy of a stockbroker's disciplinary and employment records from this site.

Investors

www.aaii.com. American Association of Individual Investors.

Mediators

The following is a list of organizations you can contact to find mediators in your area. *Caution!* Check out the background of your mediator very carefully before deciding whom to hire. I recommend interviewing at least three mediators before making your final determination. Make sure the mediator has experience in the area of family law and uses financial experts to help resolve your financial issues.

www.acresolution.org. Association for Conflict Resolution. Washington, D.C. 1-202-464-9700. The ACR is a merged organization of the American Academy of Family Mediators, The Conflict Education Network, and the Society of Professionals in Dispute Resolution.

Credit

To check your credit rating:

www.annualcreditreport.com. Free credit report from all three reporting companies.

www.equifax.com. Equifax. Atlanta, Georgia. 1-800-685-1111.

www.experian.com. Experian. Allen, Texas. 1-888-Experian.

www.transunion.com. TransUnion. Springfield, Pennsylvania. 1-800-888-4213.

www.consumer.gov/idtheft. National Web site on identity theft.

Insurance

www.naic.org. The National Association of Insurance Commissioners helps coordinate regulation of the insurance industry. Independent of any company or product, they provide a number of publications.

www.dol.gov. COBRA health care coverage

To gather quotes for insurance rates:

www.iquote.com. Insurance Quote Services. 1-800-972-1104.

www.intelliquote.com. Life Insurance Services. 1-888-622-0925

www.quotesmith.com. Quote Smith. 1-800-431-1147.

Pensions and Retirement

www.ssa.gov. This is the Web site for the Social Security Administration, where you can find your or your spouse's Social Security benefits. 1-800-772-1213.

www.pensionanalysis.com. Pension Analysis Consultants, Inc. 1-800-288-3675. One of many companies and qualified individuals that prepare pension valuation as well as corporate sponsors of a company plan.

www.pbgc.gov. Pension Benefit Guaranty Corporation.

www.military.com. Gives information on military pensions.

www.dod.mil/dfas. Main site for the Defense Finance and Accounting Service, listing local military finance centers and helpful information on military retirement benefits. You can also call the center responsible for processing payments subject to a separation agreement at 1-866-859-1845.

Miscellaneous

www.buc.com/index.cfm. Gives the value of boats.

www.nadaguides.com. Gives the value of cars, boats, and RVs.

www.finance.cch.com. Information on managing finances and retirement planning.

www.financialpsychology.com. Provides a tool to learn about your money personality.

www.amazon.com. Online retailer for books on divorce and financial planning.

www.lexisnexis.com. Subscription-based research site.

www.livingto100.com. Presents interesting information that will show how changing your lifestyle may influence your life span.

www.privacyrights.org. A nonprofit site to protect your privacy during public proceedings.

PUBLICATIONS

American Association of Retired Persons (AARP). The AARP offers four free helpful booklets:

- *Focus Your Future: A Women's Guide to Retirement Planning* (#D14559)
- *The Social Security Book: What Every Woman Absolutely Needs to Know* (#D14117)
- *Women, Pensions and Divorce, a* survey of pension issues with a section of proposed reforms
- *A Woman's Guide to Pension Rights.*

To order, write to AARP Fulfillment, 601 E. Street N.W., Washington, D.C. 20049.

Financial Planning Perspectives. A monthly column produced as a public service by the Financial Planning Association. Articles may be downloaded from this site: **www.fpanet.org/public/tools/articles/index.cfm.**

A Guide for Military Separation or Divorce. This booklet gives information on benefits to which an ex-spouse may be entitled under the Uniformed Services Former Spouses Protection Act, explains the Survivor Benefit Plan, and outlines how to prepare for divorce court, the complete survivor benefit plan, miscellaneous benefits, and other pertinent information. To obtain a copy, write to EX-POSE, P.O. Box 11191, Alexandria, VA, 22312.

Money Harmony: Resolving Money Conflicts in Your Life and Your Relationships by Olivia Mellan (New York: Walker and Company, 1995), 252 pages ($14.95 from Amazon.com).

Your Money Personality: What It Is and How You Can Profit from It by Kathleen Gurney, Ph.D. (New York: Doubleday, 1988), 366 pages ($17.95 from Financial Psychology Corporation).

Your Pension Rights at Divorce: What Women Need to Know by Ann E. Moss, J.D. To order, write Pension Rights Center, 918 16th Street N.W., Suite 704, Washington, D.C., 20006. ($16.50).

Other Sources

To receive a free packet of information on pensions from the Older Women's League, send a self-addressed, stamped envelope to the league at 666 11th Street N.W., Suite 700, Washington, D.C., 10002. A women and pensions edition of the league's newsletter has several short articles and a list of resources. Call 800-825-3695 for the current price.

Index